MW01627728

A BENEDICTINE EDUCATION

A BENEDICTINE EDUCATION

Two Essays

THE MISSION OF SAINT BENEDICT

THE BENEDICTINE SCHOOLS

John Henry Newman

≈ ≈

Edited and with a Preface by Christopher Fisher

Introduction by Margarita A. Mooney

With an Interpretive Essay by Abbot Thomas Frerking, O.S.B.

CLUNY

Providence, Rhode Island

Cluny Media edition, 2020,
published in partnership with the Portsmouth Institute

The two essays by John Henry Newman originally published
in the *Atlantis* in 1858 and 1859, and subsequently collected and published
in *Historical Sketches*, Vol. II, by Longmans, Green, and Co., in 1906.

For more information regarding this title
or any other Cluny Media publication,
please write to info@clunymedia.com, or to
Cluny Media, P.O. Box 1664, Providence, RI 02901
* VISIT US ONLINE AT WWW.CLUNYMEDIA.COM *

For more information on the Portsmouth Institute and its sponsors,
Portsmouth Abbey and Saint Louis Abbey, please visit:
* WWW.PORTSMOUTHINSTITUTE.ORG *
* WWW.PORTSMOUTHABBEY.ORG *
* WWW.STLOUISABBEY.ORG *

ISBN: 978-1952826191

Library of Congress Control Number: 2020942973

Cover design by Clarke & Clarke
Cover image: Juan Correa de Vivar, *Saint Benedict Blessing Saint Mauro,*
between 1540 and 1545, oil on panel
Courtesy of Wikimedia Commons

CONTENTS

PREFACE

The Need for a Benedictine Center

JOSEF PIEPER begins his magnum opus, *Leisure, the Basis of Culture,* as St. Thomas Aquinas might have done: with an objection. Many will argue, he says, that now (that is, post-war Europe) is not the time to talk about leisure. After all, "our hands are full and there is work for all."[1] On the contrary, he answers, it is precisely in this period of civilizational rebuilding that we must begin by restoring the meaning of leisure.

The same argument might be made of the Benedictine life in our own present day. Now, some might argue, is not the time to retreat from the world. Now is the time to go forth, to engage, to confront.

Like with Pieper's leisure, the reality is more complex, even paradoxical: Just as the difficult work of rebuilding of Western civilization requires a recovery of leisure as its source of vitality, so a broader evangelical engagement with secular society demands the cloister.

How does a Benedictine center such as the Portsmouth Institute fit into this cloistral project? Is it our recommendation that the only constructive activity is to leave the world and join a monastery?

Of course, we certainly would not object to an increase in vocations to the monastic life! We agree with Robert Cardinal Sarah, who wrote, "I am certain that the future of the Church is in the monasteries...because where prayer is, there is the future." And indeed, part of our role as a Benedictine center is to offer an encounter with the monastic life which for some young men and women may end in a religious vocation.

Yet vocations are not the only gifts which the Benedictine tradition has to offer the Church. As St. John Henry Newman argues in the two essays included in his volume, the Benedictine life is marked by a certain spiritual disposition which he calls "poetic." While this poetic disposition has its source in the cloister and is, properly speaking, Benedictine, it is not limited to the monk. Rather, the poetic disposition of the monk has long animated the spiritual vision of lay and religious Christians, including through the long "Benedictine Age" of the West which took place from roughly the eighth to the twelfth centuries. Yet the modern, technological, scientific world has lost the poetic disposition of the Benedictine. This is not only a civilizational loss, but a loss for the Christian life.

What does Newman mean by poetry? In her Introduction to the present volume, Margarita Mooney offers a more complete exploration of this question. Suffice to say for now that for Newman, poetry expresses a way of seeing the world. Newman writes of poetic perception that it

> demands, as its primary condition, that we should not put ourselves above the objects in which it resides, but at their feet; that we should feel them to be above and beyond us, that we should look up to them, and that, instead of fancying that we can comprehend them, we should take for granted that we are surrounded and comprehended by them ourselves. It implies that we understand them to be vast, immeasurable, impenetrable, inscrutable, mysterious; so that at best we are only forming conjectures about them, not conclusions, for the phenomena which they present admit of many explanations, and we cannot know the true one. Poetry does not address the reason, but the imagination and affections; it leads to admiration, enthusiasm, devotion, love. The vague, the uncertain, the irregular, the sudden, are among its attributes or sources.[2]

What Newman calls poetic we might take to be the wisdom of the heart: and indeed, St. Benedict in his (very short) *Rule* uses the word heart, or *cor* in Latin, thirty-seven times (fifty-seven when its derivations are included, such as *concordia, misericordia, discordia, corpus, and corporalis*).[3] Poetic perception is the receptive attitude of mind, which, formed in silence, is capable of apprehending the whole of reality. This is what Pieper calls the ability to "steep oneself in the whole of creation."[4] This attitude of contemplation which informs the poetic disposition is at the heart of the Christian life.

As we seek to evangelize a post-Christian culture, as we attempt with God's grace to transform our own lives and conform them more deeply to the Gospel, and as we work to restore a vibrant Christian culture, it is necessary that we recover a sense of the poetic. This is the work of the Portsmouth Institute: to recover the idea of Benedictine poetry as a means by which we can inspire transformative encounters with Christ. In many ways, this work of recovery and transformation is our answer to Rod Dreher's Benedict Option, our attempt to provide an experience of the cloister to the world. We believe that poetic perception will enliven the spiritual lives of those Christians who we receive as monastic guests at our seminars, colloquia, and retreats. And, like Pieper seeing that leisure is essential not only for the person, but for the civilization, so too do we recognize that a recovery of the fruits of the Benedictine charism will be a leaven to our personal spiritual lives and to Christian culture.

If Newman is correct that the Benedictine disposition is essentially poetic and that Benedictine poetry is the foundation of the Christian life, Christian education, and Christian civilization, and if we believe that a poetic experience is limited not only to the monk, but available to and necessary for the lay person, then what can practically be done to inspire a recovery of poetic perception?

This Preface sketches three activities or modes of being which draw on Newman's understanding of Benedictine poetry and which provide a sort of programmatic blueprint for the activities of the Portsmouth Institute. These include monastic humanism, *lectio divina,* and the liturgy. While these practices are not exclusive to the Benedictines, they do find their source in monasticism. More importantly, these three activities reveal the heart of the Benedictine life and offer a means by which the Church can recover the Benedictine poetic vision. They are also easily transferable to the lay context. The recovery and promotion of monastic humanism, *lectio divina,* and a rich liturgical life is perhaps especially important today for Catholic schools, which will find in these activities a source of renewed vision and purpose.[5]

Monastic Humanism and Poetic Vision

In today's STEM-centric educational environment, Catholic academic institutions often emphasize the Catholic tradition of scientific, analytical, and dialectical study. Newman sees this mode of learning exemplified by the Dominicans, whom he argues represent "Science," a counter-part to Benedictine "Poetry." The greatest representative of the Dominican scientific tradition is the Angelic Doctor, St. Thomas Aquinas. Indeed, a Catholic education void of the wisdom of St. Thomas Aquinas has no business calling itself Catholic. Further, what Newman calls the scientific tradition of the Dominicans, marked by analysis, definition, dialogue—which I will call the *Dominican principle*—is essential to Catholic education and the Catholic intellectual life more broadly. It is among the great pearls in the infinite treasure of the Catholic intellectual tradition. In his Interpretive Essay, which concludes the present volume, Abbot Thomas Frerking, O.S.B., provides a moving and learned reflection of the importance of the Dominican principle even in the Benedictine life. Indeed, Newman believes these two principles—Dominican science and Benedictine poetry—coexist in the life of the Church:

> Instead of passing from one stage of life to another, she [the Church] has carried her youth and middle age along with her, on to her latest time. She has not changed possessions, but accumulated them, and has brought out of her treasure-house, according to the occasion, things new and old. She did not lose Benedict by finding Dominic; and she has still both Benedict and Dominic at home, though she has become the mother of

> Ignatius. Imagination, Science, Prudence, all are good, and she has them all. Things incompatible in nature, cöexist in her; her prose is poetical on the one hand, and philosophical on the other.

Abbot Thomas convincingly argues that these two modes of being, science and poetry, not only coexist in the life of the Church but indeed may coexist in the individual person. Abbot Thomas's own life as Benedictine monk and Thomist philosopher is a beautiful witness to this reality.

Today it is equally important—perhaps even of prior importance—to recover what I will call the *Benedictine principle* in the life of the Church. The Portsmouth Institute is uniquely suited to lead that recovery. One means for recovering the poetic disposition is through what Benedictine scholar Jean Leclercq, O.S.B., calls monastic humanism.

André Gushurst-Moore, a philosopher of education and Second Master at Worth School, a Benedictine boarding school in England associated with Worth Abbey,[6] considers that Newman's understanding of Benedictine poetry

> is very much grounded in its root sense of *poiesis*. The distinction Newman makes between poetry and science is essentially one between a sacramental and an analytical dispositions, between the mysticism of St. Bernard (*credo ut experiar*) and the scholasticism of St. Anselm (*credo ut intelligam*). *Poiesis* is making; man is in the image of God in being a maker of symbols through imitation of creation. The poetic instinct involves a sacramental view of reality, such that signs, symbols, and metaphors—ways of speaking of one thing in terms of another—are never *only* representations.... A poetic view of the world is a sacramental view; a sacramental view is a mystical view. Unless our education is founded in the sacramental sense of the created world, we shall not enable persons or the culture to see things

> as they really are. This, too, is humility [St. Benedict's word for wisdom], and it will affect the way persons and communities, cities and countries interact with each other and with the natural and built environments. Nothing could be more relevant to education for today's world.[7]

Poetic perception enables the student to perceive things as they really are, to grasp the sacramental view of creation, and to thus become more humane, both as persons and as communities.

Such a poetic vision is the essence of monastic humanism. Monastic humanism is a "humanism wholly inspired by classical antiquity, a humanism whose touchstone is Christ crucified, risen from the dead, who by His example and His grace makes us renounce evil in order to lead us to the heavenly city."[8] This poetic or sacramental perception is nurtured through an encounter with literature, which is read not only as representation of reality but as revelation of truth. This is uniquely possible in a Catholic environment, where we that see Christ, through His Incarnation, "is all and is in all" (Col. 3:11). Thus, all creation, all *poiesis*, becomes sacramentalized, charged with God's grace. Through this encounter with God's grace in literature, and through an exploration into the truth, goodness, and beauty of the created order, we allow ourselves to be transformed—to experience the Benedictine vow of *conversatio morum*, or what the Gospels call *metanoia*.

For Leclercq, as for Newman, the monk sees the study of literature as primarily transformational, as it combines the monk's desire for heaven with the humanist's desire to "study the classics for the reader's personal good, [and] to enable him to enrich his personality."[9] This means that monastic humanism is both an Incarnational and eschatological education: it contains within it the firm belief that God has revealed Himself fully to each of us in the person of Jesus Christ, that we can know the truth because it has been revealed in its fulness, and that the activity of our life and our studies has an ultimate purpose, which is union with Christ. Monastic humanism is reading literature with the purpose of revealing God's providential grace within it, making us more aware of our humanity as well as the divine source of our humanity, thereby drawing our hearts closer to God and our salvation. The "Benedictine life shows that grammar [or literature] can—in no insignificant sense—lead to God."[10] In this way, monastic learning is *sapiential* instead of *sciential*—it is concerned with the wisdom of the heart, as opposed to analytical knowledge of the mind. Monastic humanism is fundamentally an education in *communion,* in Incarnation, and in love.

The Portsmouth Institute offers such encounters with monastic humanism to students, teachers, and lifelong learners in a spirit of intellectual and contemplative retreat.

In the Portsmouth Institute's PIETAS Summer Seminar, Catholic teachers from across the country gather for an encounter with literature, theology, and philosophy. By studying literature from Augustine to Dante to Flannery O'Connor, teachers encounter a form of Incarnational study that seeks Christ in all things, including the word in forms both sacred and profane. They experience for themselves the transformational power of literature, and by doing so, are able to offer such an experience to their own students. It is essential that Catholic educators encounter monastic humanism in order to experience firsthand the transformative power of literature. By doing so, we encourage schools to claim their Benedictine heritage as their own, offering students intellectual growth not only in critical thinking and analysis, but in poetry and wonder.

In the Portsmouth Institute's Oxford Summer Programme, high school students from Portsmouth Abbey School and Saint Louis Priory School encounter the poetic life in the "city of dreaming spires." By studying Shakespeare, Newman, Hopkins, Chesterton, Tolkien, and Lewis; participating in monastic liturgies and *lectio divina*; and wandering through the medieval streets and country landscapes, students immerse themselves in wonder, imagination and devotion. The Oxford Summer Programme complements formal curricular programs such as Portsmouth Abbey School's Humanities Program, which is in many ways inspired by Newman's and Leclercq's vision of monastic education.

In our colloquia and conferences for lifelong learners, guests are similarly invited into an intellectual, spiritual and moral encounter with truth, beauty, and goodness. Through the spoken word, prayer and contemplation, private reading of literature, and hospitality among fellow attendees, guests participate in the activity of monastic humanism.

Lectio Divina and the Poetic Life

The monastic practice of *lectio divina*, or divine reading, is a prayerful reading of Scripture, wherein the reader listens to the Logos, the Divine Word, speaking directly to him or her. As opposed to reading to analyze, *lectio divina* is fundamentally poetic in that it is "the cultivation of grammar, the art of reading, which is the active process of interacting with the world, so as to read things as they are, and to see our place in the story. In the widest as well as the nearest sense, Benedictine *lectio* is the beginning of the encounter with the Gospel, the completed story at the heart of the universe, written in the language of the Logos, and which can be read in the sacred Name of God, YHWH, 'I am that I am.'"[11] Little wonder, then, that Pope Benedict XVI said that "if [lectio divina] is effectively promoted, this practice will bring to the Church—I am convinced of it—a new spiritual springtime."[12]

At the heart of *lectio* is the desire for friendship *with* Christ and friendship *in* Christ. Those joined together in the communal act of reading Scripture draw closer to Christ and to one another. *Lectio* forms the heart of the reader, allowing her to open herself up to God speaking to her in her own life. Obedience—the second monastic vow—comes from the Latin *obedire,* to listen. In *lectio,* the reader listens to God speaking to him or her through Scripture, and responds by obeying His voice. *Lectio* forms the reader into a person who is receptive to hearing divine wisdom. Such a person is thus able to be transformed (*conversatio morum*) and to transform his or her community.

The Portsmouth Institute thus reserves a special place in its activities for *lectio divina.* It also supports the practice of lectio as it occurs in the context of Portsmouth Abbey and Saint Louis Priory schools. In these schools and at others in the English Benedictine Congregation, groups of friends bound by Scripture—groups of students, faculty, monks, and parents—practice *lectio divina* together. The practice of *lectio divina* in these schools and in the Portsmouth Institute is a fruit of a friendship with the Manquehue Apostolic Movement, a lay Benedictine movement in Santiago, Chile, which is devoted to sharing the practice of *lectio divina.*

Liturgy and Poetry

The intellectual, moral, and spiritual activities of a Benedictine education—its humanistic studies and its *lectio divina*—combine in the liturgy. The poetic disposition which Newman attributes to the Benedictine finds its most meaningful expression in the monastic liturgies: the Divine Office—the *opus Dei* of the monk—and Holy Mass. Thus, the liturgy is at the heart of all Portsmouth Institute activities, a reality befitting a Benedictine center for the intellectual and contemplative life. For, as Pope Benedict XVI observes,

> The saying from the Rule of St. Benedict "Nothing is to be preferred to the liturgy" (43, 3) applies specifically to monasticism, but as a way of ordering priorities it is true also for the life of the Church and of every individual, for each in his own way. It may be useful here to recall that in the word "orthodoxy," the second half, "-doxa," does not mean idea but, rather, "glory": it is not a matter of the right "idea" about God; rather, it is a matter of the right way of glorifying him, of responding to him. For that if the fundamental question of the man who begins to understand himself correctly: how must I encounter God? Thus, learning the right way of worshipping—orthodoxy—is the gift par excellence that is given to us by the faith.[13]

In the sacred liturgies, including the Divine Office and Holy Mass, the community—students, teachers, lay men and women, clergy, and religious—do what human beings are created to do: they worship God in community. In the Mass, the Divine Office, and liturgies of the Church, the community declares its purpose.

As Leclercq notes in his chapter on the "Poem of the Liturgy," the literary pursuits of the monks were always and everywhere illuminated by "the light of the liturgy":

> It is, to begin with, the general atmosphere this literature breathed, the atmosphere of Christian optimism, of faith in the redemption, which makes Christ's victory a constant and personal cause for hope. If each author, each reader, in a word each monk, believes he can attain to a certain experience of God, it is because he knows that this union between himself and the Lord is realized primarily in the mystery of the liturgy.... Ecclesiology and eschatology unite, consequently, as the two dominating themes of a literature born in the atmosphere of the liturgy.[14]

Joined together in a communion of love, the community rejoices in the love of Christ. All learning, all communal bonds, all moral development, and all spiritual purpose achieve their perfection and completion in the liturgy. From the liturgy flows meaning, informing the work of the Portsmouth Institute—its intellectual activities, its hospitality, its celebrations and its rituals—with their ultimate purpose: the love of God and neighbor. All Portsmouth Institute experiences offer these moments for liturgical prayer. The monastic *horarium* dictates the flow of the day, allowing space and time for celebration of the Divine Office and Holy Mass. In addition to encounters with the monastic liturgy, the Portsmouth institute promotes the study of liturgy and its central place in the Christian life. The poetic disposition is thus formed in liturgy.

* * *

In his *Rule*, St. Benedict describes the monastery as a *schola servitii dominici*, a school of the Lord's service. Since *schola* is the Latin term not simply for school but for leisure, we may say that a Benedictine monastery is a place of leisure in service to Christ.

The Portsmouth Institute, as an extension of two monastic communities at Portsmouth Abbey and Saint Louis Abbey, is thus a place of leisure for students, teachers, and lifelong learners. Like the cloister itself, the Portsmouth Institute builds communities of charity, bonding participants together in a shared "love of learning and desire for God." And it is a place where one might grow in contemplation and poetic perception, where through the practices of monastic humanism, liturgy, and *lectio divina*, one can learn to see the presence of God's grace in our world and in our lives. For as the dying priest says at the conclusion of George Bernanos's *A Diary of the Country Priest*: "grace is everywhere."[15] We just need the eyes to see it.

Christopher Fisher
Feast of Saints John Fisher and Thomas More
Portsmouth Abbey, Rhode Island

Notes for the Preface

1. Josef Pieper, *Leisure, the Basis of Culture*, trans. Alexander Dru (San Francisco, CA: Ignatius Press, 2009), p. 19.
2. John Henry Newman, "The Mission of Saint Benedict," in *A Benedictine Education: The Mission of Saint Benedict & The Benedictine Schools*, ed. Christopher Fisher (Providence, RI: Cluny Media, 2020), p. 20.
3. André Gushurst-Moore, *Glory in All Things: Saint Benedict & Catholic Education Today* (Brooklyn, NY: Angelico Press, 2020), p. 74.
4. Pieper, *Leisure*, p. 47.
5. For a fuller treatment of the role of Benedictine principles in Catholic education, see Gushurst-Moore, *Glory in All Things*.
6. Worth Abbey is a member of the English Benedictine Congregation, as are Portsmouth Abbey and Saint Louis Abbey. The English Benedictine Congregation is the oldest continuously operating Benedictine congregation in the world, erected by the Holy See in 1216, and includes monastic houses for men and women in the United Kingdom, the United States, Peru, and Zimbabwe.
7. Gushurst-Moore, *Glory in All Things*, p. 34.
8. Jean Leclercq, *The Love of Learning and the Desire for God: A Study of Monastic Culture* (New York: Fordham University Press, 2017), p. 40.
9. Leclercq, *Love of Learning and the Desire for God*, p. 133.
10. Gushurst-Moore, *Glory in All Things*, p. 16.
11. Ibid.
12. Pope Benedict XVI, Address, "To Participants in the International Congress for the 40th Anniversary of the Dogmatic Constitution on Divine Revelation *Dei Verbum*," September 16, 2005, https://w2.vatican.va/content/benedict-xvi/en/speeches/2005/september/documents/hf_ben-xvi_spe_20050916_40-dei-verbum.html.
13. Pope Benedict XVI, *Theology of the Liturgy: The Sacramental Foundation of Christian Existence*, ed. Michael J. Miller, trans. John Saward and Kenneth Baker (San Francisco, CA: Ignatius Press, 2014), p. xv.
14. Leclercq, *Love of Learning and the Desire for God*, p. 247.
15. Georges Bernanos, *The Diary of a Country Priest*, trans. Pamela Morris (New York: Carroll & Graf, 1987), p. 298.

INTRODUCTION

The Benedictine Charism as Poetry: Sacramental Living that Sows the Seeds of Order

WHAT DID John Henry Newman mean when he wrote in his essay "The Mission of St. Benedict" that the discriminating badge of the Benedictines is poetry? By saying that the Benedictine charism was poetry, Newman does not mean that Benedictines spent all day writing poems.

St. Benedict did not found a religious order aimed purely at mystical knowledge—experiences of God that remain in the soul, and tend towards silence. In contrast to monks who fled the world to encounter God in solitude, the *Rule* of St. Benedict was written to guide communities in living elemental aspects of Christianity—such as shared meals, shared prayer, and shared work. Life in common is the Benedictine monastic path toward God.

As the philosopher Jacques Maritain writes, "poetic experience is concerned with the created world and the enigmatic and innumerable relations of beings with each other."[1] Poetic knowledge expresses itself in work through a dynamic process: "Poetic experience is from the very start oriented toward expression, and terminates in a word uttered, or a work produced; while mystical experience tends towards silence."[2]

Poetic knowledge is therefore communication between the soul and the world, as

> the soul is known in the experience of the world and the world is known in the experience of the soul...In poetic intuition

> objective reality and subjectivity, the world and the whole of the soul, coexist inseparably. At that moment sense and sensation are brought back to the heart, blood to the spirit, passion to intuition. And through the vital and nonconceptual actuation of the intellect all the powers of the soul are also actuated in their roots.[3]

In Newman's words, the gift of the Benedictines is a way of being in the world that "lets each work, each occurrence stand by itself—which acts towards each as it comes before it, without a thought of anything else."[4] Newman even calls this approach to life a "mortification of reason,"[5] but that is not because St. Benedict and his many followers devalue scientific or conceptual knowledge reached through reason.

Rather, at times, our tendency to analyze, measure, and manipulate needs to be forgone in order to return to a childlike, simple state of perceiving reality that opens up to a sacramental way of living—seeing in visible things the invisible grace of God. The Benedictine vision reminds us that to see the totality of things and to live a contemplative life in the ordinary work of manual labor and repetitive daily routines requires an attentiveness to the present moment and commitment to particular people and places. Being present to all of reality—without having to always conceptualize our experience of analyze things scientifically—is a way of encountering God intimately and simply, like a child who wonders at the beauty of each flower and rejoices at every bird in the sky.

By calling the Benedictine way a simple, almost childlike way of living, by no means was Newman discarding the importance of Benedictine contributions to science (in particular through agriculture), as well as letters (for example, St. Bede the Venerable, the English historian and Gospel translator). Indeed, the Benedictines have plenty of cause to boast of their great saints who exemplified holiness, such as Saint Anselm or Saint Hildegard, both of whom are Doctors of the Church.

Newman contrasts the Benedictine gift of poetic living to the noble, but distinct, mission of other orders in the church that sought to be apologists for the faith, teachers in the pulpit, professors in the chairs of universities, and rulers of the church. The Benedictine way counteracts the miseries of life with beauty. Benedictines model how to have an open ear listening to God and a heart ready to receive the truth.

Newman's summary of the Benedictine way of life from his essay on the Benedictine Schools summarizes beautifully the particular gifts of the Benedictines: simplicity, commitment to place, routine, hospitality, and seeing the totality of reality. Benedictines see the sparkling of divine creation in every living organism, from the sky that covers all of creation to the microbes of the soil. As Newman writes:

> The one object, immediate as well as ultimate, of Benedictine life, as history presents it to us, was to live in purity and to die in peace. The monk proposed to himself no great or systematic work, beyond that of saving his soul. What he did more than this was the accident of the hour, spontaneous acts of piety, the sparks of mercy or beneficence, struck off in the heat, as it were, of his solemn religious toil, and done and over almost as soon as they began to be. If today he cut down a tree, or relieved the famishing, or visited the sick, or taught the ignorant, or transcribed a page of Scripture, this was a good in itself, though nothing was added to it tomorrow. He cared little for knowledge, even theological, or for success, even though it was religious. It is the character of such a man to be contented, resigned, patient, and incurious; to create or originate nothing; to live by tradition. He does not analyze, he marvels; his intellect attempts no comprehension of this multiform world, but on the contrary, it is hemmed in, and shut up within it. It recognizes but one cause in nature and in human affairs, and that is the First and Supreme; and why things happen day by day in this way, and not in that, it refers immediately to His will. It loves the country, because it is His work.[6]

What kind of education did St. Benedict himself envision? In reflecting on the schools started by St. Benedict, Newman points out that St. Benedict's schools were focused on the young. What is today known as high school or higher education hardly existed in the tumultuous times in which St. Benedict lived. Academies of higher learning were for the elite. The Benedictine way of life and Benedictine education was for the ordinary Christian, the person in adult life who would engage in manual labor.

In the twenty-first century, even pre-kindergarten instructing has often shifted to college readiness, as if what matters to toddlers are the skills that will help gain admission to a college where the nearly exclusive focus on scientific and conceptual mode of living shuts out the poetic way of living that allows us to integrate our intellect with our soul. By contrast, St. Benedict followed a kind of liberal arts model of education (teaching the subjects of the *trivium* and *quadrivium*) for the young, including the Greek and Roman classics and instruction in Scripture in his grammar schools for the young. Certainly the Benedictine poetic way of living and educating—a simple, joyful emphasis on teaching languages, learning about nature, and studying the history and stories of great civilizations of the past—mingled easily with the desire to nurture a child's wonder at the marvels of nature or history and a child's eager intuition to find symbolic meaning in all things.

All levels of education would benefit from nurturing the creative intuition that is the engine and fruit of poetic knowledge. The importance of the Benedictine charism is evident in its power to elevate the *being mode* of life and shut down (or at least slow) the *analytical mode* of life aimed at investigating means and ends, predicting outcomes, or examining premises and conclusions. Not educating the inner core of our soul from which all other capacities emanate—including our reason—leads (and has led) to dissonance, dispersion, and the fragmentation that results from a lack of direction for our drives, passions and instincts.

Pondering the Benedictine charism of poetry can positively shape the Church, schools, and culture today in (at least) three concrete ways.

First, reading and writing poems is one way to capture the complexity of objective reality and to express our own emotions—which confronts the challenge in today's culture in that many people suffer from a crisis of attention and a lack of imagination. Catholic poet and former director of the National Endowment of the Arts Dana Gioia has argued that the study of poems and the writing of poetry needs to be recovered.[7] Writing and memorizing poetry used to be an activity of common people, not academics in universities. Studying great works of literature like the *Divine Comedy* matter because stories shape our imagination and guide us when making important decisions about our lives. Great literature opens our hearts to respond to the attraction of the good. Literature lights the fire of our desire for a blessed life.

Second, reviving poetic knowledge is crucial to the advancement of scientific knowledge. Marveling at the beauty of the world—whether that be the beauty of soil or the beauty of the many mathematical calculations that make a building structurally sound—is not secondary to technological advancement, but primary. As Catholic professor of mathematics and physics Carlo Lancellotti has argued, scientific advancement is driven not primarily by technological innovation but by the creative intellect that seeks to know *why* things work, not just *how* they work. Seeking to understand why things work as they do, as Lancellotti puts it, "the ultimate motivation that has led to the triumphs of modern science is essentially aesthetic."[8] The ability to marvel at the world needs to be cultivated because it is the seed of the sustained human effort to know why things work the way they do. Math, science and engineering education that never takes students out of the controlled environment of the laboratory too often squashes the very human creativity that not only drives new scientific discoveries but also guides their application towards ends that promote human flourishing.[9]

Third, reviving poetic knowledge is crucial to liturgical renewal because poetic ways of everyday living are essential for educating the imagination and intuition as they are engaged in the liturgy. Timothy O'Malley, director of the Center for Liturgy at the University of Notre

Dame, has argued that within the Catholic Church, many do not appreciate poetic forms of knowledge, not even in the liturgy.[10] Is it surprising, then, that the failure to educate our aesthetic sensibilities leads to poorly done liturgy that is sense-numbing and unimaginative? Too many parishioners are unable to sufficiently focus their attention to enter into the contemplative space of beautiful liturgy. Aesthetic education in art, literature, and science can enliven liturgical experiences of the faithful and motivate clergy to celebrate the Mass with beauty. Liturgy well done is itself a form of aesthetic education.

A poetic, sacramental way of living and educating the young can never fully be conceptualized. It has to be lived *and* to be experienced in order to be known more fully.

In the chapter on humility from his *Rule*, St. Benedict discusses the image of the ladder (in Latin, *scala*). Benedict instructs readers that

> if we wish to reach the very highest point of humility and to arrive speedily at that heavenly exaltation to which ascent is made through the humility of this present life, we must by our ascending actions erect the ladder Jacob saw in his dream, on which Angels appeared to him descending and ascending. By that descent and ascent we must surely understand nothing else than this, that we descend by self-exaltation and ascend by humility. And the ladder thus set up is our life in the world, which the Lord raises up to heaven if our heart is humbled. For we call our body and soul the sides of the ladder, and into these sides our divine vocation has inserted the different steps of humility and discipline we must climb.

This image of the ladder inspired the name for the Scala Foundation, a non-profit initiative that aims to revive classical liberal arts education, of which I am the Founder. Scala aims to link educational philosophy to practices that educate the whole person, including integrating the search for truth with experiences of beauty. Through Scala, I have led student groups to Benedictine monasteries such as the Abbey of Regina Laudis and Portsmouth Abbey in the United States, as well as Ampleforth Abbey in the United Kingdom. Each trip combined time dedicated to forming the mind with time dedicated to immersing ourselves in the Benedictine routine of the liturgy of the hours, shared meals, manual labor and playing games. Reading Newman's *Idea of a University*, Jacques Maritain's *Education at the Crossroads*, and Luigi Giussani's *Risk of Education* while at a Benedictine monastery allowed us to immediately put into practice the ideas of some of the greatest Catholic thinkers of the nineteenth and twentieth centuries. We deepened our knowledge of the texts we read because we lived what we reading.

These trips afforded us a slice of the original beatific vision because we lived an integrated life where everything we do, think, and feel comes from the soul, the place of the direct encounter with God, and emanates out into a sacramental way of living every moment of the day. Whether we were in the classroom, the strawberry field, the chapel, or the dining hall, the Benedictine communities created a sense of harmony with nature that produced a deep inner resonance so deeply desired by today's students and their instructors.[11] The unity of all activity, interior and exterior, generates peace and gently guides students into a state of productive leisure where all of our being and doing points towards the sacred.

Anyone who has tried to follow the Benedictine routine knows that the lifestyle is too demanding and the education too holistic to be conceived of as a mystical floating above earthly realities or a retreat from the world's conflicts. The simple, daily routines of manual labor, prayer, study and a shared way of life, along with a spirit of attention to the divine in the liturgy of the hours and *lectio divina* of both Scripture and nature captivates students' hearts and prunes their minds. Poetic knowledge can guide scientific and conceptual forms of reason to be used more in harmony with our souls.

As Pope Benedict XVI notes in his address *Quaerere Deum,* the Benedictines transformed European culture slowly, but not by through a political strategy. Little wonder that he chose the name of Benedict for his papacy, as he argues that the Benedictine monastic tradition that reveres the word of God and all of creation is both "what gave Europe's culture its foundation—*the search for God and the readiness to listen to him*—[and] remains today the basis of any genuine culture."[12] The Benedictine influence on society is the result of its producing resonance and harmony in the soul which in turn sow the seeds of life-giving culture. In the past, the Benedictine commitment to preserving ideas of the past, living in community, and preserving the land to be bountiful brought order out of chaos. It surely can do so again.

The curricular fragmentation in schools at all levels and the interior dissonance of students are not unrelated. As a result, the Benedictine charism is being studied, experienced, and applied by educators who, like myself, will not become monks or nuns, but are looking for a way to purify today's educational systems. Educators need positive examples that can be drawn from the Benedictines in order to build on the good of today's culture and of current school structure. It is important to critique the obsessively achievement-oriented, narrowly pragmatic, and ultimately soul-draining forms of education, while also being inspired by models that help educators swim against the stream where an understanding of the Benedictine (and Catholic) vision is missing but its influence is nevertheless felt.

Benedictine communities are an embodiment of a tradition that has preserved a living expression of a unified, simple, yet also glorious and joyful way of Christian life and education. Monks and nuns working the land and running schools who welcome student groups for agricultural work, retreats and seminars can be hospitable guides to people from all faith backgrounds and types of schools. Benedictines offer an ancient tradition of daily living and a method of education that is also ever new and capable of bringing interior and external order to our culture and our schools.

Margarita A. Mooney, Ph.D.
Feast of Saint Matthias the Apostle
The Scala Foundation, New Jersey

Notes for the Introduction

1. Jacques Maritain, *Creative Intuition in Art and Poetry* (Providence, RI: Cluny Media, 2018), p. 216.
2. Ibid., p. 216.
3. Ibid., p. 113.
4. John Henry Newman, "The Mission of Saint Benedict," in *A Benedictine Education: The Mission of Saint Benedict & The Benedictine Schools*, ed. Christopher Fisher (Providence, RI: Cluny Media, 2020), p. 11.
5. Ibid.
6. Ibid., p. 74.
7. See Dana Gioia, *The Catholic Writer Today: And Other Essays* (Belmont, NC: Wiseblood Books, 2019).
8. Carlo Lancellotti, "The Redemption of Scientific Reason," *Church Life Journal*, November 18, 2019, at https://churchlifejournal.nd.edu/articles/the-redemption-of-scientific-reason/.
9. Margarita A. Mooney, "Engineering, Beauty and a Longing for the Infinite," *Scientific American*, October 22, 2019, at https://blogs.scientificamerican.com/observations/engineering-beauty-and-a-longing-for-the-infinite/.
10. Timothy P. O'Malley, "A Guide Through the Poetic Theology of the Triduum," *Church Life Journal*, April 10, 2020, at https://churchlifejournal.nd.edu/articles/the-poetic-theology-of-the-triduum/.
11. Margarita A. Mooney, "The Love of Learning and the Lay Desire for God," *Church Life Journal*, November 6, 2019, at https://churchlifejournal.nd.edu/articles/the-love-of-learning-and-the-lay-desire-for-god/.
12. Pope Benedict XVI, "*Quaerere Deum*," in *A Reason Open to God: On Universities, Education and Culture*, ed. Steven J. Brown (Washington, DC: Catholic University of America Press, 2013), p. 236.

First Essay

The Mission of Saint Benedict

❊ ❊ ❊

FIRST ESSAY

The Mission of St. Benedict

From the ATLANTIS *of* JANUARY 1858

§1.

AS THE physical universe is sustained and carried on in dependence on certain centres of power and laws of operation, so the course of the social and political world, and of that great religious organization called the Catholic Church, is found to proceed for the most part from the presence or action of definite persons, places, events, and institutions, as the visible cause of the whole. There has been but one Judea, one Greece, one Rome; one Homer, one Cicero; one Caesar, one Constantine, one Charlemagne. And so, as regards Revelation, there has been one St. John the Divine, one Doctor of the Nations. Dogma runs along the line of Athanasius, Augustine, Thomas. The conversion of the heathen is ascribed, after the Apostles, to champions of the truth so few, that we may almost count them, such as Martin, Patrick, Augustine, Boniface. Then there is St. Antony, the father of monachism; St. Jerome, the interpreter of Scripture; St. Chrysostom, the great preacher.

Education follows the same law: it has its history in Christianity, and its doctors or masters in that history. It has had three periods: the ancient, the medieval, and the modern; and there are three Religious Orders in those periods respectively, which succeed, one the other, on its public stage, and represent the teaching given by the Catholic Church during the time of their ascendancy. The first period is that long series of centuries, during which society was breaking or had broken up, and then slowly attempted its own re-construction; the second may be called the period of re-construction; and the third dates from the Reformation, when that peculiar movement of mind commenced, the issue of which is still to come. Now, St. Benedict has had the training of the ancient intellect, St. Dominic of the medieval; and St. Ignatius of the modern. And in saying this, I am in no degree disrespectful to the Augustinians, Carmelites, Franciscans, and other great religious families, which might be named, or to the holy Patriarchs who founded them; for I am not reviewing the whole history of Christianity, but selecting a particular aspect of it.

Perhaps as much as this will be granted to me without great hesitation. Next, I proceed to contrast these three great masters of Christian teaching with each other. To St. Benedict, then, who may fairly be taken to represent the various families of monks before his time and those which sprang from him (for they are all pretty much of one school), to this great Saint let me assign, for his discriminating badge, the element of Poetry; to St. Dominic, the Scientific element; and to St. Ignatius, the Practical.

These characteristics, which belong respectively to the schools of the three great Teachers, grow out of the circumstances under which they respectively entered upon their work. Benedict, entrusted with his mission almost as a boy, infused into it the romance and simplicity of boyhood. Dominic, a man of forty-five, a graduate in theology, a priest and a Canon, brought with him into religion that maturity and completeness of learning which he had acquired in the schools. Ignatius, a man of the world before his conversion, transmitted as a legacy to his disciples that knowledge of mankind which cannot be learned in cloisters. And thus the three several Orders were (so to say), the births of Poetry, of Science, and Practical Sense.

And here another coincidence suggests itself. I have been giving these three attributes to the three Patriarchs whom I have specified, severally, from a *bonâ-fide* regard to their history, and without at all having any theory of philosophy in my eye. But after having so described them, it certainly did strike me that I had unintentionally been illustrating a somewhat popular notion of the day, the like of which is attributed to authors with whom I have as little sympathy as with any persons who can be named. According to these speculators, the life, whether of a race or of an individual of the great human family, is divided into three stages, each of which has its own ruling principle and characteristic. The youth makes his start in life, with "*hope* at the prow, and *fancy* at the helm"; he has nothing else but these to impel or direct him; he has not lived long enough to exercise his reason, or to gather in a store of facts; and, because he cannot do otherwise, he dwells in a world which he has created. He begins with illusions. Next, when at length he looks about for some surer footing than imagination gives him, he may have recourse to reason, or he may have recourse to facts; now facts are external to him, but his reason is his own: of the two, then, it is easier for him to exercise his reason than to ascertain facts. Accordingly, his first mental revolution, when he discards the life of aspiration and affection which has disappointed him, and the dreams of which he has been the sport and victim, is to embrace a life of logic: this, then, is his second stage—the metaphysical. He acts now on a plan, thinks by system, is cautious about his middle terms, and trusts nothing but what takes a scientific form. His third stage is when he has made full trial of life; when he has found his theories break down under the weight of facts, and experience falsify his most promising calculations. Then the old man recognizes at length, that what he can taste, touch, and handle, is trustworthy, and nothing beyond it. Thus he runs through his three periods of Imagination, Reason, and Sense; and then he comes to an end, and is not—a most impotent and melancholy conclusion.

Undoubtedly a Catholic has no sympathy in so heartless a view of life, and yet it seems to square with what I have been saying of the three great Patriarchs of Christian teaching. And certainly there is a truth in it, which gives it its plausibility. However, I am not concerned here to do more than to put my finger on the point at which I should diverge from it, both in what I have been saying and what I must say concerning them. It is true then, that history, as viewed in these three Saints, is, somewhat after the manner of the theory I have mentioned, a progress from poetry through science to practical sense or prudence; but then this important *proviso* has to be borne in mind at the same time, that what the Catholic Church once has had, she never has lost. She has never wept over, or been angry with, time gone and over. Instead of passing from one stage of life to another, she has carried her youth and middle age along with her, on to her latest time. She has not changed possessions, but accumulated them, and has brought out of her treasure-house, according to the occasion, things new and old. She did not lose Benedict by finding Dominic; and she has still both Benedict and Dominic at home, though she has become the mother of Ignatius. Imagination, Science, Prudence, all are good, and she has them all. Things incompatible in nature, coexist in her; her prose is poetical on the one hand, and philosophical on the other.

Coming now to the historical proof of the contrast I have been instituting, I am sanguine in thinking that one branch of it is already allowed by the consent of the world, and is undeniable. By common consent, the palm of religious Prudence, in the Aristotelic sense of that comprehensive word, belongs to the School of Religion of which St. Ignatius is the Founder. That great Society is the classical seat and fountain (that is, in religious thought and the conduct of life, for of ecclesiastical politics I speak not), the school and pattern of discretion, practical sense, and wise government. Sublimer conceptions or more profound speculations may have been created or elaborated elsewhere; but, whether we consider the illustrious Body in its own constitution, or in its rules for instruction and direction, we see that it is its very genius to prefer this most excellent prudence to every other gift, and to think little both of poetry and of science, unless they happen to be useful. It is true that, in the long catalogue of its members, there are to be found the names of the most consummate theologians, and of scholars the most elegant and accomplished; but we are speaking here, not of individuals, but of the body itself. It is plain that the body is not over-jealous about its theological traditions, or it certainly would not suffer Suarez to controvert with Molina, Viva with Vasquez, Passaglia with Petavius, and Faure with Suarez, de Lugo, and Valentia. In this intellectual freedom its members justly glory; inasmuch as they have set their affections, not on the opinions of the Schools, but on the souls of men. And it is the same charitable motive which makes them give up the poetry of life, the poetry of ceremonies—of the cowl, the cloister, and the choir—content with the most prosaic architecture, if it be but convenient, and the most prosaic neighbourhood, if it be but populous. I need not then dwell longer on this wonderful Religion, but may confine the remarks which are to follow to the two Religions which historically preceded it—the Benedictine and the Dominican.[1]

One preliminary more, suggested by a purely fanciful analogy: As there are three great Patriarchs on the high road and public thoroughfare of Christian Education, so there were three chief Patriarchs in the first age of the chosen people. Putting aside Noe and Melchisedec, and Joseph and his brethren, we recognize three venerable fathers, Abraham, Isaac, and Jacob, and what are their characteristics? Abraham, the father of many nations; Isaac, the intellectual, living in solitary simplicity, and in loving contemplation; and Jacob, the persecuted and helpless, visited by marvellous providences, driven from place to place, set down and taken up again, ill-treated by those who were his debtors, suspected because of his sagacity, and betrayed by his eager faith, yet carried on and triumphing amid all troubles by means of his most faithful and powerful guardian-archangel.

§2.

St. Benedict, then, like the great Hebrew Patriarch, was the "Father of many nations." He has been styled "the Patriarch of the West," a title which there are many reasons for ascribing to him. Not only was he the first to establish a perpetual Order of Regulars in Western Christendom; not only, as coming first, has he had an ampler course of centuries for the multiplication of his children; but his Rule, as that of St. Basil in the East, is the normal rule of the first age of the Church, and was in time generally received even in communities which in no sense owed their origin to him. Moreover, out of his Order rose, in process of time, various new monastic families, which have established themselves as independent institutions, and are able in their turn to boast of the number of their houses, and the sanctity and historical celebrity of their members. He is the representative of Latin monachism for the long extent of six centuries, while monachism was one; and even when at length varieties arose, and distinct titles were given to them, the change grew out of him; not the act of strangers who were his rivals, but of his own children, who did but make a new beginning in all devotion and loyalty to him. He died in the early half of the sixth century; at the beginning of the tenth rose from among his French monasteries the famous Congregation of Cluni, illustrated by St. Majolus, St. Odilo, Peter the Venerable, and other considerable personages, among whom is Hildebrand, afterwards Pope Gregory the Seventh. Then came, in long succession, the Orders or Congregations of Camaldoli under St. Romuald, of Vallombrosa, of Citeaux, to which St. Bernard has given his name, of Monte Vergine, of Fontvrault; those of England, Spain, and Flanders; the Silvestrines, the Celestines, the Olivetans, the Humiliati, besides a multitude of institutes for women, as the Gilbertines and the Oblates of St. Frances, and then at length, to mention no others, the Congregation of St. Maur in modern times, so well known for its biblical, patristical, and historical works, and for its learned members, Montfaucon, Mabillon, and their companions. The panegyrists of this illustrious Order are accustomed to claim for it in all its branches as many as 37,000 houses, and, besides, 30 Popes, 200 Cardinals, 4 Emperors, 46 Kings, 51 Queens, 1,406 Princes, 1,600 Archbishops, 600 Bishops, 2,400 Nobles, and 15,000 Abbots and learned men.[2]

Nor are the religious bodies which sprang from St. Benedict the full measure of what he has accomplished—as has been already observed. His Rule gradually made its way into those various monasteries which were of an earlier or of an independent foundation. It first coalesced with, and then supplanted, the Irish Rule of St. Columban in France, and the still older institutes which had been brought from the East by St. Athanasius, St. Eusebius, and St. Martin. At the beginning of the ninth century it was formally adopted throughout the dominions of Charlemagne. Pure, or with some admixture, it was brought by St. Augustine to England; and that admixture, if it existed, was gradually eliminated by St. Wilfrid, St. Dunstan, and Lanfranc, till at length it was received, with the name and obedience of St. Benedict, in all the Cathedral monasteries[3] (to mention no others), excepting Carlisle. Nor did it cost such regular bodies any very great effort to make the change, even when historically most separate from St. Benedict; for the Saint had taken up for the most part what he found, and his Rule was but the expression of the genius of monachism in those first times of the Church, with a more exact adaptation to their needs than could elsewhere be met with.

So uniform indeed had been the monastic idea before his time, and so little stress had been laid by individual communities on their respective peculiarities, that religious men passed at pleasure from one body to another.[4] St. Benedict provides in his Rule for the case of strangers coming to one of his houses, and wishing to remain there. If such a one came from any monastery with which the monks had existing relations, then he was not to be received without letters from his Abbot; but, in the instance of "a foreign monk from distant parts," who wished to dwell with them as a guest, and was content with their ways, and conformed himself to them, and was not troublesome, "should he in the event wish to stay for good," says St. Benedict, "let him not be refused; for there has been room to make trial of him, during the time that hospitality has been shown to him: nay, let him even be invited to stay, that others may gain a lesson from his example; for in every place we are servants of one Lord and soldiers of one King."[5]

§3.

THE UNITY of idea, which, as these words imply, is to be found in all monks in every part of Christendom, may be described as a unity of object, of state, and of occupation. Monachism was one and the same everywhere, because it was a reaction from that secular life, which has everywhere the same structure and the same characteristics. And, since that secular life contained in it many objects, many states, and many occupations, here was a special reason, as a matter of principle, why the reaction from it should bear the badge of unity, and should be in outward appearance one and the same everywhere. Moreover, since that same secular life was, when monachism arose, more than ordinarily marked by variety, perturbation and confusion, it seemed on that very account to justify emphatically a rising and revolt against itself, and a recurrence to some state which, unlike itself, was constant and unalterable. It was indeed an old, decayed, and moribund world, into which Christianity had been cast. The social fabric was overgrown with the corruptions of a thousand years, and was held together, not so much by any common principle, as by the strength of possession and the tenacity of custom. It was too large for public spirit, and too artificial for patriotism, and its many religions did but foster in the popular mind division and scepticism. Want of mutual confidence would lead to despondency, inactivity, and selfishness. Society was in the slow fever of consumption, which made it restless in proportion as it was feeble. It was powerful, however, to seduce and deprave; nor was there any *locus standi* from which to combat its evils; and the only way of getting on with it was to abandon principle and duty, to take things as they came, and to do as the world did. Worse than all, this encompassing, entangling system of things, was, at the time we speak of, the seat and instrument of a paganism, and then of heresies, not simply contrary, but bitterly hostile, to the Christian profession. Serious men not only had a call, but every inducement which love of life and freedom could supply, to escape from its presence and its sway.

Their one idea then, their one purpose, was to be quit of it; too long had it enthralled them. It was not a question of this or that vocation, of the better deed, of the higher state, but of life and death. In later times a variety of holy objects might present themselves for devotion to choose from, such as the care of the poor, or of the sick, or of the young, the redemption of captives, or the conversion of the barbarians; but early monachism was flight from the world, and nothing else. The troubled, jaded, weary heart, the stricken, laden conscience, sought a life free from corruption in its daily work, free from distraction in its daily worship; and it sought employments as contrary as possible to the world's employments—employments, the end of which would be in themselves, in which each day, each hour, would have its own completeness—no elaborate undertakings, no difficult aims, no anxious ventures, no uncertainties to make the heart beat, or the temples throb, no painful combination of efforts, no extended plan of operations, no multiplicity of details, no deep calculations, no sustained machinations, no suspense, no vicissitudes, no moments of crisis or catastrophe—nor again any subtle investigations, nor perplexities of proof, nor conflicts of rival intellects, to agitate, harass, depress, stimulate, weary, or intoxicate the soul.

Hitherto I have been using negatives to describe what the primitive monk was seeking; in truth monachism was, as regards the secular life and all that it implies, emphatically a negation, or, to use another word, a *mortification*; a mortification of sense, and a mortification of reason. Here a word of explanation is necessary. The monks were too good Catholics to deny that reason was a divine gift, and had too much common sense to think to do without it. What they denied themselves was the various and manifold exercises of the reason; and on this account, because such exercises were excitements. When the reason is cultivated, it at once begins to combine, to centralize, to look forward, to look back, to view things as a whole, whether for speculation or for action; it practises synthesis and analysis, it discovers, it invents. To these exercises of the intellect is opposed simplicity, which is the state of mind which does not combine, does not deal with premisses and conclusions, does not recognize means and their end, but lets each work, each place, each occurrence stand by itself—which acts towards each as it comes before it, without a thought of anything else. This simplicity is the temper of children, and it is the temper of monks. This was their mortification of the intellect; every man who lives, must live by reason, as every one must live by sense; but, as it is possible to be content with the bare necessities of animal life, so is it possible to confine ourselves to the bare ordinary use of reason, without caring to improve it or make the most of it. These monks held both sense and reason to be the gifts of heaven, but they used each of them as little as they could help, reserving their full time and their whole selves for devotion—for, if reason is better than sense, so devotion they thought to be better than either; and, as even a heathen might deny himself the innocent indulgences of sense in order to give his time to the cultivation of the reason, so did the monks give up reason, as well as sense, that they might consecrate themselves to divine meditation.

Now, then, we are able to understand how it was that the monks had a unity, and in what it consisted. It was a unity, I have said, of object, of state, and of occupation. Their object was rest and peace; their state was retirement; their occupation was some work that was simple, as opposed to intellectual, viz., prayer, fasting, meditation, study, transcription, manual labour, and other unexciting, soothing employments. Such was their institution all over the world; they had eschewed the busy mart, the craft of gain, the money-changer's bench, and the merchant's cargo. They had turned their backs upon the wrangling forum, the political assembly, and the pantechnicon of trades. They had had their last dealings with architect and habit-maker, with butcher and cook; all they wanted, all they desired, was the sweet soothing presence of earth, sky, and sea, the hospitable cave, the bright running stream, the easy gifts which mother earth, "justissima tellus," yields on very little persuasion. "The monastic institute," says the biographer of St. Maurus, "demands *Summa Quies*, the most perfect quietness"[6]; and where was quietness to be found, if not in reverting to the original condition of man, as far as the changed circumstances of our race admitted; in having no wants, of which the supply was not close at hand; in the "nil admirari"; in having neither hope nor fear of anything below; in daily prayer, daily bread, and daily work, one day being just like another, except that it was one step nearer than the day just gone to that great Day, which would swallow up all days, the day of everlasting rest.

§4.

HOWEVER, I have come into collision with a great authority, M. Guizot, and I must stop the course of my argument to make my ground good against him. M. Guizot, then, makes a distinction between monachism in its birth-place, in Egypt and Syria, and that Western institute, of which I have made St. Benedict the representative. He allows that the Orientals mortified the intellect, but he considers that Latin monachism was the seat of considerable mental activity. "The desire for retirement," he says, "for contemplation, for a marked rupture with civilized society, was the source and fundamental trait of the Eastern monks: in the West, *on the contrary*, and especially in Southern Gaul, where, at the commencement of the fifth century, the principal monasteries were founded, it was in order to live in common, *with a view to conversation* as well as to religious edification, that the first monks met. The monasteries of Lerins, of St. Victor, and many others, were especially great schools of theology, the focus of intellectual movement. It was by no means with solitude or with mortification, but with discussion and activity, that they there concerned themselves."[7] Great deference is due to an author so learned, so philosophical, so honestly desirous to set out Christianity to the best advantage; yet, I am at a loss to understand what has led him to make such a distinction between the East and West, and to assign to the Western monks an activity of intellect, and to the Eastern a love of retirement.

It is quite true that instances are sometimes to be found of monasteries in the West distinguished by much intellectual activity, but more, and more striking, instances are to be found of a like phenomenon in the East. If, then, such particular instances are to be taken as fair specimens of the state of Western monachism, they are equally fair specimens of the state of Eastern also; and the Eastern monks will be proved more intellectual than the Western, by virtue of that greater interest in doctrine and in controversy which given individuals or communities among them have exhibited. A very cursory reference to ecclesiastical history will be sufficient to show us that the fact is as I have stated it. The theological sensitiveness of the monks of Marseilles, Lerins, or Adrumetum, it seems, is to be a proof of the intellectualism generally of the West: then, why is not the greater sensitiveness of the Scythian monks at Constantinople, and of their opponents, the Acoemetae, an evidence in favour of the East? These two bodies of Religious actually came all the way from Constantinople to

Rome to denounce one another, besieging, as it were, the Holy See, and the former of them actually attempting to raise the Roman populace against the Pope, in behalf of its own theological tenet. Does not this show activity of mind? I venture to say that, for one intellectual monk in the West, a dozen might be produced in the East. The very reproach, thrown out by secular historians against Greeks in general, of over-subtlety of intellect, applies in particular, if to any men, to certain classes or certain communities of Eastern monks. These were sometimes orthodox, quite as often heretical, but inexhaustible in their argumentative resources, whether the one or the other. If Pelagius be a monk in the West, on the other hand, Nestorius and Eutyches, both heresiarchs, are both monks in the East; and Eutyches, at the time of his heresy, was an old monk into the bargain, who had been thirty years abbot of a convent, and whom age, if not sanctity, might have saved from this abnormal use of his reason. His partizans were principally monks of Egypt; and they, coming up in force to the pseudo-synod of Ephesus, in aid of a theological thesis, kicked to death the patriarch of Constantinople, and put to flight the Legate of the Pope, all in consequence of their intellectual susceptibilities. A century earlier, Arius, on starting, carried away into his heresy as many as seven hundred nuns[8]; what have the Western convents to show, in the way of controversial activity, comparable with a fact like this? I do not insist on the zealous and influential orthodoxy of the monks of Egypt, Syria, and Asia Minor in the fourth century, because it was probably nothing else but an honourable adhesion to the faith of the Church, without any serious exercise of mind; but turn to the great writers of Eastern Christendom, and consider how many of them figure at first sight as monks—Chrysostom, Basil, Gregory Nazianzen, Epiphanius, Ephrem, Amphilochius, Isidore of Pelusium, Theodore, Theodoret, perhaps Athanasius. Among the Latin writers no great names occur to me but those of Jerome and Pope Gregory; I may add Paulinus, Sulpicius, Vincent, and Cassian, but Jerome is the only learned writer among them. I have a difficulty, then, even in comprehending, not to speak of admitting, M. Guizot's assertion, a writer who does not commonly speak without a meaning or a reason.

But, after all, however the balance of intellectualism may lie between certain convents or individuals in the East and the West, such particular instances of mental activity are nothing to the purpose, when taken to measure the state of the great body of the monks; certainly not in the West, with which in this paper I am exclusively concerned. In taking an estimate of the Benedictines, we need not trouble ourselves about the state of monachism in Egypt, Syria, Asia Minor, and Constantinople, as it existed after the fourth century, when the true monastic tradition was passing from the East to the West. In the fourth century, the Eastern Monks simply follow the defined and promulgated doctrine of the Church, and in following it are guilty of no exercise of reason; their intellectualism proper, which is foreign to the genius of their institute, begins with the fifth. Taking, then, the great tradition of St. Antony, St. Pachomius, and St. Basil in the East, and then tracing it into the West by the hands of St. Athanasius, St. Martin, and their contemporaries, we shall find no historical facts but what admit of a fair explanation, consistent with the views which we have laid down above about monastic simplicity, bearing in mind always, what holds in all matters of fact, that there never was a rule without its exceptions.

§5.

EVERY RULE has its exceptions; but, further than this, when exceptions occur, they are commonly likely to be great ones. This is no paradox; illustrations of it are to be found everywhere. For instance, we may conceive a climate very fatal to children, and yet those who survive growing up to be strong men; and for a plain reason, because those alone could have passed the ordeal who had robust constitutions. Thus the Romans, so jealous of their freedom, when they resolved on the appointment of a supreme ruler for an occasion, did not do the thing by halves, but made him a Dictator. In like manner, a mere trifling occurrence, or an ordinary inward impulse, would be powerless to snap the bond which keeps the monk fast to his cell, his oratory, and his garden. Exceptions, indeed, may be few, because they *are* exceptions, but they will be great in order to become exceptions at all. It must be a serious emergence, a particular inspiration, a sovereign command, which brings the monk into political life; and he will be sure to make a great figure in it, else why should he have been torn from his cloister at all? This will account for the career of St. Gregory the Seventh or of St. Dunstan, of St. Bernard or of Abbot Suger, as far as it was political: the work they had to do was such as none could have done but a monk with his superhuman single-mindedness and his pertinacity of purpose. Again, in the case of St. Boniface, the Apostle of Germany, and in that of others of the missionaries of his age, it seems to have been a particular inspiration which carried them abroad; and it is observable after all how soon most of them settled down into the mixed character of agriculturists and pastors in their new country, and resumed the tranquil life to which they had originally devoted themselves. As to the early Greek Fathers, some of those whom we have instanced above are only *primâ facie* exceptions, as Chrysostom, who, though he lived with the monks most austerely for as many as six years, can hardly be said to have taken on himself the responsibilities of their condition, or to have simply abandoned the world. Others of them, as Basil, were scholars, philosophers, men of the world, before they were monks, and could not put off their cultivation of mind or their learning with their secular dress; and these would be the very men, in an age when such talents were scarce, who would be taken out of their retirement by superior authority, and who therefore cannot fairly be quoted as ordinary specimens of the monastic life.

Exceptio probat regulam: let us see what two Doctors of the Church, one Greek, one Latin, both rulers, both monks, say concerning the state, which they at one time enjoyed, and afterwards lost. "You tell me," says St. Basil, writing to a friend from his solitude, "that it was little for me to describe the place of my retirement, unless I mentioned also my habits and my mode of life; yet really I am ashamed to tell you how I pass night and day in this lonely nook. I am like one who is angry with the size of his vessel, as tossing overmuch, and leaves it for the boat, and is seasick and miserable still. However, what I propose to do is as follows, with the hope of tracing His steps who has said, 'If any one will come after Me, let him deny himself.' We must strive after a quiet mind. As well might the eye ascertain an object which is before it, while it roves up and down without looking steadily at it, as a mind, distracted with a thousand worldly cares, be able clearly to apprehend the truth. One who is not yoked in matrimony is harassed by rebellious impulses and hopeless attachments; he who is married is involved in his own tumult of cares: is he without children? he covets them; has he children? he has anxieties about their education. Then there is solicitude about his wife, care of his house, oversight of his servants, misfortunes in trade, differences with his neighbours, law-suits, the merchant's risks, the farmer's toil. Each day, as it comes, darkens the soul in its own way; and night after night takes up the day's anxieties, and cheats us with corresponding dreams. Now, the only way of escaping all this is separation from the whole world, so as to live without city, home, goods, society, possessions, means of life, business, engagements, secular learning, that the heart may be prepared as wax for the impress of divine teaching. Solitude is of the greatest use for this purpose, as it stills our passions, and enables reason to extirpate them. Let then a place be found such as mine, separate from intercourse with men, that the tenor of our exercises be not interrupted from without. Pious exercises nourish the soul with divine thoughts. Soothing hymns compose the mind to a cheerful and calm state. Quiet, then, as I have said, is the first step in our sanctification; the tongue purified from the gossip of the world, the eyes unexcited by fair colour or comely shape, the ear secured from the relaxation of voluptuous songs, and that especial mischief, light jesting. Thus the mind, rescued from dissipation from without, and sensible allurements, falls back upon itself, and thence ascends to the contemplation of God."[9] It is quite clear that at least St. Basil took the same view of the monastic state as I have done.

So much for the East in the fourth century; now for the West in the seventh. "One day," says St. Gregory, after he had been constrained, against his own wish, to leave his cloister for the government of the Universal Church, "one day, when I was oppressed with the excessive trouble of secular affairs, I sought a retired place, friendly to grief, where whatever displeased me in my occupations might show itself, and all that was wont to inflict pain might be seen at one view." While he was in this retreat, his "most dear son, Peter," with whom, ever since the latter was a youth, he had been intimate, surprised him, and he opened his grief to him. "My sad mind," he said, "labouring under the soreness of its engagements, remembers how it went with me formerly in this monastery, how all perishable things were beneath it, how it rose above all that was transitory, and, though still in the flesh, went out in contemplation beyond that prison, so that it even loved death, which is commonly thought a punishment, as the gate of life and the reward of labour. But now, in consequence of the pastoral charge, it undergoes the busy work of secular men, and for that fair beauty of its quiet, is dishonoured with the dust of the earth. And often dissipating itself in outward things, to serve the many, even when it seeks what is inward, it comes home indeed, but is no longer what it used to be."[10] Here is the very same view of the monastic state at Rome which St. Basil had in Pontus, viz., retirement and repose. There have been great Religious Orders since, whose atmosphere has been conflict, and who have thriven in smiting or in being smitten. It has been their high calling; it has been their peculiar meritorious service; but, as for the Benedictine, the very air he breathes is peace.

§6.

I HAVE now said enough both to explain and to vindicate the biographer of St. Maurus, when he says that the object, and life, and reward of the ancient monachism was *summa quies*—the absence of all excitement, sensible and intellectual, and the vision of Eternity. And therefore have I called the monastic state the most poetical of religious disciplines. It was a return to that primitive age of the world, of which poets have so often sung, the simple life of Arcadia or the reign of Saturn, when fraud and violence were unknown. It was a bringing back of those real, not fabulous, scenes of innocence and miracle, when Adam delved, or Abel kept sheep, or Noe planted the vine, and Angels visited them. It was a fulfilment in the letter, of the glowing imagery of prophets, about the evangelical period. Nature for art, the wide earth and the majestic heavens for the crowded city, the subdued and docile beasts of the field for the wild passions and rivalries of social life, tranquillity for ambition and care, divine meditation for the exploits of the intellect, the Creator for the creature, such was the normal condition of the monk. He had tried the world, and found its hollowness; or he had eluded its fellowship, before it had solicited him—and so St. Antony fled to the desert, and St. Hilarion sought the sea shore, and St. Basil ascended the mountain ravine, and St. Benedict took refuge in his cave, and St. Giles buried himself in the forest, and St. Martin chose the broad river, in order that the world might be shut out of view, and the soul might be at rest. And such a rest of intellect and of passion as this is full of the elements of the poetical.

I have no intention of committing myself here to a definition of poetry; I may be thought wrong in the use of the term; but, if I explain what I mean by it, no harm is done, whatever be my inaccuracy, and each reader may substitute for it some word he likes better. Poetry, then, I conceive, whatever be its metaphysical essence, or however various may be its kinds, whether it more properly belongs to action or to suffering, nay, whether it is more at home with society or with nature, whether its spirit is seen to best advantage in Homer or in Virgil, at any rate, is always the antagonist to *science*. As science makes progress in any subject-matter, poetry recedes from it. The two cannot stand together; they belong respectively to two modes of viewing things, which are contradictory of each other. Reason investigates, analyzes, numbers, weighs, measures, ascertains, locates, the objects of its contemplation, and thus gains a scientific knowledge of them. Science results in system, which is complex unity; poetry delights in the indefinite and various as contrasted with unity, and in the simple as contrasted with system. The aim of science is to get a hold of things, to grasp them, to handle them, to comprehend them; that is (to use the familiar term), to *master* them, or to be superior to them. Its success lies in being able to draw a line round them, and to tell where each of them is to be found within that circumference, and how each lies relatively to all the rest. Its mission is to destroy ignorance, doubt, surmise, suspense, illusions, fears, deceits, according to the "Felix qui potuit rerum cognoscere causas" of the Poet, whose whole passage, by the way, may be taken as drawing out the contrast between the poetical and the scientific.[11] But as to the poetical, very different is the frame of mind which is necessary for its perception. It demands, as its primary condition, that we should not put ourselves above the objects in which it resides, but at their feet; that we should feel them to be above and beyond us, that we should look up to them, and that, instead of fancying that we can comprehend them, we should take for granted that we are surrounded and comprehended by them ourselves. It implies that we understand them to be vast, immeasurable, impenetrable, inscrutable, mysterious; so that at best we are only forming conjectures about them, not conclusions, for the phenomena which they present admit of many explanations, and we cannot know the true one. Poetry does not address the reason, but the imagination and affections; it leads to admiration, enthusiasm, devotion, love. The vague, the uncertain, the irregular, the sudden, are among its attributes or sources. Hence it is that a child's mind is so full of poetry, because he knows so little; and an old man of the world so devoid of poetry, because his experience of facts is so wide. Hence it is that nature is commonly more poetical than art, in spite of Lord Byron, because it is less comprehensible and less patient of definitions; history more poetical than philosophy; the savage than the citizen; the knight-errant than the brigadier-general; the winding bridle-path than the straight railroad; the sailing vessel than the steamer; the ruin than the spruce suburban box; the Turkish robe or Spanish doublet than the French dress coat. I have now said far more than enough to make it clear what I mean by that element in the old monastic life, to which I have given the name of the Poetical.

Now, in many ways the family of St. Benedict answers to this description, as we shall see if we look into its history. Its spirit indeed is ever one, but not its outward circumstances. It is not an Order proceeding from one mind at a particular date, and appearing all at once in its full perfection, and in its extreme development, and in form one and the same everywhere and from first to last, as is the case with other great religious institutions; but it is an organization, diverse, complex, and irregular, and variously ramified, rich rather than symmetrical, with many origins and centres and new beginnings and the action of local influences, like some great natural growth; with tokens, on the face of it, of its being a divine work, not the mere creation of human genius. Instead of progressing on plan and system and from the will of a superior, it has shot forth and run out as if spontaneously, and has shaped itself according to events, from an irrepressible fulness of life within, and from the energetic self-action of its parts, like those symbolical creatures in the prophet's vision, which "went every one of them straight forward, whither the impulse of the spirit was to go." It has been poured out over the earth, rather than been sent, with a silent mysterious operation, while men slept, and through the romantic adventures of individuals, which are well nigh without record; and thus it has come down to us, not risen up among us, and is found rather than established. Its separate and scattered monasteries occupy the land, each in its place, with a majesty parallel, but superior, to that of old aristocratic houses. Their known antiquity, their unknown origin, their long eventful history, their connection with Saints and Doctors when on earth, the legends which hang about them, their rival ancestral honours, their extended sway perhaps over other religious houses, their hold upon the associations of the neighbourhood, their traditional friendships and compacts with other great landlords, the benefits they have conferred, the sanctity which they breathe—these and the like attributes make them objects, at once of awe and of affection.

§7.

SUCH IS the great Abbey of Bobbio, in the Apennines, where St. Columban came to die, having issued with his twelve monks from his convent in Benchor, county Down, and having spent his life in preaching godliness and planting monasteries in half-heathen France and Burgundy. Such St. Gall's, on the lake of Constance, so called from another Irishman, one of St. Columban's companions, who remained in Switzerland, when his master went on into Italy. Such the Abbey of Fulda, where lies St. Boniface, who, burning with zeal for the conversion of the Germans, attempted them a first time and failed, and then a second time and succeeded, and at length crowned the missionary labours of forty-five years with martyrdom. Such Monte Cassino, the metropolis of the Benedictine name, where the Saint broke the idol, and cut down the grove, of Apollo. Ancient houses such as these subdue the mind by the mingled grandeur and sweetness of their presence. They stand in history with an accumulated interest upon them, which belongs to no other monuments of the past. Whatever there is of venerable authority in other foundations, in Bishops' sees, in Cathedrals, in Colleges, respectively, is found in combination in them. Each gate and cloister has had its own story, and time has engraven upon their walls the chronicle of its revolutions. And, even when at length rudely destroyed, or crumbled into dust, they live in history and antiquarian works, in the pictures and relics which remain of them, and in the traditions of their place.

In the early part of last century the Maurist Fathers, with a view of collecting materials for the celebrated works which they had then on hand, sent two of their number on a tour through France and the adjacent provinces. Among other districts the travellers passed through the forest of Ardennes, which has been made classical by the prose of Caesar, and the poetry of Shakespeare. There they found the great Benedictine Convent of St. Hubert [12]; and, if I dwell awhile upon the illustration which it affords of what I have been saying, it is not as if twenty other religious houses which they visited would not serve my purpose quite as well, but because it has come first to my hand in turning over the pages of their volume. At that time the venerable abbey in question had upon it the weight of a thousand years, and was eminent above others in the country in wealth, in privileges, in name, and, not the least recommendation, in the sanctity of its members. The lands on which it was situated were its freehold, and their range included sixteen villages. The old chronicle informs us that, about the middle of the seventh century, St. Sigibert, the Merovingian, pitched upon Ardennes and its neighbourhood for the establishment of as many as twelve monasteries, with the hope of thereby obtaining from heaven an heir to his crown. Dying prematurely, he but partially fulfilled his pious intention, which was taken up by Pepin, sixty years afterwards, at the instance of his chaplain, St. Beregise; so far, at least, as to make a commencement of the abbey of which we are speaking. Beregise had been a monk of the Benedictine Abbey of St. Tron, and he chose for the site of the new foundation a spot in the midst of the forest, marked by the ruins of a temple dedicated to the pagan Diana, the goddess of the chase. The holy man exorcised the place with the sign of the Cross; and, becoming abbot of the new house, filled it either with monks, or, as seems less likely, with secular canons. From that time to the summer day, when the two Maurists visited it, the sacred establishment, with various fortunes, had been in possession of the land.

On entering its precincts, they found it at once full and empty: empty of the monks, who were in the fields gathering in the harvest; full of pilgrims, who were wont to come day after day, in never-failing succession, to visit the tomb of St. Hubert. What a series of events has to be recorded to make this simple account intelligible! and how poetical is the picture which it sets before us, as well as those events themselves, which it presupposes, when they come to be detailed! Were it not that I should be swelling a passing illustration into a history, I might go on to tell how strict the observance of the monks had been for the last hundred years before the travellers arrived there, since Abbot Nicholas de Fanson had effected a reform on the pattern of the French Congregation of St. Vanne. I might relate how, when a simple monk in the Abbey of St. Hubert, Nicholas had wished to change it for a stricter community, and how he got leave to go off to the Congregation just mentioned, and how then his old Abbot died suddenly, and how he himself to his surprise was elected in his place. And I might tell how, when his mitre was on his head, he set about reforming the house which he had been on the point of quitting, and how he introduced for that purpose two monks of St. Vanne; and how the Bishop of Liege, in whose diocese he was, set himself against his holy design, and how some of the old monks attempted to poison him; and how, though he carried it into effect, still he was not allowed to aggregate his Abbey to the Congregation whose reform he had adopted; but how his good example encouraged the neighbouring abbeys to commence a reform in themselves, which issued in an ecclesiastical union of the Flemish Houses.

All this, however, would not have been more than one passage, of course, in the adventures which had befallen the abbey and its abbots in the course of its history. It had had many seasons of decay before the time of Nicholas de Fanson, and many restorations, and from different quarters. None of them was so famous or important as the reform effected in the year 817, about a century after its original foundation, when the secular canons, who anyhow had got in, were put out, and the monks put in their place, at the instance of the then Bishop of Liege, who had a better spirit than his successor in the time of Nicholas. The new inmates were joined by some persons of noble birth from the Cathedral, and by their suggestion and influence the bold measure was taken of attempting to gain from Liege the body of the great St. Hubert, the Apostle of Ardennes. Great, we may be sure, was the resistance of the city where he lay; but Abbot Alreus, the friend and fellow-workman of St. Benedict of Anian, the first Reformer of the Benedictine Order before the date of Cluni, went to the Bishop, and he went to the Archbishop of Cologne; and then both prelates went to the Emperor Louis le Debonnaire, the son of Charlemagne, whose favourite hunting ground the forest was; and he referred the matter to the great Council of Aix-la-Chapelle, whence a decision came in favour of the monks of Ardennes. So with great solemnity the sacred body was conveyed by water to its new destination; and there in the Treasury, in memorial of the happy event, the Maurist visitors saw the very chalice of gold, and the beautiful copy of the Gospels, ornamented with precious stones, given to the Abbey by Louis at the time. Doubtless it was the handiwork of the monks of some other Benedictine House, as must have been the famous Psalter, of which the visitors speak also, written in letters of gold, the gift of Louis's son, the Emperor

Lothaire; and there he sits in the first page, with his crown on his head, his sceptre in one hand, his sheathed sword in the other, and something very like a fleur-de-lys buckling on his ermine robe at the shoulder: which precious gift, that is, the Psalter with all its pictures, two centuries after came most unaccountably into the possession of the Lady Helvidia of Aspurg, who gave it to her young son Bruno, afterwards Pope Leo the Ninth, to learn the Psalms by; but, as the young Saint made no progress in his task, she came to the conclusion that she had no right to the book, and so she ended by making a pilgrimage to St. Hubert with Bruno, and, not only gave back the Psalter, but made the offering of a Sacramentary besides.

But to return to the relics of the Saint; the sacred body was taken by water up the Maes. The coffin was of marble, and perhaps could have been taken no other way; but another reason, besides its weight, lay in the indignation of the citizens of Liege, who might have interfered with a land journey, and in fact did make several attempts, in the following years, to regain the body. In consequence, the good monks of Ardennes hid it within the walls of their monastery, confiding the secret of its whereabouts to only two of their community at a time; and they showed in the sacristy to the devout, instead, the Saint's ivory cross and his stole, the sole of his shoe and his comb, and Diana, Marchioness of Autrech, gave a golden box to hold the stole. This, however, was in after times; for they were very loth at first to let strangers within their cloisters at all; and in 838, when a long spell of rain was destroying the crops, and the people of the neighbourhood came in procession to the shrine to ask the intercession of the Saint, the cautious Abbot Sewold, availing himself of the Rule, would only admit priests, and them by threes and fours, with naked feet, and a few laymen with each of them. The supplicants were good men, however, and had no notion of playing any trick: they came in piety and devotion, and the rain ceased, and the country was the gainer by St. Hubert of Ardennes. And thenceforth others, besides the monks, became interested in his stay in the forest.

And now I have said something in explanation why the courtyard was full of pilgrims when the travellers came. St. Hubert had been an object of devotion for a particular benefit, perhaps ever since he came there, certainly as early as the eleventh century, for we then have historical notice of it. His preference of the forest to the city, which he had shown in his life-time before his conversion, was illustrated by the particular grace or miraculous service, for which, more than for any other, he used his glorious intercession on high. He is famous for curing those who had suffered from the bite of wild animals, especially dogs of the chase, and a hospital was attached to the Abbey for their reception. The sacristan of the Church officiated in the cure; and with rites which never indeed failed, but which to some cautious persons seemed to savour of superstition. Certainly they were startling at first sight; accordingly a formal charge on that score was at one time brought against them before the Bishop of Liege, and a process followed. The Bishop, the University of Louvain, and its Faculty of Medicine, conducted the inquiry, which was given in favour of the Abbey, on the ground that what looked like a charm might be of the nature of a medical regimen.

However, though the sacristan was the medium of the cure, the general care of the patients was left to externs. The hospital was served by secular priests, since the monks heard no confessions save those of their own people. This rule they observed, in order to reserve themselves for the proper duties of a Benedictine—the choir, study, manual labour, and transcription of books; and, while the Maurists were ocular witnesses of their agricultural toils, they saw the diligence of their penmanship in its results, for the MSS. of their Library were the choicest in the country. Among them, they tell us, were copies of St. Jerome's Bible, the Acts of the Councils, Bede's History, Gregory and Isidore, Origen and Augustine.

The Maurists report as favourably of the monastic buildings themselves as of the hospital and library. Those buildings were a chronicle of past times, and of the changes which had taken place in them. First there were the poor huts of St. Beregise upon the half-cleared and still marshy ground of the forest; then came the building of a sufficient house, when St. Hubert was brought there; and centuries after that, St. Thierry, the intimate friend of the great Pope Hildebrand, had renewed it magnificently, at the time that he was Abbot. He was sadly treated in his lifetime by his monks, as Nicholas after him; but, after his death, they found out that he was a Saint, which they might have discovered before it; and they placed him in the crypt, and there he and another holy Abbot after him lay in peace, till the Calvinists broke into it in the sixteenth century, and burned both of them to ashes. There were marks too of the same fanatics on the pillars of the nave of the Church; which had been built by Abbot John de Wahart in the twelfth century, and then again from its foundations by Abbots Nicholas de Malaise and Romaclus, the friend of Blosius, four centuries later; and it was ornamented by Abbot Cyprian, who was called the friend of the poor; and doubtless the travellers admired the marble of the choir and sanctuary, and the silver candelabra of the altar given by the reigning Lord Abbot; and perhaps they heard him sing solemn Mass on the Assumption, as was usual with him on that feast, with his four secular chaplains, one to carry his Cross, another his mitre, a third his gremial, and a fourth his candle, and accompanied by the pealing organ and the many musical bells, which had been the gift of Abbot Balla about a hundred years earlier. Can we imagine a more graceful union of human with divine, of the sweet with the austere, of business and of calm, of splendour and of simplicity, than is displayed in a great religious house after this pattern, when unrelaxed in its observance, and pursuing the ends for which it was endowed?

§8.

THE MONKS have been accused of choosing beautiful spots for their dwellings; as if this were a luxury in ascetics, and not rather the necessary alleviation of their asceticism. Even when their critics are kindest, they consider such sites as chosen by a sort of sentimental, ornamental indolence. "Beaulieu river," says Mr. Warner in his topography of Hampshire, and, because he writes far less ill-naturedly than the run of authors, I quote him, "Beaulieu river is stocked with plenty of fish, and boasts in particular of good oysters and fine plaice, and is fringed quite to the edge of the water with the most beautiful hanging woods. In the area enclosed are distinct traces of various fishponds, formed for the use of the convent. Some of them continue perfect to the present day, and abound with fish. A curious instance occurs also of monkish luxury, even in the article of water; to secure a fine spring those monastics have spared neither trouble nor expense. About half a mile to the south-east of the Abbey is a deep wood; and at a spot almost inaccessible is a cave formed of smooth stones. It has a very contracted entrance, but spreads gradually into a little apartment, of seven feet wide, ten deep, and about five high. This covers a copious and transparent spring of water, which, issuing from the mouth of the cave, is lost in a deep dell, and is there received, as I have been informed, by a chain of small stone pipes, which formerly, when perfect, conveyed it quite to the Abbey. It must be confessed the monks in general displayed an elegant taste in the choice of their situations. Beaulieu Abbey is a striking proof of this. Perhaps few spots in the kingdom could have been pitched upon better calculated for monastic seclusion than this. The deep woods, with which it is almost environed, throw an air of gloom and solemnity over the scene, well suited to excite religious emotions; while the stream that glides by its side afforded to the recluse a striking emblem of human life: and at the same time that it soothed his mind by a gentle murmuring, led it to serious thought by its continual and irrevocable lesson."[13]

The monks were not so soft as all this, after all; and if Mr. Warner had seen them, we may be sure he would have been astonished at the stern, as well as sweet simplicity which characterized them. They were not dreamy sentimentalists, to fall in love with melancholy winds and purling rills, and waterfalls and nodding groves; but their poetry was the poetry of hard work and hard fare, unselfish hearts and charitable hands. They could plough and reap, they could hedge and ditch, they could drain; they could lop, they could carpenter; they could thatch, they could make hurdles for their huts; they could make a road, they could divert or secure the streamlet's bed, they could bridge a torrent. Mr. Warner mentions one of their luxuries—clear, wholesome water; it was an allowable one, especially as they obtained it by their own patient labour. If their grounds are picturesque, if their views are rich, they made them so, and had, we presume, a right to enjoy the work of their own hands. They found a swamp, a moor, a thicket, a rock, and they made an Eden in the wilderness. They destroyed snakes; they extirpated wild cats, wolves, boars, bears; they put to flight or they converted rovers, outlaws, robbers. The gloom of the forest departed, and the sun, for the first time since the Deluge shone upon the moist ground. St. Benedict is the true man of Ross.

> Who hung with woods yon mountain's sultry brow?
> From the dry rock who made the waters flow?
> Whose causeway parts the vale with shady rows?
> Whose seats the weary traveller repose?
> He feeds yon almshouse, neat, but void of state,
> When Age and Want sit smiling at the gate;
> Him portioned maids, apprenticed orphans blessed,
> The young who labour, and the old who rest.

And candid writers, though not Catholics, allow it. Even English, and much more foreign historians and antiquarians, have arrived at a unanimous verdict here. "We owe the agricultural restoration of great part of Europe to the monks," says Mr. Hallam. "The monks were much the best husbandmen, and the only gardeners," says Forsyth. "None," says Wharton, "ever improved their lands and possessions more than the monks, by building, cultivating, and other methods." The cultivation of Church lands, as Sharon Turner infers from Doomsday Book, was superior to that held by other proprietors, for there was less wood upon them, less common pasture, and more abundant meadow. "Wherever they came," says Mr. Soame on Mosheim, "they converted the wilderness into a cultivated country; they pursued the breeding of cattle and agriculture, laboured with their own hands, drained morasses, and cleared away forests. By them Germany was rendered a fruitful country." M. Guizot speaks as strongly: "The Benedictine monks were the agriculturists of Europe; they cleared it on a large scale, associating agriculture with preaching."[14]

St. Benedict's direct object indeed in setting his monks to manual labour was neither social usefulness nor poetry, but penance; still his work was both the one and the other. The above-cited authors enlarge upon its use, and I in what I am writing may be allowed to dwell upon its poetry; we may contemplate both its utility to man and its service to God in the aspect of its poetry. How romantic then, as well as useful, how lively as well as serious, is their history, with its episodes of personal adventure and prowess, its pictures of squatter, hunter, farmer, civil engineer, and evangelist united in the same individual, with its supernatural colouring of heroic virtue and miracle! When St. Columban first came into Burgundy with his twelve young monks, he placed himself in a vast wilderness, and made them set about cultivating the soil. At first they all suffered from hunger, and were compelled to live on the barks of trees and wild herbs. On one occasion they were for five days in this condition. St. Gall, one of them, betook himself to a Swiss forest, fearful from the multitude of wild beasts; and then, choosing the neighbourhood of a mountain stream, he made a cross of twigs, and hung some relics on it, and laid the foundation of his celebrated abbey. St. Ronan came from Ireland to Cornwall, and chose a wood, full of wild beasts, for his hermitage, near the Lizard. The monks of St. Dubritius, the founder of the Welsh Schools, also sought the woods, and there they worked hard at manufactures, agriculture, and road making. St. Sequanus placed himself where "the trees almost touched the clouds." He and his companions, when they first explored it, asked themselves how they could penetrate into it, when they saw a winding footpath, so narrow and full of briars that it was with difficulty that one foot followed another. With much labour and with torn clothes they succeeded in gaining its depths, and stooping their heads into the darkness at their feet, they perceived a cavern, shrouded by the thick interlacing branches of the trees, and blocked up with stones and underwood. "This," says the monastic account, "was the cavern of robbers, and the resort of evil spirits." Sequanus fell on his knees, prayed, made the sign of the Cross over the abyss, and built his cell there. Such was the first foundation of the celebrated abbey called after him in Burgundy.[15]

Sturm, the Bavarian convert of St. Boniface, was seized with a desire, as his master before him in his English monastery, of founding a religious house in the wilds of Pagan Germany; and setting out with two companions, he wandered for two days through the Buchonian forest, and saw nothing but earth, sky, and large trees. On the third day he stopped and chose a spot, which on trial did not answer. Then, mounting an ass, he set out by himself, cutting down branches of a night to secure himself from the wild beasts, till at length he came to the place (described by St. Boniface as "locum silvaticum in eremo, vastissimae solitudinis"), in which afterwards arose the abbey and schools of Fulda. Wunibald was suspicious of the good wine of the Rhine where he was, and, determining to leave it, he bought the land where Heidensheim afterwards stood, then a wilderness of trees and underwood, covering a deep valley and the sides of lofty mountains. There he proceeded, axe in hand, to clear the ground for his religious house, while the savage natives looked on sullenly, jealous for their hunting-grounds and sacred trees. Willibald, his brother, had pursued a similar work on system; he had penetrated his forest in every direction and scattered monasteries over it. The Irish Alto pitched himself in a wood, half way between Munich and Vienna. Pirminius chose an island, notorious for its snakes, and there he planted his hermitage and chapel, which at length became the rich and noble abbey and school of Augia Major or Richenau.[16]

The more celebrated School of Bec had a similar beginning at a later date, when Herluin, an old soldier, devoted his house and farm to an ecclesiastical purpose, and governed, as abbot, the monastery which he had founded. "You might see him," says the writer of his life, "when office was over in church, going out to his fields, at the head of his monks, with his bag of seed about his neck, and his rake or hoe in his hand. There he remained with them hard at work till the day was closing. Some were employed in clearing the land of brambles and weeds; others spread manure; others were weeding or sowing; no one ate his bread in idleness. Then when the hour came for saying office in church, they all assembled together punctually. Their ordinary food was rye bread and vegetables with salt and water; and the water muddy, for the well was two miles off."[17] Lanfranc, then a secular, was so edified by the simple Abbot, fresh from the field, setting about his baking with dirty hands, that he forthwith became one of the party[18]; and, being unfitted for labour, opened in the house a school of logic, thereby to make money for the community. Such was the cradle of the scholastic theology; the last years of the patristic, which were nearly contemporaneous, exhibit a similar scene—St. Bernard founding his abbey of Clairvaux in a place called the Valley of Wormwood, in the heart of a savage forest, the haunt of robbers, and his thirteen companions clearing a homestead, raising a few huts, and living on barley or cockle bread with boiled beech leaves for vegetables.[19]

How beautiful is Simeon of Durham's account of Easterwine, the first abbot after Bennet of St. Peter's at Wearmouth! He was a man of noble birth, who gave himself to religion, and died young. "Though he had been in the service of King Egfrid," says Simeon, "when he had once left secular affairs, and lain aside his arms, and taken on him the spiritual warfare instead, he was nothing but the humble monk, just like any of his brethren, winnowing with them with great joy, milking the ewes and cows, and in the bakehouse, the garden, the kitchen, and all house duties, cheerful and obedient. And, when he received the name of Abbot, still he was in spirit just what he was before to every one, gentle, affable, and kind; or, if any fault had been committed, correcting it indeed by the Rule, but still so winning the offender by his unaffected earnest manner, that he had no wish ever to repeat the offence, or to dim the brightness of that most clear countenance with the cloud of his transgression. And often going here and there on business of the monastery, when he found his brothers at work, he would at once take part in it, guiding the plough, or shaping the iron, or taking the winnowing fan, or the like. He was young and strong, with a sweet voice, a cheerful temper, a liberal heart and a handsome countenance. He partook of the same food as his brethren, and under the same roof. He slept in the common dormitory, as before he was abbot, and he continued to do so for the first two days of his illness, when death had now seized him, as he knew full well. But for the last five days he betook himself to a more retired dwelling; and then, coming out into the open air and sitting down, and calling for all his brethren, after the manner of his tender nature, he gave his weeping monks the kiss of peace, and died at night while they were singing lauds."[20]

§9.

THIS GENTLENESS and tenderness of heart seems to have been as characteristic of the monks as their simplicity; and if there are some Saints among them, who on the public stage of history do not show it, it was because they were called out of their convents for some special purpose, and, as I have said above, exceptions to a rule are commonly great exceptions. Bede goes out of his way to observe of King Ethelbert, on St. Austin's converting him, that "he had learned from the teachers and authors of his salvation that men were to be drawn heaven-wards, and not forced." Aldhelm, when a council had been held about the perverse opinions of the British Christians, seconding the principle which the Fathers of it laid down, that "schismatics were to be convinced, not compelled," wrote a book upon their error and converted many of them. Wolstan, when the civil power failed in its attempts to stop the slave trade of the Bristol people, succeeded by his persevering preaching. In the confessional he was so gentle, that penitents came to him from all parts of England.[21] This has been the spirit of the monks from the first; the student of ecclesiastical history may recollect a certain passage in St. Martin's history, when his desire to shield the Spanish heretics from capital punishment brought him into great difficulties[22] with the usurper Maximus.

Works of penance indeed and works of mercy have gone hand in hand in the history of the monks; from the Solitaries in Egypt down to the Trappists of this day, it is one of the points in which the unity of the monastic idea shows itself. They have ever toiled for others, while they toiled for themselves; nor for posterity only, but for their poor neighbours, and for travellers who came to them. St. Augustine tells us that the monks of Egypt and of the East made so much by manual labour as to be able to freight vessels with provisions for impoverished districts. Theodoret speaks of a certain five thousand of them, who by their labour supported, besides themselves, innumerable poor and strangers. Sozomen speaks of the monk Zeno, who, though a hundred years old, and the bishop of a rich Church, worked for the poor as well as for himself. Corbinian in a subsequent century surrounded his German Church with fruit trees and vines, and sustained the poor with the produce. The monks of St. Gall, already mentioned, gardened, planted, fished, and thus secured the means of relieving the poor and entertaining strangers. "Monasteries," says Neander, "were seats for the promotion of various trades, arts, and sciences. The gains accruing from their combined labour were employed for the relief of the distressed. In great famines, thousands were rescued from starvation."[23] In a scarcity at the beginning of the twelfth century, a monastery in the neighbourhood of Cologne distributed in one day fifteen hundred alms, consisting of bread, meat, and vegetables. About the same time St. Bernard founded his monastery of Citeaux, which, though situated in the waste district described above, was able at length to sustain two thousand poor for months, besides extraordinary alms bestowed on others. The monks offered their simple hospitality, uninviting as it might be, to high as well as low; and to those who scorned their fare, they at least could offer a refuge in misfortune or danger, or after casualties.

Duke William, ancestor of the Conqueror, was hunting in the woods about Jumieges, when he fell in with a rude hermitage.[24] Two monks had made their way through the forest, and with immense labour had rooted up some trees, levelled the ground, raised some crops, and put together their hut. William heard their story, not perhaps in the best humour, and flung aside in contempt the barley bread and water which they offered him. Presently he was brought back wounded and insensible: he had got the worst in an encounter with a boar. On coming to himself, he accepted the hospitality which he had refused at first, and built for them a monastery. Doubtless he had looked on them as trespassers or squatters on his domain, though with a religious character and object. The Norman princes were as good friends to the wild beasts as the monks were enemies: a charter still exists of the Conqueror, granted to the abbey of

Caen,[25] in which he stipulates that its inmates should not turn the woods into tillage, and reserves the game for himself.

Contrast with this savage retreat and its rude hospitality the different, though equally Benedictine picture of the sacred grove of Subiaco, and the spiritual entertainment which it ministers to all comers, as given in the late pilgrimage of Bishop Ullathorne: "The trees," he says, "which form the venerable grove, are very old, but their old age is vigorous and healthy. Their great grey roots expose themselves to view with all manner of curling lines and wrinkles on them, and the rough stems bend and twine about with the vigour and ease of gigantic pythons... Of how many holy solitaries have these trees witnessed the meditations! And then they have seen beneath their quiet boughs the irruption of mailed men, tormented by the thirst of plunder and the passion of blood, which even a sanctuary held so sacred could not stay. And then they have witnessed, for twelve centuries and more, the greatest of the Popes, the Gregories, the Leos, the Innocents, and the Piuses, coming one after another to refresh themselves from their labours in a solitude which is steeped with the inspirations and redolent with the holiness of St. Benedict."[26]

What congenial subjects for his verse would the sweetest of all poets have found in scenes and histories such as the foregoing, he who in his Georgics has shown such love of a country life and country occupations, and of the themes and trains of thought which rise out of the country! Would that Christianity had a Virgil to describe the old monks at their rural labours, as it has had a Sacchi or a Domenichino to paint them! How would he have been able to set forth the adventures and the hardships of the missionary husbandmen, who sang of the Scythian winter, and the murrain of the cattle, the stag of Sylvia, and the forest home of Evander! How could he have pourtrayed St. Paulinus or St. Serenus in his garden, who could draw so beautiful a picture of the old Corycian, raising amid the thicket his scanty pot-herbs upon the nook of land, which was "not good for tillage, nor for pasture, nor for vines!" How could he have brought out the poetry of those simple labourers, who has told us of that old man's flowers and fruits, and of the satisfaction, as a king's, which he felt in those innocent riches! He who had so huge a dislike of cities, and great houses, and high society, and sumptuous banquets, and the canvass for office, and the hard law, and the noisy lawyer, and the statesman's harangue—he who thought the country proprietor as even too blessed, did he but know his blessedness, and who loved the valley, winding stream, and wood, and the hidden life which they offer, and the deep lessons which they whisper—how could he have illustrated that wonderful union, of prayer, penance, toil, and literary work, the true "otium cum dignitate," a fruitful leisure and a meek-hearted dignity, which is exemplified in the Benedictine! That ethereal fire which enabled the Prince of Latin poets to take up the Sibyl's strain, and to adumbrate the glories of a supernatural future—that serene philosophy, which has strewn his poems with sentiments which come home to the heart—that intimate sympathy with the sorrows of human kind and with the action and passion of human nature—how well would they have served to illustrate the patriarchal history and office of the monks in the broad German countries, or the deeds, the words, and the visions of a St. Odilo or a St. Aelred!

What a poet deliberately chooses for the subject of his poems must be in its own nature poetical. A poet indeed is but a man after all, and in his proper person may prefer solid beef and pudding to all the creations of his own "fine frenzy," which, in his character of poet, are his meat and drink. But no poet will ever commit his poetical reputation to the treatment of subjects which do not admit of poetry. When, then, Virgil chooses the country and rejects the town, he shows us that a certain aspect of the town is uncongenial with poetry, and that a certain aspect of the country is congenial. Repose, intellectual and moral, is that quality of country life which he selects for his praises; and effort, and bustle, and excitement is that quality of a town life which he abhors. Herein then, according to Virgil, lies the poetry of St. Benedict, in the "secura quies et nescia fallere vita," in the absence of anxiety and fretfulness, of schemes and scheming, of hopes and fears, of doubts and disappointments. Such a life—living for the day without solicitude for the morrow, without plans or objects, even holy ones, here below; working, not (so to say) by the piece, but as hired by the hour; sowing the ground with the certainty, according to the promise, of reaping; reading or writing this present week without the consequent necessity of reading or writing during the next; dwelling among one's own people without distant ties; taking each new day as a whole in itself, an addition, not a complement, to the past; and doing works which cannot be cut short, for they are complete in every portion of them—such a life may be called emphatically Virgilian. They, on the contrary, whose duty lies in what may be called *undertakings*, in science and system, in sustained efforts of the intellect or elaborate processes of action—apologists, controversialists, disputants in the schools, professors in the chair, teachers in the pulpit, rulers in the Church—have a noble and meritorious mission, but not so poetical a one. When the bodily frame receives an injury, or is seized with some sudden malady, nature may be expected to set right the evil, if left to itself, but she requires time; science comes in to shorten the process, and is violent that it may be certain. This may be taken to illustrate St. Benedict's mode of counteracting the miseries of life. He found the world, physical and social, in ruins, and his mission was to restore it in the way, not of science, but of nature, not as if setting about to do it, not professing to do it by any set time or by any rare specific or by any series of strokes, but so quietly, patiently, gradually, that often, till the work was done, it was not known to be doing. It was a restoration, rather than a visitation, correction, or conversion. The new world which he helped to create was a growth rather than a structure. Silent men were observed about the country, or discovered in the forest, digging, clearing, and building; and other silent men, not seen, were sitting in the cold cloister, tiring their eyes, and keeping their attention on the stretch, while they painfully deciphered and copied and re-copied the manuscripts which they had saved. There was no one that "contended, or cried out," or drew attention to what was going on; but by degrees the woody swamp became a hermitage, a religious house, a farm, an abbey, a village, a seminary, a school of learning, and a city. Roads and bridges connected it with other abbeys and cities, which had similarly grown up; and what the haughty Alaric or fierce Attila had broken to pieces, these patient meditative men had brought together and made to live again.

And then, when they had in the course of many years gained their peaceful victories, perhaps some new invader came, and with fire and sword undid their slow and persevering toil in an hour. The Hun succeeded to the Goth, the Lombard to the Hun, the Tartar to the Lombard; the Saxon was reclaimed only that the Dane might take his place. Down in the dust lay the labour and civilization of centuries—Churches, Colleges, Cloisters, Libraries—and nothing was left to them but to begin all over again; but this they did without grudging, so promptly, cheerfully, and tranquilly, as if it were by some law of nature that the restoration came, and they were like the flowers and shrubs and fruit trees which they reared, and which, when ill-treated, do not take vengeance, or remember evil, but give forth fresh branches, leaves, or blossoms, perhaps in greater profusion, and with richer quality, for the very reason that the old were rudely broken off. If one holy place was desecrated, the monks pitched upon another, and by this time there were rich or powerful men who remembered and loved the past enough to wish to have it restored in the future. Thus was it in the case of the monastery of Ramsey after the ravages of the Danes. A wealthy Earl, whose heart was touched, consulted his Bishop how he could best promote the divine glory: the Bishop answered that they only were free, serene, and unsolicitous, who renounced the world, and that their renunciation brought a blessing on their country. "By their merit," he said, "the anger of the Supreme Judge is abated; a healthier atmosphere is granted; corn springs up more abundantly; famine and pestilence withdraw; the state is better governed; prisons are opened; the fetters unbound; the shipwrecked relieved." He proceeded to advise him, as the best of courses, to give ground for a monastery, and to build and endow it. Earl Alwin observed in reply, that he had inherited some waste land in the midst of marshes, with a forest in the neighbourhood, some open spots of good turf, and others of meadow; and he took the Bishop to see it. It was in fact an island in the fens, and as lonely as religious men could desire. The gift was accepted, workmen were collected, the pious peasants round about gave their labour. Twelve monks were found from another cloister; cells and a chapel were soon raised. Materials were collected for a handsome church; stones and cement were given; a firm foundation was secured; scaffolding and machinery were lent; and in course of time a sacred edifice and two towers rose over the desolate waste, and renewed the past—a learned divine from France was invited to preside over the monastic schools.[27]

§10.

HERE THEN I am led, lastly, to speak of the literary labours of the Benedictines, but I have not room to do more than direct attention to the peculiar character of their work, and must leave the subject of their schools for some future opportunity. Here, as in other respects above noticed, the unity of monachism shows itself. What the Benedictines, even in their latest literary developments, have been, in St. Maur in the seventeenth century, and at Solesme now, such were the monks in their first years. One of the chief occupations of the disciples of St. Pachomius in Egypt was the transcription of books. It was the sole labour of the monks of St. Martin in Gaul. The Syrian solitaries, according to St. Chrysostom, employed themselves in making copies of the Holy Scriptures. It was the occupation of the monks of St. Equitius and of Cassiodorus, and of the nunnery of St. Caesarius. We read of one holy man preparing the skins for writing, of another selling his manuscripts in order to gain alms for the poor, and of an abbess writing St. Peter's Epistles in letters of gold. St. David had shown the same reverence to St. John's Gospel. Abbot Plato filled his own and other monasteries with his beautifully written volumes.[28] During the short rule of Abbot Desiderius at Monte Cassino, his monks wrote out St. Austin's fifty Homilies, his Letters, his Comment upon the Sermon on the Mount, upon St. Paul and upon Genesis; parts of St. Jerome and St. Ambrose, part of St. Bede, St. Leo's Sermons, the Orations of St. Gregory Nazianzen; the Acts of the Apostles, the Epistles and the Apocalypse; various histories, including that of St. Gregory of Tours, and of Josephus on the Jewish War, Justinian's Institutes, and many ascetic and other works; of the Classics, Cicero de Naturâ Deorum, Terence, Ovid's Fasti, Horace, and Virgil. Maurus Lapi, a Camaldolese, in the fifteenth century, copied a thousand volumes in less than fifty years. Jerome, a monk in an Austrian monastery, wrote so great a number of books that, it is said, a wagon with six horses would scarcely suffice to draw them. Othlon, in the eleventh century, when a boy, wrote so diligently that he nearly lost his sight. That was in France; he then went to Ratisbon, where he wrote nineteen missals, three books of the Gospel, two books of Epistle and Gospel, and many others. Many he gave to his friends, but the list is too long to finish. The Abbot Odo of Tournay "used to exult," according to his successor, "in the number of writers which the Lord had given him. Had you gone into his cloister, you might have seen a dozen young men sitting in perfect silence, writing at tables constructed for the purpose. All Jerome's Commentaries on the Prophets, all the works of St. Gregory, all that he could find of Austin, Ambrose, Isidore, Bede, and the Lord Anselm, Abbot of Bec, and afterwards Archbishop of Canterbury, he caused to be diligently transcribed."[29]

These tranquil labourers found a further field in the illumination and binding of the transcribed volumes, as they had previously been occupied in the practice necessary for the then important art of calligraphy. It was not running hand that the monks had to learn; for it was no ephemeral expression of their own thoughts which their writing was to convey, but the formal transcript, for the benefit of posterity, of the words of inspired teachers and Doctors of the Church. They were performing what has been since the printer's work; and it is said that from the English monks is derived the small letter of the modern Roman type. In France the abbeys of Fontenelle, Rheims, and Corbie were especially famed for beauty of penmanship in the age of Charlemagne,[30] when literature was in its most depressed state. Books intended for presents, such as that which the mother of Leo the Ninth presented to St. Hubert, and, much more, if intended for sacred uses, were enriched with gold and silver plates and precious stones. Here was a commencement of the cultivation of the fine arts in those turbulent times—a quiet, unexciting occupation, which went on inside the monasteries, whatever rivalries or heresies agitated Christendom outside of them, and which, though involving, of course, an improvement in the workmanship as time went on, yet in the case of every successive specimen, whatever exact degree of skill or taste each exhibited, had its end in itself, as though there had been no other specimen before or after.

Brower, in his work on the Antiquities of Fulda, gives us a lively picture of the various tranquil occupations which were going on at one time within the monastic walls. "As industrious bees," he says, "their work never flagging, did these monks follow out their calling. Some of them were engaged in describing, here and there upon the parchment, the special letters and characters which were to be filled in; others were wrapping or binding the manuscripts in handsome covers; others were marking out in red the remarkable sentences or the heads of the chapters. Some were writing fairly what had been thrown together at random, or had been left out in the dictation, and were putting every part in fair order. And not a few of them excelled in painting in all manner of colours, and in drawing figures."[31] He goes on to refer to an old manuscript there, which speaks of the monks as decorating their church, and of their carpenters' work, sculpture, engraving, and brass work.

I have mentioned St. Dunstan in an earlier page, as called to political duties, which were out of keeping with the traditionary spirit of his Order; here, however, he shows himself in the simple character of a Benedictine. He had a taste for the arts generally, especially music. He painted and embroidered; his skill in smith's work is recorded in the well-known legend of his combat with the evil one. And, as the monks of Hilarion joined gardening with psalmody, and Bernard and his Cistercians joined field work with meditation, so did St. Dunstan use music and painting as directly expressive or suggestive of devotion. "He excelled in writing, painting, moulding in wax, carving in wood and bone, and in work in gold, silver, iron, and brass," says the writer of his life in Surius. "And he used his skill in musical instruments to charm away from himself and others their secular annoyances, and to rouse them to the thought of heavenly harmony, both by the sweet words with which he accompanied his airs, and by the concord of those airs themselves."[32] And then he goes on to mention how on one occasion, when he had hung his harp against the wall, and the wind brought out from its strings a wild melody, he recognized in it one of the antiphons in the Commune Martyrum, "Gaudete in Coelis," etc., and used it for his own humiliation.

As might be expected, the monasteries of the South of Europe would not be behind the North in accomplishments of this kind. Those of St. Gall, Monte Cassino, and Solignac, are especially spoken of as skilled in the fine arts. Monte Cassino excelled in illumination and in mosaic, the Camaldolese in painting, and the Olivetans in wood-inlaying.[33]

§11.

WHILE MANUAL labour, applied to these artistic purposes, ministered to devotion, on the other hand, when applied to the transcription and multiplication of books, it was a method of instruction, and that peculiarly Benedictine, as being of a literary, not a scientific nature. Systematic theology had but a limited place in ecclesiastical study prior to the eleventh and twelfth centuries; Scripture and the Fathers were the received means of education, and these constituted the very text on which the pens of the monks were employed. And thus they would be becoming familiar with that kind of knowledge which was proper to their vocation, at the same time that they were engaged in what was unequivocally a manual labour; and, in providing for the religious necessities of posterity, they were directly serving their own edification. And this again had been the practice of the monks from the first, and is included in the *unity* of their profession. St. Chrysostom tells us that their ordinary occupation in his time was "to sing and pray, to read Scripture, and to transcribe the sacred text."[34] As the works of the early Fathers gradually became the literary property of the Church, these, too, became the subject-matter of the reading and the writing of the monks. "For him who is going on to perfection," says St. Benedict in his Rule, "there are the lessons of the Holy Fathers, which lead to its very summit. For what page, what passage of the

Old or New Testament, coming as it does with divine authority, is not the very exactest rule of life? What book of the Holy Catholic Fathers does not resound with this one theme, how we may take the shortest course to our Creator?" But I need not here insist on this characteristic of monastic study, which, especially as regards the study of Scripture, has been treated so fully and so well by Mr. Maitland in his "Essays on the Dark Ages."

The sacred literature of the monks went a step further. They would be naturally led by their continual perusal of the Scriptures and the Fathers to attempt to compare and adjust these two chief sources of theological truth with each other. Hence resulted the peculiar character of the religious works of what may be especially called the Benedictine period, the five centuries between St. Gregory and St. Anselm. The age of the Fathers was well nigh over; the age of the Schoolmen was yet to come; the ecclesiastical writers of the intervening centuries employed themselves for the most part in arranging and digesting the patristical literature which had come down to them; they either strung together choice passages of the Fathers in *catenae,* as a running illustration of the inspired text, or they formed them into a comment upon it. The *Summae Sententiarum* of the same centuries were works of a similar character, while they also opened the way to the intellectual exercises of the scholastic period; for they were lessons or instructions arranged according to a scheme or system of doctrine, though they were still extracted from the works of the Fathers, and though the matter of those works suggested the divisions or details of the system. Moreover, such labours, as much as transcription itself, were Benedictine in their spirit, as well as in their subject-matter; for where there was nothing of original research, nothing of brilliant or imposing result, there would be nothing to dissipate, elate, or absorb the mind, or to violate the simplicity and tranquillity proper to the monastic state.

The same remark applies to a further literary employment in which the Benedictines allowed themselves, and which is the last I shall here mention, and that is the compilation of chronicles and annals, whether ecclesiastical, secular, or monastic. So prominent a place does this take in their literature, that the author of the *Asceticon,* in the fourth volume of Dom Francois's Bibliothèque des Ecrivains Bénédictins, does not hesitate to point to the historical writings of his Order as constituting one of its chief claims, after its Biblical works, on the gratitude of posterity. "This," he says, "is the praise especially due to the monks, that they have illustrated Holy Scripture, rescued history, sacred and profane, from the barbarism of the times and have handed down to posterity so many lives both of Saints and of Bishops."[35] Here again is a fresh illustration of the Benedictine character; for first, those histories are of the most simple structure and most artless composition, and next, from the circumstance of their being commonly narratives of contemporary events, or compilations from a few definite sources of information which were at hand, they involved nothing of that laborious research and excitement of mind which is demanded of the writer who has to record a complex course of history, extending over many centuries and countries, and who aims at the discovery of truth, in the midst of deficient, redundant, or conflicting testimony. "The men who wrote history," says Mr. Dowling, speaking of the times in question, "did not write by rule; they only put down what they had seen, what they had heard, what they knew. Very many of them did what they did as a matter of moral duty. The result was something *sui generis*; it was not even what *we* call history at all. It was, if I may so speak, something more, an actual admeasurement rather than a picture; or, if a picture, it was painted in a style which had all the minute accuracy and homely reality of the most domestic of the Flemish masters, not the lofty hyperbole of the Roman school, nor the obtrusive splendour, not less unnatural, of the Venetian. In a word, history, as a subject of criticism, is an art, a noble and beautiful *art*; the historical writings of the middle ages is *nature*."[36]

Mention is made in this passage of the peculiarity in monastic historiography, that it proceeded from the motive of religious duty. This must always have been the case in consequence of the monastic profession; however, we have here, in addition to the presumption, actual evidence, and not on one occasion only, of the importance which the Benedictine Order attached to these notices and memorials of past times. In the year

1082, for instance, the Abbot Marquand of New Corbie, in Saxony, seems to have sent an order to all churches and monasteries subject to his rule to send to him severally the chronicles of their own places. Abbot Wichbold repeated the order sixty years later, and Abbot Thierry in 1337 addressed to the provosts and rectors subject to him a like injunction.[37] Again, in 1481 the Abbot of Erfurdt addressed a letter to the Fathers of the Reform of Bursfeld, with the view of persuading them to take part in a similar work. "If you were to agree among yourselves," he says, "and make a statute to the effect that every Prelate is under an obligation to compose annals and histories of his monastery, what could be better, what more useful, what more interesting, whether for knowing or for reading?"[38]

It is easier to conjecture what those literary works would be, in which a Benedictine would find himself at liberty to engage, than to pretend to point out those from which his vocation would debar him; yet Mabillon, equally with de Rancé, implied that all subjects do not come alike to him. Here we are recalled to the well-known controversy between these two celebrated men. The Abbot of La Trappe, the Cistercian de Rancé, writing to his own people, put forth some statements on the subject of the studies proper to a monk, which seemed to reflect upon the learned Maurists. Mabillon, one of them, replied, in a learned vindication of himself and his brethren. The Abbot had maintained that study of whatever kind should be kept in strict subordination to manual labour, and should not extend to any books except the Scriptures and the ascetic treatises of the Fathers. Mabillon, on the other hand, without denying the necessity of manual labour, to which the Maurists themselves devoted an hour a day, seemed to allow to the Benedictine the free cultivation of the intellect, and an unlimited range of studies. When they explained themselves, each combatant would appear to have asserted more than he could successfully maintain; yet after all there was a considerable difference of view between them, which could not be removed. The critical question was whether certain historical instances, which Mabillon urged in his favour, were to be considered exceptions or not to the rule of St. Benedict. I have certainly maintained in an earlier page of this Essay that such instances as

Alcuin, Paschasius, or Lanfranc are no fair specimens of the Benedictine profession, and must not be taken to represent the monks generally. Lest, however, in saying this, I may be thought to be evading the testimony of history, as adduced by a writer, authoritative at once by his learning and as spokesman of the great Congregation of St. Maur, I think it well to extract in my behalf some of his own admissions, which seem to me fully to bear out what I have been laying down above about the spirit and mission of his Order.

For instance, he frankly concedes, or rather maintains, that the scholastic method of teaching theology and philosophy is foreign to the profession of a Benedictine, as such. "Why," he asks, "need we cultivate these sciences in the way of disputation? Why not as positive sciences, explaining questions and resolving doubts as they occur? Why is it not more than enough for religious pupils to be instructed in the more necessary principles of the science, and thereby to make progress in the study of the Scriptures and the Fathers? What need of this perpetual syllogizing in form, and sharp answers to innumerable objections, as is the custom in the schools?" Elsewhere he contrasts the mode of teaching a subject, as adopted by the early Fathers, with that which the Schoolmen introduced. "The reasonings of the Fathers," he says, "are so full, so elegantly set forth, as to be everywhere redolent of the sweetness and vigour of Christian eloquence, whereas scholastic theology is absolutely dry and sterile." Elsewhere he says that "in the study of Holy Scripture consists the entire science of monks." Again, he says of Moral Theology, "As monks are rarely destined to the cure of souls, it does not seem necessary that they should give much time to the science of Morals." And though of course he does not forbid them the study of history, which we have seen to be so congenial to their calling, yet he observes of this study, when pursued to its full extent, "It seems to cause much dissipation of mind, which is prejudicial to that inward compunction of heart, which is so especially fitting to the holy life of a monk." Again, observing that the examination of ancient MSS. was the special occupation of the Maurists in his time, he says, "They who give themselves to this study have the more merit with

God, in that they have so little praise with men. Moreover, it obliges them to devote the more time to solitude, which ought to be their chief delight. I confess it is a most irksome and unpleasant labour; however, it gives much less trouble than transcription, which was the most useful work of our early monks." Elsewhere, speaking of the celebrated Maurist editions of the Fathers, he observes, "Labour, such as this, which is undergone in silence and in quietness, is especially compatible with true tranquillity of mind and the mastery of the passions, provided we labour as a duty, and not for glory."[39]

I trust the reader will be so good as to keep in mind that I am all along speaking of the Benedictine life *historically*, and as I might speak of any other historical *fact*; not venturing at all on what would be the extreme presumption of any quasi-doctrinal or magisterial exposition of it, which belongs to those only who have actually imbibed its tradition. This being clearly understood, I think I may interpret Mabillon to mean that (be the range of studies lawful to a monk what it may) still, whatever literary work requires such continuous portions of time as not to admit of being suspended at a moment's notice, whatever is so interesting that other duties seem dull and heavy after it, whatever so exhausts the power of attention as to incapacitate for attention to other subjects, whatever makes the mind gravitate towards the creature, is inconsistent with monastic simplicity. Accordingly, I should expect to find that controversy was uncongenial to the Benedictine, because it excited the mind, and metaphysical investigations, because they fatigued it; and, when I met such instances as St. Paschasius or St. Anselm, I should deal with them as they came and as I could. Moreover, I should not look to a Benedictine for any elaborate and systematic work on the history of doctrine, or of heresy, or for any course of patristical theology, or any extended ecclesiastical history, or any philosophical disquisitions upon history, as implying a grasp of innumerable details, and the labour of using a mass of phenomena to the elucidation of a theory, or of bringing a range of multifarious reading to bear upon one point; and that, because such efforts of mind require either an energetic memory devoted to matters of time and place, or, instead of the tranquil and plodding study of one book after another, the presence of a large library, and the distraction of a vast number of books handled all at once, not for perusal, but for reference. Perhaps I am open to the charge of refining, in attempting to illustrate the principle which I seem to myself to detect in the Benedictine tradition; but the principle itself which I have before me is clear enough, and is expressed in the advice which is given to us by a sacred writer: "The words of the wise are as goads, and nails deeply fastened in; *more than these, my son, require not*: of making many books there is no end, and much study is an affliction of the flesh."

To test the truth of this view of the Benedictine mission, I cannot do better than appeal as a palmary instance to the Congregation of St. Maur, an intellectual school of Benedictines assuredly. Now what, in matter of fact, is the character of its works? It has no Malebranche, no Thomassin, no Morinus; it has no Bellarmine, no Suarez, no Petavius; it has no Tillemont or Fleury—all of whom were more or less its contemporaries; but it has a Montfaucon, it has a Mabillon, it has a Sainte Marthe, a Coustant, a Sabbatier, a Martene—men of immense learning and literary experience; it has collators and publishers of MSS. and of inscriptions, editors of the text and of the versions of Holy Scripture, editors and biographers of the Fathers, antiquarians, annalists, paleographists—with scholarship indeed, and criticism, and theological knowledge, admirable as often as elicited by the particular subject on which they are directly employed, but conspicuously subordinate to it.

If we turn to other contemporary Congregations of St. Benedict we are met by the same phenomenon. Their labours have been of the same modest, patient, tranquil kind. The first name which occurs to me is that of Augustine Calmet, of the Congregation of St. Vanne. His works are biblical and antiquarian—a literal Comment on Scripture with Dissertations, a dictionary of the Bible, a Comment on the Benedictine Rule, a history of Lorraine. I cast my eyes round the Library, in which I happen at the moment to be writing; what Benedictine authors meet them? There is Ceillier, also of the Congregation of St. Vanne; Bertholet, of the same Congregation; Cardinal Aguirre of Salamanca; Cressy of Douai; Pez of Mölk on the Danube; Lumper of St. George in the Hercynian Forest; Brockie of the Scotch College at Ratisbon; Reiner of the English Congregation. Their Works are of the same complexion—historical, antiquarian, biographical, patristical—calling to mind the line of study traditionally pursued by a modern ecclesiastical congregation, the Italian Oratory. I do not speak of Ziegelbauer, Francois, and other Benedictines, who might be added, because they have confined themselves to Benedictine Antiquities, and every Order will write about itself.

And so of the Benedictine Literature from first to last. Ziegelbauer, who has just been mentioned, has written four folio volumes on the subject. Now one of them is devoted to a catalogue and an account of Benedictine authors; of these, those on Scripture and Positive Theology occupy one hundred and ten pages; those on history, three hundred; those on scholastic theology, twelve; those on polemics, twelve; those on moral theology, six. This surprising contrast may be an exaggeration of the fact, because there is much of repetition and digression in his survey, and his biographical notices vary in length; but, after all allowances for such accidental unfairness in the list, the result must surely be considered as strikingly confirmatory of the account which I have been giving.

§12.

BUT I must cut short an investigation which, though imperfect for the illustration of its subject, is already long for the patience of the reader. All human works are exposed to vicissitude and decay; and that the great Order of which I have been writing should in the lapse of thirteen centuries have furnished no instances of that general law is the less to be expected, in proportion to the extent of its territory, the independence of its separate houses, and the local varieties of its constitution. To say that peace may engender selfishness, and humility become a cloak for indolence, and a country life may be an epicurean luxury, is only to enunciate the over-true maxim, that every virtue has a vice for its first cousin. *Usum non tollit abusus*; and the circumstance that Benedictine life admits of being corrupted into a mode of living which is not Benedictine, but its very contradictory, cannot surely be made an argument against its meritorious innocence, its resolute cheerfulness, and its strenuous tranquillity. We are told to be like little children; and where shall we find a more striking instance than is here afforded us of that union of simplicity and reverence, that clear perception of the unseen, yet recognition of the mysterious, which is the characteristic of the first years of human existence? To the monk heaven was next door; he formed no plans, he had no cares; the ravens of his father Benedict were ever at his side. He "went forth" in his youth "to his work and to his labour" until the evening of life; if he lived a day longer, he did a day's work more; whether he lived many days or few, he laboured on to the end of them. He had no wish to see further in advance of his journey than where he was to make his next stage. He ploughed and sowed, he prayed, he meditated, he studied, he wrote, he taught, and then he died and went to heaven. He made his way into the labyrinthine forest, and he cleared just so much of space as his dwelling required, suffering the high solemn trees and the deep pathless thicket to close him in. And when he began to build, his architecture was suggested by the scene—not the scientific and masterly conception of a great whole with many parts, as the Gothic style in a later age, but plain and inartificial, the adaptation of received fashions to his own purpose, and an addition of chapel to chapel and a wayward growth of cloister, according to the occasion, with half-concealed shrines and unexpected recesses, with paintings on the wall as by a second thought, with an absence of display and a wild, irregular beauty, like that of the woods by which he was at first surrounded. And when he would employ his mind, he turned to Scripture, the book of books, and there he found a special response to the peculiarities of his vocation; for there supernatural truths stand forth as the trees and flowers of Eden, in a divine disorder, as some awful intricate garden or paradise, which he enjoyed the more because he could not catalogue its wonders. Next he read the Holy Fathers, and there again he recognized a like ungrudging profusion and careless wealth of precept and of consolation. And when he began to compose, still he did so after that mode which nature and revelation had taught him, avoiding curious knowledge, content with incidental ignorance, passing from subject to subject with little regard to system, or care to penetrate beyond his own homestead of thought—and writing, not with the sharp logic of disputants, or the subtle analysis of philosophers, but with the one aim of reflecting in his pages, as in a faithful mirror, the words and works of the Almighty, as they confronted him, whether in Scripture and the Fathers, or in that "mighty maze" of deeds and events, which men call the world's history, but which to him was a Providential Dispensation.

Here the beautiful character in life and death of St. Bede naturally occurs to the mind, who is, in his person and his writings, as truly the pattern of a Benedictine as is St. Thomas of a Dominican; and with an extract from the letter of Cuthbert to Cuthwin concerning his last hours, which, familiarly as it is known, is always pleasant to read, I break off my subject for the present.

"He was exceedingly oppressed," says Cuthbert of St. Bede,

> with shortness of breathing, though without pain, before Easter Day, for about a fortnight; but he rallied, and was full of joy and gladness, and gave thanks to Almighty God day and night and every hour, up to Ascension Day; and he gave us, his scholars, daily lectures, and passed the rest of the day in singing the Psalms, and the night too in joy and thanksgiving, except the scanty time which he gave to sleep. And as soon as he woke, he was busy in his customary way, and he never ceased with uplifted hands giving thanks to God. I solemnly protest, never have I seen or heard of any one who was so diligent in thanksgiving.
>
> He sang that sentence of the blessed Apostle Paul, "It is a dreadful thing to fall into the hands of the Living God," and many other passages of Scripture, in which he warned us to shake off the slumber of the soul, by anticipating our last hour. And he sang some verses of his own in English also, to the effect that no one could be too well prepared for his end, viz.,

in calling to mind, before he departs hence, what good or evil he has done, and how his judgment will lie. And he sang too the antiphons, of which one is, "O King of Glory, Lord of Angels, who this day hast ascended in triumph above all the heavens, leave us not orphans, but send the promise of the Father upon us, the Spirit of Truth, alleluia." And when he came to the words, "leave us not orphans," he burst into tears, and wept much. He said, too, "God scourgeth every son whom He receiveth," and, with St. Ambrose, "I have not so lived as to be ashamed to have been among you, nor do I fear to die, for we have a good Lord."

In those days, besides our lectures and the Psalmody, he was engaged in two works; he was translating into English the Gospel of St. John, as far as the words, "But what are these among so many," and some extracts from the *Notae*[40] of Isidore. On the Tuesday before Ascension Day he began to suffer still more in his breathing, and his feet were slightly swollen. However, he went through the day, dictating cheerfully, and he kept saying from time to time, "Take down what I say quickly, for I know not how long I am to last, or whether my Maker will not take me soon." He seemed to us to be quite aware of the time of his going, and he passed that night in giving of thanks, without sleeping. As soon as morning broke, that is on the Wednesday, he urged us to make haste with the writing which we had begun. We did so till nine o'clock, when we walked in procession with the Relics of the Saints, according to the usage of that day. But one of our party said to him, "Dearest Master, one chapter is still wanting; can you bear our asking you about it?" He answered, "I can bear it; take your pen and be ready, and write quickly." At three o'clock he said to me, "Run fast, and call our priests, that I may divide among them some little gifts which I have in my box." When I had done this in much agitation, he spoke to each, urging and entreating them all to make a point of saying Masses and prayers for him. Thus he passed the day in joy until

> the evening, when the above-named youth said to him, "Dear Master, there is yet one sentence not written"; he answered, "Write quickly." Presently the youth said, "Now it is written"; he replied, "Good, thou hast said the truth; *consummatum est*; take my head into thy hands, for it is very pleasant to me to sit facing my old praying place, and thus to call upon my Father." And so, on the floor of his cell, he sang, "Glory be to Father, Son, and Holy Ghost," and, just as he had said "Holy Ghost," he breathed his last, and went to the realms above."

It is remarkable that this flower of the Benedictine school died on the same day as St. Philip Neri (May 26); Bede on Ascension Day, and Philip on the early morning after the feast of Corpus Christi. It was fitting that two saints should go to heaven together, whose mode of going thither was the same; both of them singing, praying, working, and guiding others, in joy and exultation, till their very last hour.

Notes for The Mission of Saint Benedict

1. Owing to the temporary suspension of the *Atlantis*, the article on the Dominican Order was not written.
2. Helyot, Hist. Mon. Ziegelbauer, Litt. Hist. Soame's Mosheim, vol. ii., p. 26. Brockie. Praef. ad Regul. Buckingham's Bible in the Middle Ages, p. 81, etc., etc.
3. Butler, June 22.
4. Thomassin, Disc. Eccl., t. i., p. 705. Calmet, Reg. Ben., t. ii., p. 25. Mabillon, Acta Saec. iv., p. 1, praef., p. xxx. Annal., t. i., praef., § 19.
5. Reg., c. 61.
6. Mabillon, Act Benedict., t. iv., p. 1, p. xxxvii.
7. History of Civilization, vol. ii., p. 65, Bohn; and so Ampère.
8. Epiph. Haer., 69.
9. Ep. 2. *Vid.* Supr. p. 63.
10. Dial., i. 1. *Vid.* Essays, vol. ii., p. 284.
11. Me verò primùm dulces ante omnia Musae...
    Accipiant, *coelique vias et sidera monstrent*, etc., etc.
    Sin, has ne possim naturae accedere partes,
    Frigidus obstiterit circùm praecordia sanguis,
    Rura mihi et rigui placeant in vallibus amnes, etc.
    And so again:
    Felix, qui potuit rerum cognoscere *causas*, etc.
    Fortunatus et ille, Deos qui novit agrestes, etc.
12. Voyage Littéraire. *Vid.* also Calmet, Lorraine, t. i., p. 1043. Moreri, art. S. Hubert. Gallia Christ., t. iii. p. 966. Mabillon, Annal. Bened., t. ii., pp. 16, 441, 606. Bucherii, Gest. Tungr. etc., t. i., p. 153. Helyot, Ordres Mon., t. vi., p. 296.
13. Vol. i., p. 237, etc.
14. Hallam, Middle Ages, vol. iii., p. 436. Forsyth, Antiqu., vol. i., pp. 37, 44, 179. Turner, Anglo-Sax., vol. ii., p. 167. Murdoch's Mosheim, vol. ii., p. 21, etc. Guizot, Hist. Civil., vol. ii., p. 75, Bohn.
15. Neander, Memorials, pp. 436, 451, 473, Bohn. Rader, Bavaria Sacra. Calles, Arm. Germ., t. i., pp. 200, 276, 317, 318. Guizot, Civil., vol. ii., p 134. Whitaker's Cornwall, vol. ii., p. 196. Fosbroke, Antiq. p. 16.
16. Meyrick's Willibald, p. 68. Bavaria Sacra, p.119. Petri, Suevia Eccles., p. 96. Calles Ann. Germ., t. i., p. 191.
17. Butler's Lives, Aug. 20.
18. Apud. Mabillon Act. Bened.
19. Thomass. Disc. Eccl. t. iii., p. 513.
20. P. 93. The passage seems taken from Bede.
21. Bede, Hist. Eccles., i. 26. William of Malmesb. Ponfic. Angl.
22. *Vid.* Supr. p. 198.
23. Eccl. Hist., vol. vii., p. 331, Bohn.

24. Duchesne, Script. North., p. 236.
25. Turner, Middle Ages, vol. v., p. 89.
26. P. 37.
27. *Vid.* Turner, Anglo-Saxons, vol. iii., p. 468.
28. Pallad, c. 39. Cassian, Inst., iv., 12. Calmet, Reg., t. ii., p. 150. Thomassin, Disc. Eccl., t. iii., p. 505. Ziegelbaum, Hist. Litt. Bened., t. ii., p. 510.
29. Annal. Camald., t. vii., p. 300: *vid.* other instances in Maitland's Dark Ages, and Buckingham's Bible in the Middle Ages, who, however, is deficient in references.
30. Guizot's Hist. Civil., vol. ii., p. 236, Bohn.
31. See p. 45.
32. *Vid*, also Whitaker's Cornwall, vol. i., p. 167, and the whole chapter.
33. Meehan's Marchese, p. xxiv.
34. Hist. Litter. de St. Maur. 1770, p. 21.
35. P. 379. Printing, another tranquil work, was introduced into Italy by the Benedictines of Subiaco. *Vid.* Dr. Ullathorne's Pilgrimage.
36. Introd. Eccles. Hist., p. 56.
37. Ziegelbaur, t. ii., p. 401.
38. *Ibid.*, t. i., p. 424. For lists of monastic histories, *vid.* Mr. Dowling, Introd. E. H., p. 260; the Asceticon as above, § 26. Ziegelbaur, t. ii., p. 398. Balmez., Prot. and Cath., p. 195.
39. Stud. Monast., ed. 1732; t. i., pp. 52, 135; t. ii., p. 2; t. i., pp. 145, 147, 191, 64.
40. The Bollandists have not been able to determine which of St. Isidore's works is here intended. "Notae" means "Musical Notes," according to Du Cange. According to Leboeuf in Ampère, Hist. Litter. t. iii., p. 253, the word means "penmanship."

Second Essay

The Benedictine Schools

❊ ❊ ❊

SECOND ESSAY

The Benedictine Schools

From the Atlantis *of* January 1859

§1.

We read in history of great commanders, who, when an overwhelming force was directed against them on the plain, and success was for the time impossible, submitted to necessity, and, with plans afterwards to be developed, retired up the mountain passes in their rear, where nature had provided a safe halting-place for brave men who could not advance, and would not turn in flight. There, behind the lofty crag, the treacherous morass, and the thick wood, they nursed their confidence of victory, and waited patiently for an issue, which was not less certain because it was delayed. On came the haughty foe, with cries of defiance; and when at length he thought he had them at his mercy, he found that first he must do battle with the adamantine rocks, which sternly rose up in defence of fugitives who had invoked their aid. Then he stood for a while irresolute, till the difficulties of his position ended his deliberation, and forced upon him a retreat in his turn, while the lately besieged hosts were once more in motion, and pressed upon the baffled foe, who had neither plan of campaign nor base of operations to fall back upon.

Such is the history of Christian civilization. It gave way before the barbarians of the north and the fanatics of the south; it fled into the wilderness with its own books and those of the old social system which it was succeeding. It obeyed the direction given it in the beginning—when persecuted in one place, to flee away to another; and then at length the hour of retribution came, and it advanced into the territories from which it had retired. St. Benedict is the historical emblem of its retreat, and St. Dominic of its return.

I do not say that its retreat in the first centuries was made with the intent of its return in the medieval. There was no oracular voice which proclaimed what would be the course and fortune of the war; no secret tradition which whispered to the initiated the tactic that ought to be pursued. It is a sufficient explanation of the double movement, that they who feel their weakness are used to give way, and they who feel their strength are used to push forward. The corruptions of Roman society caused Christians to despair of ever mending it, and to look out for that better world which was destined to supersede it. The evil which they experienced, the good for which they sighed, the promise in which they confided, wrought in them the persuasion that the end of all things was at hand; and this persuasion made them patient under inconveniences which they felt to be only temporary. "Behold, my brethren," says Pope Gregory about the year 600, "we already see with our eyes what we are used to hear in prophecy. Day by day is the world assaulted by fresh and thickening blows. Out of that innumerable Roman *plebs* what a mere remnant are ye at this day! Yet incessant scourges are still in action; sudden adversities thwart you; new and unforeseen slaughters wear you away. For, as in youth, the body is in vigour, the chest is strong, the neck muscular, and the arms plump, but in old age the stature is bent, the neck is withered and stooping, the chest pants, the energies are feeble, and breath is wanting for the words; so the world too once was vigorous, robust for the increase of its kind, green in its health, and opulent in its resources, but now on the contrary it is laden with the weight of years, and is fast sinking into the grave by its ever-multiplying maladies. Beware, then, of giving your heart to that which, as even your senses tell you, cannot last for ever."[1] Commonly the presentiment wore a more definitely supernatural expression than is found in this extract. Not sense merely, but the prophecies were directly invoked, which spoke of that great enemy of the Church, who was to be the herald of the Second Advent; and the rudiments of a new order of things were descried in the manifest tokens of an expiring world.

In all times, indeed, the multitude, whether from religious feeling or from superstition, is prone to portend some impending catastrophe from the occurrence of any startling phenomenon of nature. An eclipse, a comet, a volcanic eruption, is to them the omen of coming evil. But in the early centuries of the Church the expectation extended to the learned and the saintly. It was the posture of mind of confessors and doctors. As St. Gregory looked out for Antichrist in the sixth century, so had the Martyrs of Lyons in the second, St. Cyprian in the third, St. Hilary and St. Chrysostom in the fourth, and St. Jerome in the fifth. It was the sober judgment of the wisest and the most charitable, that the world was too bad to mend, and that destruction was close upon it.

What would be the practical result of such a belief? That which I have partly described in my remarks on the mission of St. Benedict; evidently, to leave the world to itself. Evils which threaten to continue we try to remedy; but what was the use of spending one's strength in reforming a state of things which would go to pieces, if let alone, and, if ever so much meddled with, would go to pieces too, nay, the sooner, perhaps, for the meddling? Hence it was the prevalent disposition, as I have said, of Christians of the first centuries, and no irrational disposition, either to leave the world or to put up with it, not to set about influencing it. "Let us go hence," said the Angels in the doomed sanctuary of the chosen people. "Come ye out of her, my people," was the present bidding of inspiration. Those who would be perfect obeyed it, and became monks. Monachism therefore was a sort of recognized emigration from the old world. St. Antony had found out a new coast, the true *eldorado* or gold country; and on the news of it thousands took their departure year after year for the diggings in the desert. The monks of Egypt alone soon became an innumerable host. As times got worse, Basil in the East, and Benedict in the West, put themselves at the head of fresh colonies, bound for the land of perpetual peace. There they sat them down, over against Babylon, and waited for the coming judgment and the end of all things. Those who remained in the world, waited too. To undergo patiently what was—to make the best of it, to use it, as far as it could be used, for religious purposes—was their wisdom and their resolve. If they took another course, they would be wasting strength and hope upon a shadow, and losing the present for a future which would never come. They had no large designs or profound policy. It was their aim that things should just last their time. They patched them up as best they might, they made shift, and lived from hand to mouth; and they followed events, rather than created them. Nor, when they undertook great labours and began works pregnant with consequences, did they perceive whither they were going.

How different in this respect is the spirit of the first Gregory, already cited, from that of Hildebrand, the seventh! Gregory the First did not understand his own act, when he converted the Anglo-Saxons; nor Ambrose, when he put Theodosius to penance. The great Christian Fathers laid anew the foundations of the world, while they thought that its walls were tottering to the fall, and that they already saw the fires of judgment through the chinks. They refuted Arianism, which they named the forerunner of the last woe, with reasonings which were to live for ages; and they denounced the preachers of a carnal millennium, without anticipating that wonderful temporal reign of the saints which was to be manifested in medieval times. They propounded broad principles, but did not carry them out into their inevitable consequences. How slow were they to define doctrine, when disputes arose about its meaning or its bearing! How patient they seem to us of imperial encroachments on ecclesiastical rights, when we view them by the side of the great Popes who came after them! How tamely do they conduct themselves when the civil magistrate interferes with their jurisdiction, or takes the initiative in points of discipline or order, in questions of property, and matrimonial causes! How contented or resigned are they to avail themselves of such education as the state provided for their use; sending their children to the pagan schools, before they have teachers of their own, and, even when at length they have them, adopting the *curriculum* of studies which those pagan schools had devised!

In fact, in the minds of those high saints, "the wish was father to the thought." Religious men will always desire, will always be prone to believe, the approach of that happier order of things, which sooner or later is to be. This hope was the form in which the deep devotion of those primitive times showed itself; and if it did not continue in its full expression beyond them, this was because experience had thrown a new light upon the course of Divine Providence in the world. With the multitude, indeed, as I have said, who know little of history, and in whom religious fear is a chief element, the anticipation of the Last Day revived, and revives, from time to time. At the end of the tenth century, when a thousand years had passed over the Church, the sense of impending destruction was so vivid as even to affect the transfer and disposal of property, and the repair of sacred buildings. However, when we seek in theologians for the apprehension, we shall find that it is a characteristic of the old Empire far more than of the barbarian kingdoms which succeeded to it. The barbarian world was young, as the Roman world was effete. Youth is the season of hope; and, according as things looked more cheerful, so did they look more lasting, and today's sunshine became the sufficient promise of a long summer. A fervent preacher here or there, St. Norbert or St. Vincent Ferrer, may have had forebodings of the end of all things; or an astrologer or a schismatizing teacher may have traded on the belief; but the men of gravity and learning after the time of Gregory the First, for the most part, set their faces against speculations about the future.

Bede, after speaking of the six ages of the world, says, that "as no one of the former ages has consisted exactly of a thousand years, it follows that the sixth too, under which we live, is of uncertain length, known to Him alone who has bidden His servants watch. For," he continues, "whereas all saints naturally love the hour of His advent, and desire it to be near, still, we run into danger if we presume to conclude or to proclaim, either that the hour is near or that it is far off."[2] Raban and Adson, who witnessed or heard of the splendours of Charlemagne, go so far as to indulge the vision of a great king of the Franks, who, in time to come, is to reign religiously, ere the fulfilment of the bad times of the end.[3] Theodulf indeed predicts that they were coming; but, even when the popular excitement was at its height, in the last years of the tenth century, Richard and Abbo of Fleury, and the Adson above mentioned, set themselves against it. Hardly was the dreaded crisis over, when men took heart, and began to restore and decorate the Churches; hardly had the new century run its course, when Pope Paschal the Second held a Council at Florence against Raynerius, the archbishop of that city, who had preached of the coming end.[4] Such was the change of sentiment which followed after the Pontificate of St. Gregory, the last and saddest of a line of Fathers, who thought the world was on the verge of dissolution.

The names which I have been introducing show that, among these converts to a more hopeful view of things, were Benedictine monks, members of those very associations which had given up the world as lost, and had quitted it accordingly. And the position which they occupy in their own body is sufficient evidence that what they held, their brethren held also; and that the actual changes which had taken place in the framework of society had been followed by a change of sentiment in these religious bodies. When we look into history, to see where these preachers of new hopes were, as well as who, we find the fact plain beyond all denial; for it is the monk Alcuin who was Charlemagne's instructor, and head of the school of the palace; the monk Theodulf who was a political *employé* of the same Emperor, and bishop of Orleans; and the monk Raban who was archbishop of Mayence. How could the cloister-loving monk have come to such places of station, unless he had experienced some singular change in his sentiments? And these instances, it must be allowed, are only samples of a phenomenon which is not uncommon in these centuries. Here then we have something to explain. Why should Benedictines leave those sweet country-homes which St. Benedict bequeathed to them for the haunts of men, the seats of learning, archiepiscopal sees, and king's courts? St. Jerome had said, when Monachism was young: "If the priest's office be your choice, if a bishop's work or dignity be your attraction, live a town life, and save your soul in saving others. But, if you wish to be a monk, that is a solitary, in fact as well as in name, what have you to do with towns?" "A monk's office," he says elsewhere, "is not a teacher's but a mourner's, who bewails either himself or the world."[5] This, doubtless, was the primary aim and badge of the religious institute; and if, among uncongenial offices, there were one more uncongenial to it than another, it was that of a ruler or a master of the faithful. The monk did not lecture, teach, controvert, lay down the law, or give the word of command; and for this simple reason, because he did not speak at all, because he was bound to silence. He who had given up the use of his tongue, could neither be preacher nor disputant. It follows, we repeat, that a singular change must have taken place by the ninth century in the ecclesiastical position of a monk, when we find instances of his acting so differently from St. Jerome's teaching and example in the fifth.

I touched, in the Essay to which I have already referred, upon this seeming anomaly in the history of the Benedictines, while I was describing them in outline; if I did not then dwell upon it and investigate its limits, this was because I thought it advisable first to trace out the general idea of the monastic state, with as little interruption as was possible, without risking the confusion which would arise in my delineation from a premature introduction of the historical modifications to which that idea has actually been subjected. Now, however, the time has come for taking up what in that former sketch I passed over; and I propose accordingly here, after a brief reference to the circumstances under which these modifications appeared, and to the extent to which they spread, to direct attention to the principal instance of them, viz., the literary employments of the monks, and to show how singularly, after all, these employments, as carried out, were in keeping with the main idea of the monastic rule, even though they seem at first sight scarcely contained in its letter. I stated, on that former occasion, that the substance of the monastic life was *summa quies*; that its object was rest, its state retirement, and its occupations such as were unexciting and had their end in themselves. That the literature in question was consistent with these conditions will be clearly seen, when I come to describe it; first, however, let me consider the circumstances which called for it, and the hold which it had upon the general body.

§2.

IT IS rare, indeed, to find the profession and the history of any institution running exactly in one and the same groove. The political revolutions which issued in the rule of Charlemagne, changing, as they did, the currents of the world, and the pilotage of St. Peter's bark, became a severe trial of the consistency of an Order, like the Benedictine, of which the maxims and the aims are grave, definite, and fixed. Demands of action and work would be made on it, by the exigencies of the times, at variance with its genius, and it would find itself in the dilemma of failing in efficiency on the one hand, or in faithfulness to its engagements on the other. It would be incurring either the impatience of Society, which it disappointed, or the remonstrances of its own subjects, whom it might be considered to betray.

And indeed a greater shock can hardly be fancied than that which would overtake the peaceful inhabitant of the cloister, on his finding that, after all, he so intimately depended still upon this moribund world, which he had renounced for ever, that the changes which were taking place in its condition were affecting his own. Such men, whether senators like Paulinus, or courtiers like Arsenius, or legionaries like Martin, had one and all, in their respective places and times, left the responsibilities of earth for the anticipations of heaven.[6] They had sought, in the lonely wood or the silent mountain top, the fair uncorrupted form of nature, which spoke only of the Creator. They had retired into deserts, where they could have no enemies but such as fast and prayer could subdue. They had gone where the face of man was not, except as seen in pale, ascetic apparitions like themselves. They had secured some refuge, whence they might look round at the sick world in the distance, and see it die. But, when that last hour came, it did but frustrate all their hopes, for, instead of an old world at a distance, they found they had a young world close to them. The old order of things died, sure enough; but then a new order took its place, and they themselves, by no will or expectation of their own, were in no small measure its very life. The lonely Benedictine rose from his knees and found himself a city. This was the case, not merely here or there, but everywhere; Europe was new mapped, and the monks were the principle of mapping. They had grown into large communities, into abbeys, into corporations with civil privileges, into land-holders with tenants, serfs, and baronial neighbours; they had become centres of population, the schools of the most cherished truths, the shrines of the most sacred confidences. They found themselves priests, rulers, legislators, feudal lords, royal counsellors, missionary preachers, controversialists; and they comprehended that unless they fled anew from the face of man, as St. Antony in the beginning, they must bid farewell to the hope of leading St. Antony's life.

In this choice of difficulties, when there was a duty to stay and a duty to take flight, the monastic bodies were not unwilling to come to a compromise with the age, and, reserving their fidelity to St. Benedict, to undertake those functions to which both the world and the Church called them. Such, that is, for the most part, was the resolve of those who found themselves in this perplexity; but it could not be supposed that there were no Antonies on earth still, and that these would be satisfied to adopt it. On the contrary, there were holy men who were but impelled into a reaction of the most rigid asceticism by this semblance of a reconciliation between their brethren and the world. Such was St. Romuald in the tenth century, the founder of the Camaldolese, who, through a long life of incredible austerities, was ever forming new monastic stations, and leaving them when formed, from love of solitude. Such St. Bruno, the founder of the Carthusians, whose conversion, as described in the well-known legend, points to the union in his day of intellectual gifts and dissoluteness of life. "Come, dear friend," he is represented as saying to some companions, concerning the awful death which he had witnessed, "what is to become of us? If a man of this doctor's rank and repute, of such literary, such scientific attainments, of such seeming-virtuous life, of so wide a reputation, is thus indubitably damned, what is to become of poor creatures of no estimation, such as we are?"[7] Such, again, was St. Stephen of Grandimont, who, when two Cardinals came to see and wonder at him in his French desert, excused himself by saying, "How could we serve churches and undertake cures who are dead to the world, and have every member of our body cut off from this life, with neither feet to walk, nor tongues to speak withal?"[8] These, and others such, sought out for themselves a seclusion and silence, most congenial to the original idea of monachism, but incompatible with those active duties—missions, the pastoral office, teaching in the schools, and disputations with heresy—which at the time there were none but monks to fulfil.

Would that nothing worse than the demand of such sacred duties brought the monasteries into the world, and drove these reformers into the desert! The law of God was often broken by the monks, as well as the rule of St. Benedict. Grave moral disorders arose within their walls; and that partly indeed from the seductions of ease, wealth, and the homage of mankind, but in a great measure also from the political troubles of the times, which exposed them to the tyranny of the military chief or the violence of the marauder. Relaxation will easily take place in a religious community, when, from whatever circumstance, it cannot observe its rule; and what orderly observance could there be when the country round about was the seat of war and rapine? Nay, a simpler process of monastic degeneracy followed from the high hand of military power. Kings seized the temporalities of the abbeys for their favourites, and made licentious soldiers bishops and abbots; and these, by their terrors and their bribes, fostered a lax irreligious party in the heart of these communities up and down the country. This part of the history, however, does not concern us in these pages, which are devoted to the consideration of the real work of the Benedictine, not to the injuries or interruptions which it has sustained, or to corruptions which are not its own.

On the other hand, not kings alone interfered with St. Benedict. A not less forcible overruling of his tradition took place from another quarter, where there was authority for the act, and where nothing would be done except on religious principles and with religious purposes. It was a more serious interference, for the very reason that it was a legal one, proceeding from the Church herself. According to the maxim, "sacramenta propter homines," she has never hesitated to consider, in this sense of the maxim, that "the end justifies the means"; and since Regulars of whatever sort are her own creation, she can of course alter, or adapt, or change, or bring to nought, according as her needs require, the institutions which she has created. Necessity has no law, and charity has no reserves; and she has acted accordingly. She brought the Benedictine from his cloister into the political world; but, as far as she did so, let it be observed, it was her act and not his. If then, on account of the necessities of the day, she has overruled his resolve, and made him do what neither his tradition nor his wishes suggested, such instances cannot fairly be taken, either as specimens of Benedictine work, or as modifications of the Benedictine idea.

And such cases abound. St. Benedict himself had with difficulty contemplated a priest as being in the ranks of his children; laying it down in his Rule, "If a priest asks to be received in any monastery, his request must not quickly be granted; but if he persists, the whole discipline of the rule is binding on him without any relaxation" (C. 60). But Pope Gregory, who had himself been torn violently from the cloister to fill the Pontifical throne, spared his religious brethren as little as he had been spared himself. He made a number of them bishops. From his own convent on the Caelian he sent Augustine and his companions to be apostolic missionaries to the Anglo-Saxons, and he designed to put the entire episcopate and priesthood of the newly-converted race and thereby their secular concerns, into the hands of the monks.[9] As to the Archbishops of Canterbury, they actually were monks down to the twelfth century.[10] This is but a specimen of what was largely carried out by the Holy See on the continent in the centuries which followed Gregory; but, I repeat, the Pope's action is external to the Benedictines, who are as little compromised by his consecrating hand as by the iron glove of the feudal tyrant.

To whatever extent, however, these innovations went, whether they were simple profanations, or were made and ratified by the wise policy of those who had a right to make them, and whatever show they make in history from the circumstance of their necessary connection with public events, with principal cities, and with prominent men, we cannot speak of them as constituting any great exception to the monastic discipline, or as exerting any considerable influence on the monastic spirit, till we have surveyed the religious institutions of Christendom as a whole, and measured them by the side of the general view thus obtained. I had occasion in my former Essay to speak of the condition of the early monks, their various families, the rise of the Benedictines, and the process of assimilation and absorption, by which at length St. Benedict gathered under his own rule the disciples of St. Martin, St. Caesarius, and St. Columban. And even when the whole monastic body was Benedictine, it was not on that account moulded upon one type, or dependent upon one centre. As it had not spread out from one origin, so neither was it homogeneous in its construction nor simple and concordant in its action. It propagated itself variously, and had much of local character in its secondary dispositions. We cannot be certain what it was in one place by knowing what it was in another. One house attained more nearly to what may be called its normal idea than another, and therefore we have no right to argue that such quasi-secularizations as I have noticed extended much further than those particular cases which history has handed down to us.

And then, on the other hand, we must bear in mind how vast was the whole multitude of persons who professed the monastic life, and, compared with it, how small was the number of those who were called away to active political duties or who gave themselves to literature or science. They might all be subtracted from the sum total of religious, and, as far as number goes, they would not have been missed. I have already referred to the exuberance of Egyptian monachism. Antony left to Pachomius the rule of 50,000. Posthumus of Memphis presided over 5,000; Ammon over 3,000. In the one city of Oxyrinchus there were 10,000. Hilarion in Syria had from 2,000 to 3,000. Martin of Gaul was followed to the grave by 2,000 of his disciples. At that date the sees of the whole of Christendom, according to Bingham, did not go much beyond 1,700.[11] If every bishop then had been a monk, the general character of monastic life would not have been much affected. In a later age, the monastery of Bangor contained 2,000; that of Banchor, county Down, according to St. Bernard, "many thousand monks," one of whom founded as many as

100 monasteries in various places.[12] Again, the Episcopal Sees of France are given in the *Gallia Christiana* as one hundred and sixty, including the provinces of Utrecht, Cologne, and Treves; and precisely that number of monastic houses is said to have been founded in that country by St. Maur alone, in the very first years of the Benedictines. Trithemius, at the end of the fifteenth century, numbers the Benedictine convents as 15,000[13]; and, though we are not to suppose that each of them had the 2,000 subjects which we find at Bangor, the lowest average will swell the sum total of monks to a vast multitude. In the beginning of the previous century, a census of the Benedictines was taken by John XXII to which Helyot refers, according to which the Order, from its commencement up to that time, had had 22,000 archbishops and bishops, and of saints alone, 40,000. Vague calculations or statements are sufficient to represent general truths; it is difficult to determine what is the percentage of heroic virtue in a population of regulars; if we say at random, as many saints as one in the hundred, even at this rate the number of Benedictines would reach 4,000,000, and the Episcopal portion would be only the one hundred and eightieth part of the whole Order.

More data, then, than we need, will be left to us in history, to determine the monastic vocation, even though we strike out from the list of its disciples every monk who took any secular office, as of prelate, lecturer, or disputant; nay, though we formed all those who undertook such duties into evidence of an opposite mode of life. But in fact, these very men, who in one way or another were engaged in work, which St. Benedict has not recognized by name, are themselves specimens of fidelity to their founder, and impress the Benedictine type of sanctity upon their literary or political undertakings. The proverb, "naturam expellas furcâ," etc., holds true of religion. Whatever has life has in it a conservative principle, and a power of assimilation. Where the religious spirit was strong, it would overcome obstacles in its exercise, and revive after overthrows, and would make for itself preternatural channels for its operations, when its legitimate course was denied to it. Neither the functions of an Apostle, nor of a schoolmaster, are much akin to those of a monk; nevertheless, in a given individual, they may be reconciled, or the one merged in the other. The Benedictine missionary soon relapsed into the laborious husbandman; the champion of the faith flung his adversary, and went back to his plough or his pen; the bishop, like Peter Damian, effected, or like Boniface, contemplated, a return in his old age to the cloister which he had left. As to the schools of learning, it will be my business now to show how undisputatious was the master, and how unexciting the studies.

§3.

THE RISE and extension of these Schools seems to me as great an event in the history of the Order as the introduction of the sacerdotal office into the number of its functions. If Pope Gregory took a memorable step in turning the monks of his convent into missionary bishops, charged with the conversion of England, much more remarkable was the act of Pope Vitalian, in sending the old Greek monk Theodore to the same island, to fill the vacant see of Canterbury. I call it more remarkable, because it introduced an actual tradition into the Benedictine houses, and consecrated a system by authority. It is true that from an early date in the history of monachism, extensive learning had been combined with the profession of a monk. St. Jerome was only too fond of the Cicero and Horace, whom he put aside; and, if out of the whole catalogue of ecclesiastics I had to select a literary Father, the monk Jerome, *par excellence,* would be he. In the next century Claudian Mamercus, of Vienne, employed the leisure which his monastic profession gave him to gain an extensive knowledge of Greek and Latin literature. He collected a library of Greek, Roman, and Christian books, "quam totam, monachus," says Sidonius of him, "virente in aevo, secretâ bibit institutione."[14] And in the century after, Cassiodorus, the contemporary of St. Benedict, is well known for combining sacred and classical studies in his monastery. The tradition, however, of the cloister was up to that time against profane literature, and Theodore reversed it.

Theodore made his appearance at the end of the century which the missionary Augustine opened, and just about the time when the whole extent of England had been converted to the Christian faith. He brought with him Greek as well as Latin Classics, and set up schools for both the learned languages in various parts of the country. Henceforth the curriculum of the Seven Sciences is found in the Benedictine Schools. From Theodore[15] proceeded Egbert and the school of York; from Egbert came Bede and the school of Jarrow; from Bede, Alcuin and the schools of Charlemagne at Paris, Tours, and Lyons. From these came Raban and the school of Fulda; from Raban, Walafrid and the school of Richenau, Lupus and the school of Ferrières. From Lupus, Heiric, Remi, and the school of Rheims; from Remi, Odo of Cluni; from the dependencies of Cluni, the celebrated Gerbert, afterwards Pope Sylvester the Second, and Abbo of Fleury, whom I have already introduced to the reader's notice, though not by name, in the former part of this sketch, as repaying a portion of the debt which the Franks owed to the Anglo-Saxons by opening the schools of Ramsey Abbey, after the inroad of the Danes.

In addressing myself, then, at length, to the question, how such studies can be considered in keeping with the original idea of the monastic state, I think it right to repeat an explanation which I made at an earlier stage of the discussion, to the effect that I am proposing nothing more than a survey of the venerable order of St. Benedict from without; and I claim leave to do as much as this by the same right by which the humblest among us may freely and without offence gaze on sun, moon, and stars, and form his own private opinion, true or false, of their materials and their motions. And with this proviso, I remind the reader, if I have not sufficiently done so already, that the one object, immediate as well as ultimate, of Benedictine life, as history presents it to us, was to live in purity and to die in peace. The monk proposed to himself no great or systematic work, beyond that of saving his soul. What he did more than this was the accident of the hour, spontaneous acts of piety, the sparks of mercy or beneficence, struck off in the heat, as it were, of his solemn religious toil, and done and over almost as soon as they began to be. If today he cut down a tree, or relieved the famishing, or visited the sick, or taught the ignorant, or transcribed a page of Scripture, this was a good in itself, though nothing was added to it tomorrow. He cared little for knowledge, even theological, or for success, even though it was religious. It is the character of such a man to be contented, resigned, patient, and incurious; to create or originate nothing; to live by tradition. He does not analyze, he marvels; his intellect attempts no comprehension of this multiform world, but on the contrary, it is hemmed in, and shut up within it. It recognizes but one cause in nature and in human affairs, and that is the First and Supreme; and why things happen day by day in this way, and not in that, it refers immediately to His will.[16] It loves the country, because it is His work; but "man made the town," and he and his works are evil. This is what may be called the Benedictine idea, viewed in the abstract; and, as being such, I gave it, in my former Essay, the title of "poetical," when contrasted with that of other religious orders; and I did so, because I considered I saw in it a congeniality, *mutatis mutandis*, with the spirit of a great Roman Poet, who has perhaps a better title to that high name than any one else, at least in this respect, as having received a wider homage than others, and that among nations in time, place, and character, further removed from each other.[17]

Now, supposing the historical portrait of the Benedictine to be such as this, and that we were further told, that he was concerned with study and with teaching, and then were asked, keeping in mind the notion of his poetry of character, to guess what books he studied and what sort of pupils he taught, we should without much difficulty conclude that Scripture would be his literature, and that children would be the members of his school.[18] And, if we were further asked what was likely to be, after Scripture, the subject-matter of the schooling imparted to these boys, probably we should not be able to make any guess at all; but we surely should not be very much surprised to be told that the same spirit which led him to prefer the old basilicas for worship instead of any new architecture of his own inventing, and to honour his emperor or king with spontaneous loyalty more than by theological definitions, had also induced him, in the matter of education, to take up with the old books and subjects which he found ready to his hand in the pagan schools, as far as he could religiously do so, rather than to venture on any experiments or system of his own.[19] This, as I have already intimated, was the case. He adopted the Roman curriculum, professed the Seven Sciences, beginning with Grammar, that is, the Latin classics, and, if he sometimes finished with them, it was because his boys left him ere he had time to teach them more. The subjects he chose were his fit recompense for choosing them. He adopted the Latin writers from his love of prescription, because he found them in possession. But there were in fact no writings, after Scripture, more congenial, from their fresh and natural beauty and their freedom from intellectualism, to the monastic temperament. Such were his schoolbooks; and as "the boy is father of the man," the little monks, who had heard them read or pored over them, when they grew up filled the atmosphere of the monastery with the tasks and studies with which they had thus been imbued in their childhood.

For so it was, strange as it seems to our ideas, these boys were monks[20]—monks as truly as those of riper years. About St. Benedict's time the Latin Church innovated upon the discipline of former centuries, and allowed parents not only to dedicate their infants to a religious life, but to do so without any power on the part of those infants, when they came to years of reason, to annul the dedication. This discipline continued for five or six centuries, beginning with the stern Spaniards, nor ending till shortly before the pontificate of Innocent the Third. Divines argued in behalf of it from the case of infant baptism, in which the sleeping soul without being asked, is committed to the most solemn of engagements; from that of Isaac on the Mount, and of Samuel, and from the sanction of the Mosaic Law; and they would be confirmed in their course by the instances of compulsion, not uncommon in the early centuries, when high magistrates or wealthy heads of families were suddenly seized on by the populace or by synods, and, against their remonstrances, tonsured, ordained, and consecrated, before they could well take breath and realize to themselves their change of station. Nor must we forget the old Roman law, the spirit of which they had inherited, and which gave to the father the power even of life and death over his refractory offspring.

However, childhood is not the age at which the severity of the law would be felt, which bound a man by his parent's act to the service of the cloister. While these oblates were but children, they were pretty much like other children; they threw a grace over the stern features of monastic asceticism, and peopled the silent haunts of penance with a crowd of bright innocent faces. "Silence was pleased," to use the poet's language, when it was broken by the cheerful, and sometimes, it must be confessed, unruly voices of a set of school-boys. These would sometimes, certainly, be inconveniently loud, especially as St. Benedict did not exclude from his care lay-boys, destined for the world. It was more than the devotion of some good monks could bear; and they preferred some strict Reform, which, among its new provisions, prohibited the presence of these uncongenial associates. But, after all, it was no great evil to place before the eyes of austere manhood and unlovely age a sight so calculated to soften and to cheer. It was not adolescence, with its curiosity, its pride of knowledge and its sensitiveness, with its disputes and emulations, with its exciting prizes and its impetuous breathless efforts, which St. Benedict undertook to teach; he was no professor in a University. His convent was an infant school, a grammar school, and a seminary; it was not an academy. Indeed, the higher education in that day scarcely can be said to exist. It was a day of bloodshed and of revolution; before the time of life came when the University succeeds the School, the student had to choose his profession. He became a clerk or a monk, or else he became a soldier.

The fierce northern warriors, who had won for themselves the lands of Christendom with their red hands, rejoiced to commit their innocent offspring to the custody of religion and of peace. Nay, sometimes with the despotic will, of which I have just now spoken, they dedicated them, from or before their birth, to the service of Heaven. They determined that some at least of their lawless race should be rescued from the contamination of blood and licence, and should be set apart in sacred places to pray for their kindred. The little beings,[21] of three or four or five years old, were brought in the arms of those who gave them life to accept at their bidding the course in which that life was to run. They were brought into the sanctuary, spoke by the mouth of their parents, as at the font, put out their tiny hand for the sacred corporal to be wrapped round it, received the cowl, and took their place as monks in the monastic community. In the first ages of the Benedictine Order, these children were placed on a level with their oldest brethren. They took precedence according to their date of admission, and the grey head gave way to them in choir and refectory, if junior to them in monastic standing. They even voted in the election of abbot, being considered to speak by divine instinct, as the child who cried out, "Ambrose is Bishop."[22] If they showed waywardness in community meetings, inattention at choir, ill behaviour at table, which certainly was not an impossible occurrence, they were corrected by the nods, the words, or the blows of the grave brother who happened to be next them: it was not till an after time that they had a prefect of their own, except in school hours.

That harm came from this remarkable discipline is only the suggestion of our modern habits and ideas; that it was not expedient for all times, follows from the fact that at a certain date it ceased to be permitted. However, that, in those centuries in which it was in force, its result was good, is seen in the history of the heroic men whom it nurtured, and might have been anticipated from the principle which it embodied. The monastery was intended to be the paternal home, not the mere refuge of the monk: it was an orphanage, not a reformatory; father and mother had abandoned him, and he grew up from infancy in the new family which had adopted him. He was a child of the house; there were stored up all the associations of his wondering boyhood, and there would lie the hopes and interests of his maturer years. He was to seek for sympathy in his brethren, and to give them his own sympathy in return. He lived and died in their presence. They prayed for his soul, cherished his memory, were proud of his name, and treasured his works. A pleasing illustration of this brotherly affection meets us in the life of Walafrid Strabo, Abbot of Richenau, whose poems, written by him when a boy of fifteen and eighteen, were preserved by his faithful friends, and thus remain to us at this day. Walafrid is but one out of many, whose names are known in history, dedicated from the earliest years to the cloister. St. Boniface, Apostle of Germany, was a monk at the age of five; St. Bede came to Wiremouth at the age of seven; St. Paul of Verdun is said by an old writer to have left his cradle for the cloister; St. Robert entered it as soon as he was weaned; Pope Paschal the Second was taken to Cluni, Ernof to Bec, the Abbot Suger to St. Denis, from their "most tender infancy."

§4.

INFANTS CAN but gaze about at what surrounds them, and their learning comes to them through their eyes. In the instances I have been considering, their minds would receive the passive impressions which were made on them by the monastic scene, and would be moulded by the composed countenances and solemn services which surrounded them. Such was the education of these little ones, till perhaps the age of seven; when, under the title of "pueri,"[23] they commenced their formal schooltime, and committed to memory their first lesson. That lesson was the Psalter—that wonderful manual of prayer and praise, which, from the time when its various portions were first composed down to the last few centuries, has been the most precious *viaticum* of the Christian mind in its journey through the wilderness. In early times St. Basil speaks of it as the popular devotion in Egypt, Africa, and Syria; and St. Jerome had urged its use upon the Roman ladies whom he directed. All monks were enjoined to know it by heart; the young ecclesiastics learned it by heart; no bishop could be ordained without knowing it by heart; and in the parish schools it was learned by heart. The Psalter, with the Lord's Prayer and Creed, constituted the *sine quâ non* condition of discipleship. At home pious mothers, as the Lady Helvidia, the mother of St. Leo the Ninth, taught their children the Psalter. It was only, then, in observance of a universal law[24] that the Benedictine children were taught it—they mastered it, and then they passed into the secular schoolroom, and were introduced to the study of grammar.[25]

By Grammar, it is hardly necessary to say, was not meant, as now, the mere analysis or rules of language, as denoted by the words etymology, syntax, prosody; but rather it stood for scholarship, that is, such an acquaintance with the literature of a language as is implied in the power of original composition and the *vivâ voce* use of it. Thus Cassiodorus defines it to be "skill in speaking elegantly, gained from the best poets and orators"; St. Isidore, "the science of speaking well"; and Raban, "the science of interpreting poets and historians, and the rule of speaking and writing well." In the monastic school, the language of course was Latin; and in Latin literature first came Virgil; next Lucan and Statius; Terence, Sallust, Cicero; Horace, Persius, Juvenal; and of Christian poets, Prudentius, Sedulius, Juvencus, Aratus. Thus we find that the monks of St. Alban's, near Mayence, had standing lectures in Cicero, Virgil, and other authors. In the school of Paderborne there were lectures in Horace, Virgil, Statius, and Sallust. Theodulf speaks of his juvenile studies in the Christian authors, Sedulius and Paulinus, Aratus, Fortunatus, Juvencus, and Prudentius, and in the classical Virgil and Ovid. Gerbert, afterwards Sylvester the Second, after lecturing his class in logic, brought it back again to Virgil, Statius, Terence, Juvenal, Persius, Horace, and Lucan. A work is extant of St. Hildebert's, supposed to be a school exercise; it is scarcely more than a cento of Cicero, Seneca, Horace, Juvenal, Persius, Terence, and other writers. Horace he must have almost known by heart.

Considering the number of authors which have to be studied in order to possessing a thorough knowledge of the Latin tongue, and the length to which those in particular run which are set down in the above lists, we may reasonably infer, that with the science of Grammar the Benedictine teaching began and ended, excepting of course such religious instruction as is rather the condition of Christian life than the acquisition of knowledge. At fourteen, when the term of boyhood was completed,[26] the school-time commonly ended too, the lay youths left for their secular career, and the monks commenced the studies appropriate to their sacred calling. The more promising youths, however, of the latter class were suffered or directed first to proceed to further secular studies; and, in order to accompany them, we must take some more detailed view of the curriculum, of which Grammar was the introductory study.

This curriculum,[27] derived from the earlier ages of heathen philosophy, was transferred to the use of the Church on the authority of St. Augustine, who in his *de Ordine* considers it to be the fitting and sufficient preparation for theological learning. It is hardly necessary to refer to the history of its formation; we are told how Pythagoras prescribed the study of arithmetic, music, and geometry; how Plato and Aristotle insisted on grammar and music, which, with gymnastics, were the substance of Greek education; how Seneca speaks, though not as approving, of grammar, music, geometry, and astronomy, as the matter of education in his own day; and how Philo, in addition to these, has named logic and rhetoric. Augustine, in his enumeration of them, begins with arithmetic and grammar, including under the latter history; then he speaks of logic and rhetoric; then of music, under which comes poetry, as equally addressing the ear; lastly, of geometry and astronomy, which address the eye. The Alexandrians, whom he followed, arranged them differently; viz., grammar, rhetoric, and logic or philosophy,[28] which branched off into the four mathematical sciences of arithmetic, music, geometry, and astronomy. And this order was adopted in Christian education, the first three sciences being called the Trivium, the last four the Quadrivium.

Grammar was taught in all these schools; but for those who wished to proceed further than the studies of their boyhood, seats of higher education had been founded by Charlemagne in the principal cities of his Empire, under the name of public schools,[29] which may be considered the shadow, and even the nucleus of the Universities which arose in a subsequent age. Such were the schools of Paris, Tours, Rheims, and Lyons in France; Fulda in Germany; Bologna in Italy. Nor did they confine themselves to the Seven Sciences above mentioned, though it is scarcely to be supposed that, in any science whatever, except Grammar, they professed to impart more than the elements. Thus we read of St. Bruno of Segni (A.D. 1080), after being grounded in the "litterae humaniores," as a boy, by the monks of St. Perpetuus near Aste, seeking the rising school of Bologna for the "altiores scientiae."[30] St. Abbo of Fleury (A.D. 990), after mastering, in the monastery of that place, grammar, arithmetic, logic, and music, went to Paris and Rheims for philosophy and astronomy; and afterwards taught himself rhetoric and geometry. Raban (A.D. 822) left the school of Fulda for a while for Alcuin's lectures, and learned Greek of a native of Ephesus. Walafrid (A.D. 840) passed from Richenau to Fulda. St. William (A.D. 908), dedicated by his parents to St. Benedict at St. Michael's near Vercellae, proceeded to study at Pavia. Gerbert (A.D. 990), one of the few cultivators of physics, after Fleury and Orleans, went to Spain.[31] St. Wolfgang (A.D. 994), after private instruction, went to Richenau. Lupus (A.D. 840), after Ferrières, was sent for a time to Fulda. Fulbert too of Chartres (A.D. 1000), though not a monk, may be mentioned as sending his pupils in like manner to finish their studies at schools of more celebrity than his own.[32]

History furnishes us with specimens of the subjects taught in this higher education. We read of Gerbert lecturing in Aristotle's Categories and the Isagogae of Porphyry; St. Theodore taught the Anglo-Saxon youths Greek and mathematics; Alcuin, all seven sciences at York; and at some German monasteries there were lectures in Greek,[33] Hebrew, and Arabic. The monks of St. Benignus at Dijon gave lectures in medicine; the abbey of St. Gall had a school of painting and engraving; the blessed Tubilo of that abbey was mathematician, painter, and musician.[34] We read of another monk of the same monastery, who was ever at his carpentry when he was not at the altar; and of another, who worked in stone. Hence Vitruvius was in repute with them. Another accomplishment was that of copying manuscripts, which they did with a perfection unknown to the scholastic age which followed them.[35]

These manual arts, far more than the severer sciences, were the true complement of the Benedictine ideal of education, which, intellectually considered, was, after all, little more than a fair or a sufficient acquaintance with Latin literature. Such is the testimony of the ablest men of the time. "To pass from Grammar to Rhetoric, and then in course to the other liberal sciences," says Lupus, speaking of France, is "fabula tantum."[36] "It has ever been the custom in Italy," says Glaber Radulphus, writing of the year 1000, "to neglect all arts but Grammar."[37] Grammar, moreover, in the sense in which we have defined it, is no superficial study, nor insignificant instrument of mental cultivation, and the school-task of the boy became the life-long recreation of the man. Amid the serious duties of their sacred vocation the monks did not forget the books which had arrested and refined their young imagination. Let us turn to the familiar correspondence of some of these more famous Benedictines, and we shall see what were the pursuits of their leisure, and the indulgences of their relaxation. Alcuin, in his letters to his friends, quotes Virgil again and again; he also quotes Horace, Terence, Pliny, besides frequent allusions to the heathen philosophers. Lupus quotes Horace, Cicero, Suetonius, Virgil, and Martial. Gerbert quotes Virgil, Cicero, Horace, Terence, and Sallust. Petrus Cellensis quotes Horace, Seneca, and Terence. Hildebert quotes Virgil and Cicero, and refers to Diogenes, Epictetus, Croesus, Themistocles, and other personages of ancient history. Hincmar of Rheims quotes Horace. Paschasius Radbert's favourite authors were Cicero and Terence. Abbo of Fleury was especially familiar with Terence, Sallust, Virgil, and Horace; Peter the Venerable, with Virgil and Horace; Hepidann of St. Gall took Sallust as a model of style.[38]

Nor is their anxiety less to enlarge the range of their classical reading. Lupus asks Abbot Hatto through a friend for leave to copy Suetonius's Lives of the Caesars, which is in the monastery of St. Boniface in two small *codices*. He sends to another friend to bring with him the Catilinarian and Jugurthan Wars of Sallust, the *Verrines* of Cicero, and any other volumes which his friend happens to know either that he has not, or possesses only in faulty copies, bidding him withal beware of the robbers on his journey. Of another friend he asks the loan of Cicero's *de Rhetoricâ,* his own copy of which is incomplete, and of Aulus Gellius. In another letter he asks the Pope for Cicero's *de Oratore,* the Institutions of Quintilian, and the commentary of Donatus upon Terence. In like manner Gerbert tells Abbot Gisilbert that he has the beginning of the *Ophthalmicus* of the philosopher Demosthenes, and the end of Cicero's *Pro rege Deiotaro;* and he wants to know if he can assist in completing them for him. He asks a friend at Rome to send him by Count Guido the copies of Suetonius and Aurelius, which belong to his archbishop and himself; he requests Constantine the lecturer (scholasticus) at Fleury, to bring him Cicero's *Verrines* and *de Republicâ*, and he thanks Remigius, a monk of Treves, for having begun to transcribe for him the Achilleid of Statius, though he had been unable to proceed with it for want of a copy. To other friends he speaks of Pliny, Caesar, and Victorinus. Alcuin's Library contained Pliny, Aristotle, Cicero, Virgil, Statius, and Lucan; and he transcribed Terence with his own hand.

Not only the memory of their own youth, but the necessity of transmitting to the next generation what during it they had learned themselves, kept them loyal to their classical acquirements. They were, in this aspect of their history, not unlike the fellows in our modern English universities, who first learn and then teach. It is impossible, indeed, to overlook their resemblance generally to the elegant scholar of a day which is now waning, especially at Oxford, such as Lowth or Elmsley, Copleston or Keble, Howley or Parr, who thought little of science or philosophy by the side of the authors of Greece and Rome. Nor is it too much to say that the Colleges in the English Universities may be considered in matter of fact to be the lineal descendants or heirs of the Benedictine schools of Charlemagne.[39] The modern of course has vastly the advantage in the comparison; for he is familiar with Greek, has an exacter criticism and purer taste, and a more refined cultivation of mind. He writes, verse at least, far better than the Benedictine, who had commonly little idea of it; and he has the accumulated aids of centuries in the shape of dictionaries and commentaries. I am not writing a panegyric on the classical learning of the dark age, but describing what it was; and, with this object before me, I observe that, whatever the monks had not, a familiar knowledge and a real love they had of the great Latin writers, and I assert, moreover, that that knowledge and love were but in keeping with the genius and character of their institute. For they instinctively recognized in the graceful simplicity of Virgil or of Horace, in his dislike of the great world, of political contests and of ostentatious splendour, in his unambitious temper and his love of the country, an analogous gift to that religious repose, that distaste for controversy, and that innocent cheerfulness which were the special legacy of St. Benedict to his children. This attachment to the classics is well expressed by a monk of Paderborn,[40] who, when he would describe the studies of the place, suffers his prose almost to dissolve into verse, as he names his beloved authors.

Viguit Horatius, magnus et Virgilius,
Crispus et Sallustius, et urbanus Statius.
Ludusque fuit omnibus, insudare versibus,
Et dictaminibus jucundisque cantibus.

The latter of these stanzas, as they may be called, illustrates what we have wished to express, in speaking of the classical temperament of the Benedictines. As far as they allowed themselves in any recreation, which was not of a sacred nature, they found it in these beautiful authors, who might be considered as the prophets of the human race in its natural condition. How strongly they contrast in this respect with the scholastic age which swallowed them up! Amid the religious or ecclesiastical matters which were the subject of their correspondence, questions of grammar and criticism are mooted, and a loving curiosity about the nicety of languages is temperately indulged. Whether *rubus* is masculine or feminine is argued from analogy and by induction; Ambrose makes it feminine, and the names of trees, which have no plurals, are feminine, as *populus, fraxinus*; on the other hand Virgil makes it masculine, and Priscian allows it to be an exception to the rule. Again, is it *dispexeris* or *despexeris*? Priscian says *despicio*, and makes *de* answer to the Greek (*kata*), *down*; but the Greek in the Psalm is, not (*katide̱is*), but (*huperide̱is*), *above*. Again, is the penultima of *voluerimus* long or short? Long, says Servius on Virgil.[41] They carry their fidelity to the Classics into their own poetical compositions; far from resigning themselves to that merely rhythmical versification, which is ever grateful to the popular ear, which had been in use from the Augustan age, and which afterwards developed into *rhyme*,[42] they rather affect the archaisms and the licences of the classical times. "Contraria rerum," "genus omne animantum," "retundier," "formarier," "benedicier," "scribier," "indupediret," "indunt," savour of Ennius or Lucretius rather than of Virgil. They keep to the Augustan metres, and they are never unwilling to use them. Their theological treatises begin, their epistles to kings end, with hexameters and pentameters. They moralize, they protest, they soothe their sorrows, they ask favours, they compile chronicles, they record their journeys in heroics, elegiacs, and epigrams. They are versifiers, one and all, or at least those whose names or works are best known in history, or in our libraries. The habit was formed at school, and it endured through life. Some indeed, as Lupus or Gerbert, had too many occupations to indulge in it; but others, as Theodulf, bishop of Orleans, return to it in the evening of life, after the manner of Gregory Nazianzen in patristic times, or Lord Wellesley in our own. Bede, Alcuin, Aldhelm, Raban, Theodulf, Hildebert, Notgar, Adelhard, Walafrid, Agobard, Florus, Modoin, Heiric, Gerbert, Angilbert, Herman, Abbo, Odo, Hucbald, Lupus, Fridouard, Paschasius, with many others, all wrote verse. I am not insinuating that they wrote it so happily as the Patriarch of Constantinople or the Governor-General of India; on the contrary, it was not their *forte*; but Florus, for instance, is eloquent, and Walafrid Virgilian.[43] Their subjects, when most sacred, are such as the great phenomena of nature, the country, woods, mountains, flocks, and herds, plants, flowers, and others which I have called Benedictine. I have no space for extracts; but here is one, as a specimen of what I mean, when I speak of the alliance of St. Benedict and Virgil. It is the conclusion of the Hortulus of Walafrid, and presents us with a very pretty picture of an old monk amid children and fruit trees:

> Haec tibi servitii munuscula vilia parvi
> Strabo tuus, Grimalde pater! ...
> Ut, cùm conseptu viridis consederis horti,
> Inter apricatas frondenti germine malos,
> Persicus imparibus crines ubi dividit umbris,
> Dum tibi cana legunt tenerâ lanugine poma

> Ludentes pueri, schola laetabunda tuorum,
> Atque volis ingentia mala capacibus indunt,
> Grandia conantes includere corpora palmis,
> Quo moneare habeas nostri, pater alme, laboris,
> Dum relegis quae dedo volens, interque legendum
> Et vitiosa secas bonus, et meliora reformas.

I have taken a liberty with the last line, which any how is somewhat feeble.

Their prose is superior to their verse; it has little claim indeed to the purity of taste and of vocabulary, which we call classical; but it is good Latin both in structure and in idiom. At any rate the change is wonderful, when we pass from the Benedictine centuries to the Dominican which followed.

In so speaking I have no disrespectful meaning as regards those great authors whose Latinity happens not to be equal to their sanctity or their intellectual power. Their merit, in respect to language, is of a different kind; it consists in their success in making the majestic and beautiful Latin tongue minister to scientific uses, for which it was never intended. But, because they have this merit of their own, that is no reason why we should deny to the writers who preceded them the praise of being familiar with the ancient language itself, a praise which is justly theirs, though seldom allowed to them. The writers of the Benedictine centuries are supposed to have the barbarism, without the science, of the Dominican period; and modern critics, who wish to be fair, seem to consider it a great concession, if they grant that an age must at least have some smattering in classical literature, which, as the foregoing pages show, is ever quoting it and referring to it. Thus Mr. Hallam, in the opening chapter of his Literature of Europe, can but say, "Alcuin's own poems *could at least not* have been written by one *unacquainted* with Virgil." Again: "From this time, though *quotations* from the Latin poets, especially Ovid and Virgil, and *sometimes* from Cicero, are *not very* frequent, they occur sufficiently to show that manuscripts had been brought to *this* side of the Alps" (p.

7). Some pages lower he says, quoting some of St. Adelhard's verses, "the quotation from Virgil in the ninth century *perhaps deserves remark, though* in one of Charlemagne's monasteries it is not by any means *astonishing*"; as if Virgil were not the text-book in the northern schools, as my foregoing quotations make clear, and ignorance, in that day, when it was to be found, had not its special seat in the southern side of the Alps, rather than in France and Germany. Passages such as these in men of wide research are simply perplexing. I ask myself whether I have rightly understood their words, or whether I read wrongly the historical facts which they profess to be generalizing. Perhaps it is that I assume without warrant that the quotations of Alcuin and the rest are *bonâ fide* such, and not derived, as some have said, from catenas of passages, commonplace books, or traditionary use[44]; but such an account of them is absolutely inconsistent, first, with the testimonies which I have above cited, as to the actual studies of the young, and next, with the literary habits which those studies actually formed in the persons who were exercised in them. Can it be that critics of the nineteenth century, possessing the fine appreciation of classical poetry, imparted in the public schools of England, glance their eye over the rude versification of Theodulf or Alcuin, and consider it the measure of the secular learning which gave it birth? M. Guizot, Protestant as he is, is a fairer and kinder judge of the cloister literature than Mr. Hallam or Dean Milman.

§5.

AND NOW, to prevent misapprehension of my meaning in this review of the Benedictine Schools, I have two remarks to make before I bring it to an end, one on each side of the description to which that review has led me.

On the one hand, the classical studies and tastes which I have been illustrating, even though foreign to the monastic masses, as they may be called—even though historically traceable to the mission of St. Theodore from the Holy See to England—must still be regarded a true offspring of the Benedictine discipline, and in no sense the result of seasons or places, of relaxation and degeneracy. At first sight, indeed, there is some plausibility in saying that with the change of times a real change came over a portion of the great family of monks, and that however usefully employed, Cassiodorus or Theodore, Alcuin or Walafrid, did certainly fall from their proper vocation, and did really leave it to Romuald and others like him, to be, not only the most faithful imitators, but the only true children of the ancient monachism. And, in confirmation of this view, it might be added that the same circumstances which led the monks to literary pursuits, led them to political entanglements also, and that in the same persons, as Theodulf, Lupus, and Gerbert, learning and secular engagements were combined; and that, as no one would say that the cares of office were proper to a monk's vocation, as little could be fairly included in it classical attainments. Whatever be the best mode of treating this difficulty, which of course demands a candid and equitable consideration, here, in addition to what I have said by the way, I shall make one answer of a different kind, which seems to me conclusive, and there leave the question. When, then, I am asked whether these studies are but the accidents and the signs of a time of religious declension, I reply that they are found in those very persons, on the contrary, who were pre-eminent in devotional and ascetic habits, and who were so intimately partakers in the spirit of mortification, whether of St. Benedict or St. Romuald, that they have come down to us with the reputation of saints—nay, have actually received canonization or beatification. Theodore himself is a saint; Alcuin and Raban are styled "beati"; Hildebert is "venerable"; Bede and Aldhelm are saints; and we can say the same of St. Angilbert, St. Abbo, St. Bertharius, St. Adalhard, St. Odo, and St. Paschasius Radbert. At least Catholics must feel the full force of this argument; for they cannot permit themselves to attribute any dereliction of vocation to those, whom the Church holds up as choice specimens of divine power, and, as being such, sealed by miracle for eternal bliss.

This is my remark on one side the question; on the other, it must not of course be supposed—indeed my last remark negatives the idea—that critical scholarship or classical erudition was the business of life, even in the case of this minority of the monastic family, who took so prominent a part in the education of their time. I have distinctly said that, after their school years, the monks were as little taken up with the classics, *exceptis excipiendis,* as members of parliament or country gentlemen at the present day. They had their serious engagements, as statesmen have now, though of a different kind, and to these they gave themselves. Theology was their one study; to theology secular literature ministered, first as an aid and an ornament, then as a relaxation, amid the mental exertion which it involved. Nor was this literature cultivated without some holy jealousy on the part of the cultivators; "nuces pueris"—there was a time of life when it ought to be put aside; there was even a danger of its seductiveness. Alcuin himself, if we may trust the account, reproved on one occasion the study, at least of the poets; and in one of his extant letters he complains of a former pupil, then raised to the episcopate, for preferring Virgil to his old master Flaccus, that is, to himself, and prays that "the four Gospels, not the twelve AEneids, may fill his breast" (Ep. 129). St. Paschasius, too, in spite of his love for Terence and Cicero, expresses a judgment, in one passage of his comment upon Ezekiel (*Bibl. Max. P.* t. xiv., p. 788), against the elder monks being occupied with the heathen poets and philosophers. Lanfranc, when an Irish Bishop asked him some literary question, made answer, "Episcopale propositum non decet operam dare hujusmodi studiis; we passed in these our time of youth, but, when we took on ourselves the pastoral care, we bade them farewell" (*Ep.* 33). The instance of Pope Gregory is well known: when the Bishop of Vienne had been led to lecture in the classics, he wrote, "A fact has come to our ears, which we cannot name without a blush, that you, my brother, lecture on literature" (grammatica) (*Ep.* xi. 54). Such occupations, indeed, were in those centuries generally and reasonably held to be inconsistent with the calling of a Bishop.[45] St. Jerome speaks as strongly in an earlier age.

What was true of the Bishop was on the whole true of the monk also; he might perhaps have special duties as the *scholasticus* of his monastery, but ordinarily, while his manual labour was either in the field or in the *scriptorium*, so his intellectual exercises were for the most part combined with his devotional, and consisted in the study of the sacred volume. This was mainly what at that time was meant by theology. "Theologia, hoc est, Scripturarum meditatio," says Thomassin (*Disc. Eccl.* t. ii., p. 288). Their theology was a loving study and exposition of Holy Scripture, according to the teaching of the Fathers, who had studied and expounded it before them. It was a loyal adherence to the teaching of the past, a faithful inculcation of it, an anxious transmission of it to the next generation. In this respect it differed from the theology of the times before and after them. Patristic and scholastic theology each involved a creative action of the intellect; that this is the case as regards the Schoolmen need not be proved here; nor is it less true, though in a different way, of the theology of the Fathers. Origen, Tertullian, Athanasius, Chrysostom, Augustine, Jerome, Leo, are authors of powerful, original minds, and engaged in the production of original works. There is no greater mistake, surely, than to suppose that a revealed truth precludes originality in the treatment of it. The contrary is acknowledged in the case of secular subjects, in which it is the very triumph of originality, not to invent or discover what is not already known, but to make old things read as if they were new, from the novelty of aspect in which they are placed. This faculty of investing with associations, of applying to particular purposes, of deducing consequences, of impressing upon the imagination, is creative; and though false associations, applications, deductions, and impressions are often made, and were made by some theologians of the early Church, such as Origen and Tertullian, this does but prove that originality is not co-extensive with truth. And so in like manner as to Scripture; to enter into the mind of the sacred author, to follow his train of thought, to bring together to one focus the lights which various parts of Scripture throw upon his text, and to give adequate expression to the thoughts thus evolved, in other words, the breadth of view, the depth, or the richness, which we recognize in certain early expositions, is a creation. Nor is it an inferior faculty to discriminate, rescue, and adjust the truth, which a fierce controversy threatens to tear in pieces, at a time when the ecclesiastical atmosphere is thick with the dust of the conflict, when all parties are more or less in the wrong, and the public mind has become so bewildered as not to be able to say what it does or what it does not hold, or even what it held before the strife of ideas began. In such circumstances, to speak the word evoking order and peace, and to restore the multitude of men to themselves and to each other, by a reassertion of what is old with a luminousness of explanation which is new, is a gift inferior only to that of revelation itself.

This gift is not the characteristic of the history, nor is it akin to the spirit or the object, as I have described them, of the Benedictine Order. At the time of which I am writing, the Christian athlete, after running one length of the stadium, was taking breath before commencing a second course: the Christian combatant was securing his conquests in the wide field of thought by a careful review and catalogue of them, before going forth to make new ones. He was fitly represented, therefore, at such a season, by the Benedictine, faithful, conscientious, affectionate, and obedient, like the good steward who keeps an eye on all his master's goods, and preserves them from waste or decay. First, then, he compared, emendated, and transcribed the text of Scripture; next he transcribed the Fathers who directly or indirectly commented on it; then he attached to its successive portions such passages from the Fathers as illustrated them; then he fused those catenated passages into one homogeneous comment of his own: and there he stopped. He seldom added anything original. In such a task the skill would lie in the happy management and condensation of materials brought together from very various quarters, and here he would find the advantage of the literary habits gained in his early education. A taste for criticism would be another result of it, which we see in Bede, and which would result in so much of leaning to the literal interpretation of Scripture as was consistent with the profession of editing and republishing, as it may be called, the comments of the Fathers. We see this tendency in Alcuin, Paschasius, and especially in Druthmar. Indeed, Alcuin's greatest work was the revision of the Scripture text.[46] Other commentators were Ansbert, Smaragdus, Haymo, Remi, and the Irish Sedulius, if he was a Benedictine. The most widely celebrated, however, of these works was the *Glossa Ordinaria* of Walafrid, which was in great measure an abridgement of Raban's Catena and became a standard authority in the centuries which followed.

§6.

BUT TIMES were approaching when such peaceful labours were not sufficient for the Church's need, and when theology required to be something more than the rehearsal of what her champions had achieved and her sages had established in ages passed away. As the new Christian society, which Charlemagne inaugurated, grew, its intellect grew with it, and at last began to ask questions and propose difficulties, which *catenae* and commentaries could not solve. Hard-headed objectors were not to be subdued by the reverence for antiquity and the amenities of polite literature; and, when controversies arose, the Benedictines found themselves, from the necessity of the times, called to duties which were as uncongenial to the spirit of their founder as the political engagements of St. Dunstan or St. Bernard. Nor must it be supposed that the other parts of Christendom did not furnish matters demanding keen theological acumen, even though none had arisen in the Frankish Churches themselves. And here, I conceive, we have this remarkable confirmation of the identity of the Benedictine character, that, in proportion as these matters were in substance already decided by the Fathers, they acquitted themselves well in the controversy, and in proportion as these matters demanded some original explanations, the monastic disputants were less successful. And in speaking of them, I speak of course of their age itself, of which they were the leading teachers, and which they represent. And I speak, not of individual monks, who would have the natural talents, the intellectual acuteness and subtlety of other men, but of the action of the monasteries, considered as bodies and historically, which is the true measure of the mental discipline to which their Rule subjected them. I speak of those whose direct duty lay, by virtue of their vocation, not in confronting doubts but in suppressing them, and who were not likely on the whole to succeed in exercises of reason in which they had no practice.

One of the countries to which I allude, as being at the era of Charlemagne the seat of theological error, was Spain, then under the power of the Saracens. The victorious infidels, in spite of their general toleration of Catholicism, of course could not avoid inflicting on it the most serious injuries. One of these was the decay or destruction of its schools,[47] and the want of education in its priesthood, which was the consequence. Another injury lay in the circumstance that Mahometanism, being a misbelief or heresy, more than a direct denial of the faith, might think it had a right to interfere with it, and had a tendency to corrupt it by the insinuation of its own opinions and traditions about Christian facts and doctrines. Mahomet is said to have been indebted to the teaching of a Nestorian monk, and the demolition of images was one of the watchwords of his armies. Now, from Spain at this time proceeded the heresy of the Adoptionists, which is of a Nestorian character; and it was in Spain that Claudius of Turin matured those uncatholic opinions, especially on the subject of images, which have given him a place in ecclesiastical history.

The conflict with Nestorianism had been completed long before the time of Charlemagne; accordingly the theologians of the age, in refuting it, had but to repeat the arguments which they found ready for them in the pages of the Fathers. Alcuin was one of those who undertook the controversy, and proved himself abundantly prepared for the work. "Paulinus and Alcuin," says Professor Döllinger, "proved their point with a degree of theological acumen, and with a knowledge of the Fathers, which in that age may surprise us."[48]

Such was their success, when the doctrine in question had already been defined; but, on the other hand, the question with which Claudius's name is connected, the honour due to images, was still *sub judice,* and when the ecumenical decision came from Nicaea, from whatever cause, the Franks misunderstood and disputed it. The same great council of Frankfort, which condemned the Adoptionists, acted as a protection to the Iconoclasts of Constantinople. I am far indeed from insinuating that the Fathers of the Frankish churches really differed from the definition which came to them from the East; but even for a century afterwards those churches regarded it, to say the least, with dissatisfaction.

Meanwhile the spirit of inquiry was alive and operative even within the hearts of these peaceful monastic communities themselves. We find it, as it would seem, in one of the immediate friends and pupils of Alcuin. Fredegis, of the school of York, to whom he addressed various of his letters and works, and whom he made his successor at Tours, has left behind him an argumentative fragment of so strange a nature that it has been thought a mere exercise in disputation and not a portion of a serious work.[49] He starts, moreover, with a proposition in favour of the supremacy of reason as contrasted with authority, which, though admitting of a Catholic explanation, is capable also of being made the basis of a philosophy to which I shall immediately have occasion to allude.[50] Soon after, Gotteschalc, a monk of Orbais, taught that the decree of divine predestination has direct reference to the lost as well as the saved; and about the same time Ratramn of the monastery of Corbie, opposed the Catholic doctrine of the Holy Eucharist. But these intellectual movements within the Benedictine territory were eclipsed by a manifestation of the sceptical spirit which came from a country, where from its prevalent religious temperament such a phenomenon was little to have been expected.

There was a portion of the Western Church which had never been included in the Roman Empire, and but partially, if at all, included within the range of the Benedictine discipline. While that discipline made its way northward, became the instrument of Anglo-Saxon conversion, and even supplanted the rule of Columban in the French monasteries, the countrymen of Columban remained faithful to their old monachism, descended southwards a second time, and retaliated on the convents of the continent by a fresh introduction of themselves and their traditions. At this period, whatever may have been their literary attainments, they were most remarkable for a bold independence of mind, a curiosity, activity, and vigour of thought, which contrasted strongly with the genius of Bede and Raban. Their strength lay in those exercises of pure reason which go by the name of "philosophy," or of "wisdom." Thus in an ancient writer the Irish

Scots are spoken of as "*sophiâ* clari."[51] By Heric of Auxerre, in the passage so often quoted, they are described as "*philosophorum greges*," venturing across the stormy sea to the wide continent of Europe. And so in the legendary account, by a monk of St. Gall, of the Irish scholars who accosted the Frankish Emperor, they are represented as crying out, "Who wants *wisdom*? who will buy *wisdom*?" Dunstan, again, is said to have learned "*philosophy*" in Ireland; and Benedict of Aniane, the second founder of the Benedictines, is expressly described as looking with suspicion on their syllogistic method, which was so hostile to the habits of mind which his own Order cultivated. These Irish scholars, indeed, were too sincere Catholics, viewing them in the mass, to warrant this jealousy; but it was not without foundation, as we shall see, as regards individuals, and at least would be amply justified in the judgments of those who differed so much from them in mental characteristics as did the Benedictines. On the other hand, there was much in the Anglo-Saxon temper intimately congenial with the latter: then, as now, the occupants of the British soil seem to have been practical rather than speculative, fond of hard work rather than of hard thought, tenacious of what they had received, jealous of novelty, the champions of law and order. Thus the English and Irish may be said so far to represent respectively the two great Orders which came in succession on the stage of ecclesiastical history; and, as they were not without their collisions at home, so we detect some instances, and may conjecture others, of their rivalry as missionaries and teachers in central Europe. We read, for instance, in the history of St. Boniface, that one of his antagonists, in his organization of the Churches which he had founded in Germany, was an Irish priest of the name of Clement. Boniface relates, if his account is to be received to the letter, that this priest neither allowed the authority of Jerome, Augustine, or Gregory, nor of the sacred canons; that he maintained the marriage of bishops; argued from Scripture in defence of marriage with a sister-in-law, and taught a sort of universalism. Also he had to report to Pope Zacharias the false teaching of another Scottish or Irish priest, named Samson, in relation to the Sacraments.[52] Another Irishman, with whom Boniface had a quarrel, was Virgil, afterwards Bishop of

Salzburgh, who has been acknowledged, as well as Boniface, for a saint. He offended Boniface by maintaining what seems like a doctrine of the existence of *antipodes*.

The antagonism between the two schools extended into the next century. Of course John Scotus Erigena, whom Charles the Bald placed in the chair of Alcuin in the School of the Palace, is the palmary specimen of the philosophical party among the Irish monks. This remarkable man, while acknowledging the authority of Revelation, propounded it as a first principle of his speculations, as Fridegis had done before him, that reason must come first, and authority second. Such a proposition indeed was faulty only in its application; for St. Austin himself had laid it down in his treatise *de Ordine*. It is self-evident, that we should not know what was revelation and what was not, unless we used our reason to decide the point. Whatever we are obliged in the event to learn from external sources, our process of inquiry must begin from within. The ancient Father to whom I have referred propounds both the principle and the sense in which it is true. "We learn things necessarily in two ways," he says, "by authority and by reason. Tempore auctoritas, re autem ratio prior est"; but Erigena, as is generally agreed, accounted reason, not only as the ultimate basis of religious truth, but the direct and proper warrant for it; and, armed with this principle, he proceeded to take part in the two controversies which I have already had occasion to mention, the Predestinarian and the Eucharistic. "The writings have come to us," says the church of Lyons, speaking of his tendencies, like Clement's, to universalism, "the writings have come to us, vaniloqui et garruli hominis, who, disputing on divine prescience and predestination with human, or, as he boasts, philosophical reasonings, without any deference to Scripture, or regard to the authority of the Holy Fathers, has dared to define by his own independent assertion what is to be held and followed." Thus Erigena adopted Clement's argumentative basis as well as his doctrine. His views upon reason and authority are distinctly avowed in the first book of his work, *De divisione naturae*. "You are not ignorant," he argues, "that what is prius naturâ ranks higher than what is prius tempore. We have been taught," referring apparently to St. Austin, "that reason is prior in nature, authority in time; now, whereas nature was created together with time, authority did not begin with the beginning of time and nature; on the other hand, reason had its origin with nature and time in the first beginning of things." The Scholar replies to him, "Reason itself teaches this; for authority has proceeded from right reason, reason by no means from authority. For all authority which is not approved by right reason is weak; whereas right reason, when it is fortified in its own strength, settled and immovable, need not be corroborated by the concurrence of any authority" (*Lib.* 1, n. 71). In like manner, in the commencement of his work on Predestination, while appealing to St. Austin, he makes philosophy and religion convertible terms.[53]

Erigena was succeeded in the Schola Palatii by Mannon, who inherited his master's doctrine. He himself had called Plato the greatest of philosophers, and Aristotle the most subtle of investigators; and, according to the testimony of Friar Bacon, he was a successful interpreter of the latter writer; and Mannon, in like manner, has left commentaries on Plato's *de Legibus* and *de Republicâ* and on Aristotle's Ethics. About the same time flourished in France another Irishman, named Macarius; and he too showed the same leaning towards pantheism which has been imputed to Erigena.[54] From him this error was introduced into the monastery of Corbie. At a latter date we hear of one Patrick, who from his name may be considered as an Irishman, holding the same heterodox opinion about the Eucharist which Ratramn and Erigena advanced.[55]

As to the two controversies, which have been mentioned more than once, while they exemplify to us the *scholasticismus ante scholasticos* then in action, they afford fresh illustrations also of the insufficiency of such instruments as the Church at that time had in her service to meet this formidable antagonist of her religious supremacy. No mind equal to Erigena appeared on the side of traditionary teaching; and the vigour with which the Adoptionists were condemned and the *Filioque* inserted in the Creed did not manifest itself in the dealing of the Frankish Synods with the bold doctrine of Gotteschalc and Ratramn. Gotteschalc, as I have said, was a monk of Orbais. We suddenly find him asserting categorically that the reprobate have been predestined to damnation from eternity. Raban and the Synod of Mentz condemned this doctrine. Hincmar and the Synod of Quiercy condemn it also; and Pardulus, bishop of Laon, writes against it. Then Lupus writes, if not in defence of Gotteschalc, at least not in accordance with Hincmar, who, in distress for a champion, has recourse to no other than Erigena, and Erigena, as might be expected from what has been said above, proceeds to commit himself to an extreme doctrine of universalism, as Gotteschalc had to an extreme predestinarianism. Upon this, Florus and Prudentius write against Erigena; and Remigius, explaining or espousing the thesis of Gotteschalc, writes against the three Epistles of Raban, Hincmar, and Pardulus. Hincmar replies in a second Synod of Quiercy; and the Bishops of Lorraine rejoin in the Synod of Valence. The controversy ceases rather than terminates at the Synod of Savonnières, in which all parties were represented, and in which four important articles were received, bearing indirectly on the subject of dispute, but leaving without distinct notice the original position of Gotteschalc.

In the Eucharistic controversy, which lasted through several centuries, the Benedictine Paschasius, supported by Haimo, Hincmar, and Ratherius, expounded the traditionary doctrine afterwards defined: but his statements were met by the dissent, or the hesitation, as it would appear, of men of his own schools, Raban, Ratramn, Amalarius, Heribald, Heriger, Druthmar, and Florus. At the end of two centuries indeed appeared the great Benedictines Lanfranc and Anselm, who dealt successfully with this as well as other controversies. But it must be recollected that, though their school of Bec is confessedly the historical fountain-head of the new theology which was making its way into Christendom, it is as far from a specimen of the Benedictine character in matters of teaching, as imperial minds such as their brother-monk and contemporary, Hildebrand, can be considered in ecclesiastical politics.

§7.

AND THUS the period, properly Benedictine, ended; this honour being shown by Providence to the great Order from which it is named, in reward for its long and patient services to religion, that, though its monks were not to be immediately employed by the Church in the special sense in which they had been her ministers for some hundreds of years, still they should be the first to point out, and that they should hansel, those new weapons, which Orders of a different genius were destined to wield against a new description of opponents.

Nor is it without significancy that the Anglo-Saxon Church, itself the creation of the Benedictines, and the seat from which their influence went out for the education or conversion of Europe, from the Baltic to the Bay of Biscay, should have its share in this honour; and that, as Theodore was brought all the way from Tarsus to Canterbury, so Lanfranc from Lombardy and Anselm from Piedmont should successively fill the archiepiscopal throne of Theodore.

Notes for The Benedictine Schools

1. Hom. i. 1.
2. De Rat. Temp. 66, 67. Elsewhere, he speaks of *futura* tempora sub Antichristo, in Sam. iv., 2, p. 300.
3. Raban, de Antichr. opp. t. vi., p. 178. Adson, ap. Alcuin, t. ii., p. 529.
4. So Malvenda, t. i. p. 118, calling the prelate "Fluentinus"; *vid.* Ughelli, t. iii., p. 77.
5. Ad Paulin. Ep. 58; adv. Vigil. fin.
6. "Omnibus idem propositus scopus erat, idemque finis, nempe secessus à saeculi tumultu et corruptelis." Mabillon, Annal. t. i., p. 215.
7. Marten. Ampl. Coll. t. vi., p. 153.
8. Ibid., p. 1063.
9. Thomassin. Disc. Eccl. t. i., p. 674.
10. "Uno excepto, qui ob hanc praesumptionem et alia depositus per Romanum Pontificem fuit." Eadmer ap. Nat. Alex. t. vi., p. 599. St. Thomas in consequence made himself a monk, when he came to the see.
11. Thomassin. Disc. Eccles, t. i., p. 702. Gibbon, ch. 37. Bingh. Antiqu. b. 9.
12. Camden, Hist. vol. iii., p. 618.
13. Milman, Latin Christ. vol. i., p. 398.
14. Mabillon Annal. Bened. t. i., p. 32.
15. *Vid.* Daniel, Etudes Classiques, p. 100, etc.; Launoy, de Scholis, Opp. t. iv., 1.
16. Quoties videtur contra naturam aliquid evenire, quodammodo non contra naturam est, quia rerum natura hoc habet eximium, ut à quo est, semper ejus obtemperet jussis. Paschas. p. 155, Opp. ed. 1618.
17. This analogy between the monastic institute and Virgil is recognized by Cassiodorus, who, after impressing on his monks, in the first place, the study of Holy Scripture and the Fathers, continues, "However, the most holy Fathers have passed no decree, binding us to repudiate secular literature; for in fact such reading prepares the mind in no slight measure for understanding the sacred writings." Presently, "In some cases indeed, Frigidus obstiterit circum praecordia sanguis," so as to hinder a man's perfect mastery whether of human or divine letters; but even with but a poor measure of knowledge, *he may be able to choose the life which follows in the next verse,* "Rura mihi et rigui placeant in vallibus amnes"; for "*it is even congenial to monks to have the care of a garden, to till the land, and to take interest in a good crop of apples.*"—De Inst. div. litt. 28. Here, by the bye, is in fact the same contrast between the "Felix qui" and the "Fortunatus et ille," which I have suggested to the reader in my former article (*Supr.* p. 387, note). Mr. Keble, in a passage of his beautiful Prelections, p. 648, considers Virgil to allude to Lucretius in the "Felix," and to ascribe to himself the "Fortunatus."
18. "Mos in Benedictino ordine usatissimus scholas instituere, et pueros cùm pietate tum litteris imbuere." Dachery in Lanfranc. Opp. p. 28. Brower. Antiqu. Fuld., pp. 35–38.
19. On the monastic schools taking up the imperial, *vid.* Guizot, Civil, vol. ii., p. 100, etc. *Vid.* also Ampère, Hist. Lit., t. ii., p. 277.

20. Thomass. Disc. Eccles., t. i., 821.
21. Calmet, Reg. Bened., t. ii., pp. 2, 4, 116, 278, 325–6, 380, 385. *Vid.* also Thomassin. Disc. Eccl., t. i., p. 821, and Magagnotti's Dissert. in Fleury's Disc. Pop. Dei.
22. Calmet, t. ii., p. 324. This early dedication of the monk might tend to suggest or defend the abuse of boy priests. *Vid.* St. Bernard, de Off. Ep. 7.
23. Calmet, t. i., p. 495.
24. Thomass. Disc., t. ii., p. 280, etc.
25. The following sketch is drawn up from the works of the Benedictines, in Bibl. Max. Patr., tomm. 14, 15, 17, 18, 21; Mabillon's Acta SS. Bened.; Ceillier's Auteurs, tomm. 18–20; Neander's Hist., vol vi., (Bohn); Guizot, Hist. Civil., vol. ii., (Bohn); Ampère, Hist. Lit. t. iii., and two recent works, Mgr. Landriot's Ecoles Littéraires, and P. Daniel's Etudes Classiques, to which I am much indebted for many points of detail. *Vid.* also M. l'Abbé Lalanne's Influence des Pères, and P. Cahour's Etudes Classiques.
26. Calmet, Reg., t. i., p. 495.
27. Brucker, Phil. t. iii., p. 594, etc. Appul. Florid. iv. 20.
28. The Quadrivium was called "philosophy." Ampère, t. iii., p. 267.
29. Charlemagne's schools taught Grammar, Rhetoric, Leges, Canones, Theology biblical and patristical. *Vid.* Thomass. Disc. t. iii., pp. 271–294; Ampère Hist., t. iii., p. 267.
30. Vit. ap. Brun. Opp. ed. 1759.
31. Brucker, t. iii., p. 646.
32. Thomass. Disc. t. ii., pp. 296–8.
33. Fredegodus of Canterbury (A.D. 960) wrote in Greek. *Vid.* Cave's Hist. Litt. in nom. In the Life of St. Odo of Canterbury we read that his patron Athelm "Graecâ et Latinâ linguâ magistris edocendum eum tradidit, quarum linguarum *plerisque* tunc temporis in gente Anglorum usus erat, à discipulis beatae memoriae Theodori archiepiscopi profectus. Factusque est in utrâque linguâ valdè gnarus, ita ut posset poemata fingere, continuare prosam, et omnia, quicquid ei animo sederet, luculentissimo sermone proferre." Mabillon, Act. Saec. v., p. 289.
34. I quoted in my former article a passage from Brower on the art cultivated at Fulda. For a parallel in the East, *vid.* the account of the monks of Theodore Studita, Vit. p. 29, Sismond.
35. Guizot, Civil., t. ii., p. 236; Hallam, Lit. i., 1, 87.
36. Ep. 1.
37. Muratori, Dissert. xliii., p. 831.
38. The School of Ouen produced 500 writers in 50 years. Landriot, p. 138. *Vid.* the curious Letter of Gunzo, Marten., Ampl. Coll. t. i., col. 294.
39. *Vid.* infr. vol. iii., pp. 225, 6.
40. *Vid.* Daniel. p. 115. Landriot, p. 139.
41. Alcuin, Ep. 23; Lupus, Ep. pp. 5, 8, 20, 34.
42. *Vid.* Muratori Dissert. 40.
43. Du Pin, however, says, "Theodulf's poems are very fine." Cent. viii., p. 126, ed. 1699. "Tolerable poetry," says Dr. Murdock, on Mosheim, vol. ii., p. 151.

44. "Bede...had some familiarity with Virgil, Ovid, Lucan, Statius, and even Lucretius... It may be questioned, however, whether many of the citations from ancient authors, often adduced from medieval writers, as indicating their knowledge of such authors, are more than traditionary, almost proverbial, insulated passages, brilliant fragments, broken off from antiquity, and reset again and again by writers borrowing them from each other, but who had never read another word of the lost poet, orator, or philosopher."—Milman, Latin Christ. vol. ii., p. 39.
45. *Vid.* Thomass. Disc. Eccl., t. ii., pp. 268–286.
46. "Codex, Alcuini labor, in Vallicellensi Bibliothecâ asservatur." Baron. an. 778.
47. "The Spanish Latin of that period was unquestionably extremely corrupt." Neander Hist., vol vi., p. 118.
48. Cox's Translation, vol. iii., p. 60.
49. *Vid.* Ittig. Biblioth., p. 313.
50. *Vid.* Neander, vol. vi., p. 161; Baluz. Miscell., t. ii., p. 56.
51. Brucker Philos., t. iii., p. 574.
52. Boniface, Epp. 82, p. 237.
53. Guizot Civil., t. ii., p. 375.
54. Lanigan Hist., vol. iii., p. 320.
55. *Vid.* Rather. Ep. apud Dach. Spic., t. i., p. 375.

INTERPRETIVE ESSAY

Saint John Henry Newman on Benedictine Life and on Benedictine Schools

by Abbot Thomas Frerking, O.S.B.

I. Monastic Life Rooted in the First Church of Jerusalem

THE EARLIEST monks traced their origin and their vocation to the first Church of Jerusalem. Thus John Cassian, the great monastic Father who in his writings in the early fifth century transmitted to the West the teaching of the earliest monastic Fathers in Egypt, writes as follows:

> And so the system of coenobites took its rise in the days of the preaching of the Apostles. For such was all that multitude of believers in Jerusalem, which is thus described in the Acts of the Apostles: "But the multitude of believers was of one heart and one soul, neither said any of them that any of the things which he possessed was his own, but they had all things common. They sold their possessions and property and divided them to all, as any man had need." And again: "For neither was there any among them that lacked; for as many as possessed fields or houses, sold them and brought the price of the things that they sold and laid them before the feet of the Apostles: and distribution was made to every man as he had need."[1] The whole Church, I say, was then such as now are those few who can be found with difficulty in coenobia. But when at the death of the

Apostles the multitude of believers began to wax cold, and especially that multitude which had come to the faith of Christ from diverse foreign nations, from whom the Apostles out of consideration for the infancy of their faith and their ingrained heathen habits, required nothing more than that they should "abstain from things sacrificed to idols and from fornication, and from things strangled, and from blood,"[2] and that liberty which was conceded to the Gentiles because of the weakness of their newly-born faith, also had by degrees begun to mar the perfection of that Church which existed at Jerusalem, and the fervour of that early faith cooled down with the daily increasing number both of natives and foreigners, then not only those who had accepted the faith of Christ, but even those who were the leaders of the Church relaxed somewhat of that strictness. For some fancying that what they saw permitted to the Gentiles because of their weakness, was also allowable for themselves, thought that they would suffer no loss if they followed the faith and confession of Christ keeping their property and possessions. But those who still had the fervour of the apostles, mindful of that former perfection, left their cities and intercourse with those who thought that carelessness and a laxer life was permissible to themselves and the Church of God, and began to live in more remote places in the countryside around the towns, and there, in private and on their own account, to practise those things which they had learnt to have been ordered by the apostles throughout the whole body of the Church in general: and so that whole system of which we have spoken grew up from those disciples who had separated themselves from the evil that was spreading. And these, by degrees as time went on, were separated from the great mass of believers because they abstained from marriage and cut themselves off from intercourse with their kinsmen and the life of this world, and were termed monks or solitaries from the strictness of their single and solitary life. Whence it followed

> that from the communion of their life together they were called coenobites and their abodes and dwelling places coenobia. That then alone was the earliest kind of monks, which is first not only in time but also in grace, and which continued inviolable for a very long period up to the time of Abbot Paul and Antony; and even to this day we see its traces remaining in strict coenobia.[3]

The disciples "who still had the fervor of the apostles" began to cut themselves off physically from the life of the world in the late third century, and we know that no later than the early fourth century they began to be called, as Cassian says, "monks," *monachi* in Latin, *monazontes* in Greek. The period of these earliest monks may be considered to run from the late third century up to about 600 A.D., by which time they had given the essential form to all subsequent Christian monasticism in both the East and the West. If we wish, then, to understand the essence of monasticism, it is important for us to see what these earliest monks understood the essential elements of the first Church of Jerusalem to be. And since the first Church was the response to the preaching of the apostles, we need first to consider what the earliest monks understood the essential elements of the content of that preaching to be. What they understood those essential elements of the content of that preaching to be are the various doctrinal and moral teachings which are presented in the New Testament as coming from the Lord and his apostles and which appear when the various writings of the New Testament are read as in harmony with one another because ultimately coming from one Author, viz., the Holy Spirit. Such a reading of the New Testament is generally not found in the works of Biblical criticism of the past two centuries, but it is the reading that we must adopt in order to grasp the understanding of the early monks, and so it is that reading which will be adopted in this essay.

We note first that the proclamation of Saint Peter on the first Pentecost after the Resurrection of the Lord, just after the Holy Spirit has been poured out on the apostles and disciples, is presented by Saint Luke as the first expression of the apostolic preaching, and we shall see that it contains explicitly or implicitly almost all the essential elements of the content of that preaching. Saint Peter's proclamation is as follows:

> Men of Judea and all who dwell in Jerusalem, let this be known to you, and give ear to my words.... [T]his [which you see and hear] is what was spoken by the prophet Joel:
>
> > "And in the last days it shall be, God declares,
> > that I will pour out my Spirit upon all flesh,
> > and your sons and your daughters shall prophesy,
> > and your young men shall see visions,
> > and your old men shall dream dreams;
> > yea, and on my menservants and my maidservants in those days
> > I will pour out my Spirit; and they shall prophesy.
> > And I will show wonders in the heaven above
> > and signs on the earth beneath,
> > blood, and fire, and vapor of smoke;
> > the sun shall be turned into darkness
> > and the moon into blood,
> > before the day of the Lord comes,
> > the great and manifest day.
> > And it shall be that whoever calls on the name of the Lord shall be saved."
>
> Men of Israel, hear these words: Jesus of Nazareth, a man attested to you by God with mighty works and wonders and signs which God did through him in your midst, as you yourselves know—this Jesus, delivered up according to the definite plan and foreknowledge of God, you crucified and killed by the hands of lawless men. But God raised him up, having loosed the pangs of death, because it was not possible for him to be held by it. For David says concerning him,

> "I saw the Lord always before me,
> for he is at my right hand that I may not be shaken;
> therefore my heart was glad, and my tongue rejoiced;
> moreover my flesh will dwell in hope.
> For thou wilt not abandon my soul to Hades,
> nor let thy Holy One see corruption.
> Thou hast made known to me the ways of life;
> thou wilt make me full of gladness with thy presence."
>
> Brethren, I may say to you confidently of the patriarch David that he both died and was buried, and his tomb is with us to this day. Being therefore a prophet, and knowing that God had sworn with an oath to him that he would set one of his descendants upon his throne, he foresaw and spoke of the resurrection of the Christ, that he was not abandoned to Hades, nor did his flesh see corruption. This Jesus God raised up, and of that we all are witnesses. Being therefore exalted at the right hand of God, and having received from the Father the promise of the Holy Spirit, he has poured out this which you see and hear. For David did not ascend into the heavens; but he himself says,
>
> "The Lord said to my Lord, Sit at my right hand,
> till I make thy enemies a stool for thy feet."
>
> Let all the house of Israel therefore know assuredly that God has made him both Lord and Christ, this Jesus whom you crucified.[4]

Saint Peter declares to the people that what they were hearing and seeing was what had been spoken by the prophet Joel. Thus, the people were witnessing the beginning of the fulfilment by God of what he had spoken through Joel, that in the last days, the days before the great Day of the Lord, he would pour out his Spirit on all flesh, that the sons and daughters of Israel would prophesy, see visions, dream dreams, that he would show wonders in the heaven and signs on the earth, and that whoever would call on the name of the Lord would be saved. These, then, were the last days before the coming of the Day of the Lord.

From the prophets, the people would know that the Day of the Lord is the Day when God will come for the Judgment of all humankind and the inauguration of his eternal Kingdom in power and glory.[5] From the prophet Daniel in particular they would know that on that Day all the dead shall rise, that all the dead and all the living shall be judged, that the righteous will go into everlasting life and shall shine like the brightness of the firmament and like the stars for ever and ever, and that the wicked will go into shame and everlasting contempt.[6] This Day of the Lord will be the end of the days of this world, and the beginning of the eternal Kingdom of God in power and glory, with the righteous, "the saints of the Most High," joyfully acknowledging the royal rights of God and joyfully sharing in his reign, with all the powers of the wicked now forever bound and thus destroyed, and with the final states of the righteous and the wicked perduring everlastingly,[7] with a new heaven and a new earth to suit and manifest this Kingdom of God,[8] and with all this constituting the world to come.

From various places in the Scriptures, that is, the Old Testament, Saint Peter's hearers would also know that in the Kingdom of God the essential reward of the righteous will be God himself. This truth emerges very notably in many of the Psalms. Thus: "One thing have I asked of the Lord, that will I seek after; that I may dwell in the house of the Lord all the days of my life, to behold the beauty of the Lord. . . ."[9] Again, "As a hart longs for flowing streams, so longs my soul for thee, O God. My soul thirsts for God, for the living God. When shall I come and behold the face of God?"[10] Again, Psalm 63:1–8. Again, Psalm 16:1–11. And the extraordinary Psalm 73:23–28:

> Nevertheless I am continually with thee;
> thou dost hold my right hand.
> Thou dost guide me with thy counsel,

> and afterward thou wilt receive me to glory.
> Whom have I in heaven but thee?
> And there is nothing upon earth that I desire besides thee.
> My flesh and my heart fail,
> but God is the strength of my heart and my portion for ever.
> For lo, those who are far from thee shall perish;
> thou dost put an end to those who are false to thee.
> But for me it is good to be near God;
> I have made the Lord GOD my refuge,
> that I may tell of all thy works.

Further, the truth is found in the Scriptures that one attains God, is united with God, by knowledge and love. That the love of God unites one to God is apparent in all the Psalm texts just quoted, and everywhere in the Scriptures, and this is of course summed up in the great commandment of the love of God: "Hear, O Israel: The LORD our God is one LORD; and you shall love the LORD your God with all your heart, and with all your soul, and with all your might."[11] But also knowledge of God, provided that it is together with love of God, unites one to God. Thus: "For I desire steadfast love, and not sacrifice, the knowledge of God, rather than burnt offerings."[12] And: "Thus says the LORD: 'Let not the wise man glory in his wisdom, let not the mighty man glory in his might, let not the rich man glory in his riches; but let him who glories, glory in this, that he understands and knows me, that I am the LORD who practice steadfast love, justice, and righteousness in the earth; for in these things I delight, says the LORD.'"[13]

The knowledge spoken of in these texts can be attained by the righteous in this life. But Saint Peter's hearers would also know that there are suggestions here and there in the Scriptures that there is a kind of knowledge of God which will be given only in the age to come, in the Kingdom of God in power and glory. Thus Isaiah, in a passage describing the Kingdom in power, prophesies that "the earth shall be full of the knowledge of the LORD as the waters cover the sea"[14]; the immensity of this knowledge, like the immensity of the sea, surely cannot be attained in this world. Habbakuk, apparently drawing on this passage, says, going further: "the earth will be filled with the knowledge of the glory of the LORD as the waters cover the sea"[15]; this is the knowledge of the *glory* of the Lord, that is, of his divinity; it is knowledge as deep as the depths of the sea. Jeremiah prophesies: "And no longer shall each man teach his neighbor and each his brother, saying, 'Know the LORD,' for they shall all know me, from the least of them to the greatest, says the LORD"[16]; the knowledge is immediately given by God. And the Book of Wisdom, speaking of the departed souls, declares: "Those who trust in him will understand truth, and the faithful will abide with him in love, because grace and mercy are upon his elect, and he watches over his holy ones."[17]

Saint Peter's hearers will also know that a metaphor frequent in the Scriptures for knowing God is *seeing God*. As in the case of knowing God, so in the case of seeing God there is a kind of seeing God which is very great and is reserved for the Kingdom of God in power and glory. Isaiah speaks of it: "the glory of the LORD shall be revealed, and all flesh shall see it together"[18]; "Hark, your watchmen lift up their voice, together they sing for joy; for eye to eye they see the return of the LORD to Zion"[19]; "I am coming to gather all nations and tongues; and they shall come and shall see my glory."[20] Daniel's vision of the coming of the Kingdom of God in power and glory suggests that "the holy ones of the Most High" will see "the One most venerable" in a way not possible outside of the Kingdom of God in power and glory.[21] For example, in verse 9, thrones are placed at the side of the throne of the One most venerable, and it appears that the holy ones of the Most High sit on these thrones and share in the judgment of all humankind given by the One most venerable; apparently they see him as ones sitting beside him and as ones who know his mind. There are texts in the Scripture which would have suggested to Saint Peter's hearers that this kind of seeing God is to be called "seeing God face to face." For example, Deuteronomy 34:10 reads: "And there has not arisen a prophet since in Israel like Moses, whom the LORD knew face to face." And in Exodus 33:11: "the LORD used to speak to Moses face to face, as a man speaks to his friend." Other texts teach that no human being can see the face of God in this life and still live (e.g., Exodus 19:21), so Moses's seeing the face of God must have been miraculous, but the texts we first considered in this paragraph suggest that this glorious gift is extended to all who will find a place in the Kingdom of God in power and glory.

Saint Peter's hearers know well, then, that one attains God, is united with God, by knowledge and love. But they know well also the even more fundamental truth, that this knowledge and love are mutual, and that moreover God's knowledge and love of us calls forth our knowledge and love of him, and indeed is the very cause of our being. This truth is attested from one end of the Scriptures to the other. On the sixth day of creation, "God saw everything that he had created, and behold, it was very good"[22]; very good because everything God created he created out of his goodness, his generosity, his love. And Wisdom 11:24: "For thou lovest all things that exist, and hast loathing for none of the things which thou hast made, for thou wouldst not have made anything if thou hadst hated it." Again, for God's knowledge of us, see Psalm 139; for his love of us, Psalm 103. And that God's knowledge and love of us call forth our knowledge and love of him, or rather, give that knowledge and love of him to us, note how this truth is manifested in all the descriptions of the great calls of God to a human being narrated in the Scriptures: God calls Abraham, out of sheer knowledge and love for him, and Abraham responds with faith and obedience, which is to say, with faith and love of God's holy will;[23] God calls Moses from the burning bush, and Moses responds with obedience to the mission he is given, and with knowledge of the divine Name[24]; the same truth is manifested in all the calls of the prophets.

Saint Peter's hearers would know that this mutual knowledge and love between God and man must be based on their in some sense having something in common, on there being a sharing, a communion, of something between them. They would know from the very beginning of the Scriptures that this something is what makes man to be "in our image, after our likeness," in the image and after the likeness of God,[25] and they would understand that this is man's actions of knowing and of freely willing, which are not found in other animals, who therefore are not in the image and after the likeness of God. What God has shared with man, then, is knowing and willing, but God's knowing and willing is infinitely greater than man's. And yet, it seems from the Scriptures that what God has shared with the righteous is something more than this, that he has given to the righteous a share in his very own being, his very own life. Solomon in the Song of Songs teaches that an analogue to the sharing between God and the righteous is the sharing between the lover and the beloved. And Hosea is the first of the prophets, followed by many others, to teach that the analogue to the sharing between God and the righteous is marriage. Thus he prophesies:

> And I will betroth you to me for ever; I will betroth you to me
> in righteousness and in justice, in steadfast love, and in mercy.
> I will betroth you to me in faithfulness; and you shall know the
> LORD.
> And I will have pity on Not pitied,
> and I will say to Not my people, "You are my people";
> and he shall say, "Thou art my God." [26]

Saint Peter's hearers would know that this prophecy can be understood as partially fulfilled in this age; the communion between God and the righteous in this age is already great. But they would understand it also to refer to a perfect fulfillment in the Kingdom of God in power and glory. And since, as we have seen, in the Kingdom the knowledge of God which the righteous will have will be much greater, or rather, of an entirely different and greater order, than in this age, so too the fulfilment of their love of God, and the sharing, the communion of God with the righteous, will be of an entirely different and greater order.

But finally, one further immensely important point: from the Scriptures Saint Peter's hearers would know that God will exercise his Judgment and his Kingship through another,[27] who will be a descendant of David, who will be a King sitting on David's throne, who will thus be anointed, who will be known as "the Anointed One," that is, the "Messiah," the "Christ," and of whose Kingdom there will be no end.[28] Moreover, the Messiah is himself a great mystery. For, on the one hand, he is a descendant of David, and therefore a man, a "son of man" in the Hebrew idiom, *the* Man, *the* Son of Man, as Daniel calls him,[29] and yet, on the other hand, he is seen by Daniel coming on the clouds of heaven, as if he has some heavenly origin, and Isaiah gives him the most astonishing and mysterious names: "God-with-us,"[30] "Wonderful Counselor," "Mighty God," "Everlasting Father," "Prince of Peace."[31]

With this introduction to his proclamation, Saint Peter will already have the rapt attention of his hearers, at least of those who were being saved. For, if these are the last days, then one must do everything possible to be prepared at every moment for the coming of the Day of the Lord, and for calling on the Lord's name in order to be saved. For one's ultimate longing is, yes, to be saved from the punishment of the wicked and to enter into the joy, the blessedness, of the righteous, which is God, and seeing him, knowing him, loving him, being in communion with him for all eternity. But even further, the core of one's ultimate longing is, in that communion, to give oneself to him utterly, and eternally, out of love. So the hearers, at least those destined to be saved, as they listen to Saint Peter, will already be filled with an enormous vision, and with an enormous longing, and hope, and love, and joy.

Now Saint Peter continues, speaking of great glories. Jesus of Nazareth, he says, pointed out to you, shown forth to you, revealed to you by wonders and signs exactly such as Joel prophesied for the last days, wonders and signs which God did through him in your midst, as you know—"this Jesus, delivered up according to the definite plan and foreknowledge of God, you crucified and killed by the hands of lawless men. But God raised him up" (the first proclamation of the Resurrection) "having loosed the pangs of death, because it was not possible for him to be held by it." And why not possible? Because David, the great prophet, knowing that God had sworn with an oath to him that he would set one of his descendants upon his throne, foresaw and spoke of the Resurrection of the Christ, the Messiah, that he would not be abandoned to Hades, nor would his flesh see corruption. David the prophet foresaw that the descendent of his who was the Christ would, profoundly mysteriously yet according to the definite plan and foreknowledge of God, be put to death, but then, magnificently, gloriously, be raised up by God from death, not being held by Hades nor his flesh being corrupted.

Still further, David foresaw that God, after raising the Christ from death, would exalt him to the right hand of God, where he would be seated, God making his enemies a stool for his feet, and would thus be revealed as being *Lord,* rightly called "Lord," the word which throughout the Scriptures was used to stand for the name of God, the Tetragrammaton, which was never to be pronounced by anyone except the High Priest, and then only on the Day of Atonement. Moreover, if, as the prophets had foretold, God will exercise his Judgment and his Kingship through the Christ, who is now known also to be the Lord, then God will also fulfill through the Lord Christ his promise of pouring out his Spirit upon all flesh. And now Peter repeats the great proclamation, adding that the apostles are eyewitnesses of it: "This Jesus God raised up, *and of that we all are witnesses.*" Witnesses also, as Peter and the apostles will further proclaim, of his exaltation, his Ascension, into heaven. And so Peter declares, "Let all the house of Israel therefore know assuredly that God has made him both Lord and Christ, this Jesus whom you crucified." Therefore, it is also Jesus, Lord and Christ, who is pouring out the Spirit on the apostles and disciples, as the people are hearing and seeing.

In the way he says this, Peter also gives the first revelation of the Most Holy Trinity, drawing on the teaching of the Lord Jesus Christ himself. "Being therefore exalted at the right hand of God, and having received from the Father the promise of the Holy Spirit, he has poured forth this which you see and hear." There is, then, the Father, who is himself Lord, who is himself God; there is the Lord Jesus Christ, who is himself Lord, who is himself God, who must then be the Son of the Father; there is the Spirit, whom Peter now calls the Holy Spirit, because if he is of the

Father, as Joel says, that is, proceeds from the Father; and if the Father has given to the Lord Jesus Christ the Son that the Spirit is of him, as the Lord taught Peter and the apostles, that is, proceeds from him, then he, the Spirit, proceeding from both the Father and the Son, must himself be Lord, must himself be God, and so is to be called "Holy" in the sense in which that term applies to the Lord, to God, alone. And the Lord Jesus Christ is now pouring him out, as the people see and hear.

What is the reaction of those of his hearers who are being saved to all that Peter has proclaimed? It is, first, faith. Luke in his account calls them "they that received his word,"[32] i.e., they who by grace believed to be true what Peter had revealed to them and what, by implication, he said had been promised to them. We have already seen that, from the moment of the first part of Peter's proclamation that the last days before the Day of the Lord have come, those of his hearers who are being saved are already filled with an enormous vision, that of what is to occur in the last days and on the Day of the Lord itself; with an enormous longing, that they might be saved; with an enormous hope, that they will be saved if they call on the name of the Lord; with an enormous love, wishing with all one's heart to give oneself utterly to the Lord in communion with him; and with an enormous joy, the joy that accompanies this love. But now, after the completion of Peter's proclamation, the vision has been enormously enlarged, to include the first vision of who the Christ is and of his extraordinarily being both a son of man and Lord—the first vision of the Incarnation; to include the first vision of the Most Holy Trinity; to include the first vision that the Spirit is the Holy Spirit the Lord, who is coming to dwell in us; to include the first vision that Jesus, Christ and Lord, since he has not yet come for the final Judgment and for inaugurating the Kingdom of God in power, will be coming again—his Second Coming—to do so. Enormously greater, then, is also the longing, the hope, the love, and the joy.

But, at the same time, those of Saint Peter's hearers who are being saved will have one other reaction. They will realize that the leaders of their people, and many of their people, did not recognize, indeed rejected,

Jesus; that in fact they had him crucified, that even those who had hoped in him hoped in him no more. Many of them will realize they personally had some part, greater or lesser, in all this, and will be cut to the heart, filled with the most profound grief and detestation of their sin. Even if some had no part, and had still the hope that somehow Jesus would return and do all that he had promised, they will realize that still they are sinners, and need to be purified of their sins before they can go to him, who will be their Judge, and they are cut to the heart, filled with the most profound grief and detestation of their sin.

And so, those who were being saved, those who believed by faith what Peter revealed, and who were filled both with enormous longing, hope, love, and joy, and also are cut to the heart, say to Peter, and the rest of the apostles, "Brethren, what shall we do?"[33]

And now Peter's great exhortation: "Repent, and be baptized every one of you in the name of Jesus Christ for the forgiveness of your sins; and you shall receive the gift of the Holy Spirit. For the promise is to you and to your children and to all that are far off, every one whom the Lord our God calls to him." And, Saint Luke tells us, "he testified with many other words and exhorted them, saying, 'Save yourselves from this crooked generation.'"[34]

What were these many other words that Saint Peter used? Saint Luke does not tell us. But we can gather a good deal about what the content of these "many other words" was by considering the topics it would have been necessary for Saint Peter to address before any of his hearers were baptized, and by considering what the teaching on these topics was not only of Saint Peter but of the other Apostles, including Saint Paul, as these teachings are passed on to us by the New Testament.

First, then, Saint Peter had called upon his hearers to repent, and so he must have explained to them, or rather, reminded them, that this they could do if they added to their grief and their detestation of their sin the intention of not sinning again and the hope of forgiveness, thus transforming their grief and detestation into contrition, into repentance; otherwise, their grief and detestation would be such as of those who despair.

Then, he had called upon his hearers to be baptized in the name of Jesus Christ for the forgiveness of their sins. And here Saint Peter must have explained to them what Baptism was, and how it could forgive sins. He must have begun by explaining what he had not explained in his proclamation, viz., how it could be "by the determinate counsel and foreknowledge of God" that the Christ and the Lord was delivered up to be crucified, and then he must have explained how Baptism was connected with this.

As to what he might have said with regard to the first matter, consider what he himself says in his First Letter: "For Christ also died for sins once for all, the righteous for the unrighteous, that he might bring us to God..."[35] Saint Paul reports the following to have been the first teaching he himself received, originating from the first Church of Jerusalem: "For I delivered to you as of first importance what I also received, that Christ died for our sins in accordance with the scriptures, that he was buried, that he was raised on the third day in accordance with the scriptures..."[36]

Then consider also what Saint Paul says in the Letter to the Romans: "since all have sinned, and fall short of the glory of God, they are justified by his grace as a gift, through the redemption which is in Christ Jesus, whom God put forward as an expiation by his blood, to be received by faith."[37] Jesus's death was, then, a sacrifice of expiation to free all humankind, past, present, and future, from sin, the sacrifice which fulfilled all previous sacrifices and put an end to any future sacrifices. Peter alludes to all this in his second great proclamation, after the healing of the man lame from birth, when he calls Jesus God's "servant," undoubtedly alluding by that title to the prophecy in Isaiah of the sacrificial death of Jesus to redeem us from our sins.[38] Here then is the reason why Jesus's death occurred "by the determinate counsel and foreknowledge of God"; his sacrificial death was at the center of God's unspeakably merciful plan to redeem from sin the entire human race.

But, this redemption must be received by each individual human being by Baptism received in faith. And how does Baptism accomplish this? Surely Saint Peter would have explained what is expressed by Saint Paul in this way:

> Do you not know that all of us who have been baptized into Christ Jesus were baptized into his death? We were buried therefore with him by baptism into death, so that as Christ was raised from the dead by the glory of the Father, we too might walk in newness of life.
>
> For if we have been united with him in a death like his, we shall certainly be united with him in a resurrection like his. We know that our old self was crucified with him so that the sinful body might be destroyed, and we might no longer be enslaved to sin. For he who has died is freed from sin. But if we have died with Christ, we believe that we shall also live with him. For we know that Christ being raised from the dead will never die again; death no longer has dominion over him. The death he died he died to sin, once for all, but the life he lives he lives to God. So you also must consider yourselves dead to sin and alive to God in Christ Jesus.[39]

Thus, by Baptism we participate, share, in Christ's death, by which he obtained the forgiveness of all the sins of humanity and humanity's no longer being enslaved to sin. And hence, by sharing in his death, our old self was crucified with him, the sinful body was destroyed, we are no longer enslaved to sin, and we are justified, absolved, freed from sin. This is why Saint Peter says, "Be baptized...for the forgiveness of your sins." Saint Paul further explains that by Baptism, we also participate in, share in, Christ's resurrection. Immediately upon receiving Baptism our bodies are not glorified as is Christ's risen body, but on the Day of the Lord, by our Baptism, our bodies will be raised from death and then glorified. But now, in these last days, immediately upon receiving Baptism our souls are raised from the death of the soul, which is sin, to newness of life. What is this newness of life?

Saint Peter, in his Second Letter, gives this extraordinary teaching: our newness of life, given through Baptism, consists in this, that we actually become "sharers in the divine nature."[40] This share in the divine nature will be called, in the later tradition, sanctifying grace. Saint Peter's hearers would already know from the Scriptures of the Old Covenant that the righteous in some way share in God's life, that from this communion arise mutual knowledge and love, God's knowledge and love being first and principal, and giving and calling forth our own. But Saint Peter tells them that now, in these last days, by Baptism we are made sharers in his divine nature, in his very divinity, and by the faith Saint Peter is exhorting them to receive as a gift from God, they can know that this one divine nature is the nature of the Father and of the Son and of the Holy Spirit. So by Baptism we are brought into a sharing, a communion, with the Father and the Son and the Holy Spirit of their one divine nature, a true sharing and communion, although one in which we do not yet see what this nature is in itself. But still, from this communion, given by God, there arises a greater and new kind of mutual knowledge and love: we now are brought into knowledge and love of God's inner life, of the Three Persons, and God's knowledge and love of us is now greater because of these unspeakable gifts he has given us.

If we receive Baptism and this gift of loving God, then our faith, itself given us by God in order to draw us to Baptism, becomes living faith, that is, faith working by love of God, and our love of God also extends to our neighbor, because God loves all human beings, and also because he has commanded that we must do so, too. This love of God, and neighbor on account of God, the tradition will call charity, given us by Baptism. But further, as Saint John will teach, if we love God, then we will keep all his commandments, and this we can only do if we have all the virtues, which are simply the ways in which charity operates with regard to this or that matter. Therefore, Baptism also gives, in addition to the share in the divine nature, to charity, and to living faith, all the other virtues. And further, Saint Peter will surely have taught his hearers what Saint Paul will emphasize, that the communion between us and the Lord Jesus Christ effected by Baptism is like that of a Body with its Head, and that by this communion we share in the seven spirits possessed by the Christ,[41] what will later be called the gifts of the Holy Spirit. We must, however, by grace freely choose to use these virtues and gifts infused in us by Baptism, and in order to do that, we must, by grace, progressively uproot the old tendencies to sin which remain in us after Baptism, which the Lord chose to leave in us after Baptism in order that we may by grace fight hard against them and so by grace attain even higher levels of virtue than we would have done had we not had to fight against these tendencies. Therefore, the claim to these graces must also be given by Baptism.

All of this Saint Peter must have explained to his hearers, at least in an elementary way. And surely he would also have explained that all these effects of Baptism, both the forgiveness of sin and the sanctification coming from sharing in the Lord's resurrection, are effected in us by the Holy Spirit, for the Lord said that we are to be baptized by water and the Spirit. Saint Paul refers to the operation of the Holy Spirit in sanctifying us with this great teaching: "God's love has been poured into our hearts through the Holy Spirit which has been given to us."[42] Here, because of the centrality of charity in the sanctification, Saint Paul refers in effect to all of it by saying simply that the love of God has been poured into our hearts by the Holy Spirit. But he adds that the Holy Spirit not only works sanctification in us, but also comes to dwell in us, has been given to us, as we saw, by the Father and by the Lord Jesus. There is, therefore, in Baptism already a first gift of the Holy Spirit, by which he dwells in us as our sanctifier. Saint Peter must have explained all this, but also added that there is a second and perfect gift of the Holy Spirit which comes by the laying on of hands, what will in the later tradition be called Confirmation, by which the Holy Spirit dwells in us with, in addition to his gift of sanctification, his gift of the strengthening of that sanctification, especially for the courageous outward confession of the faith. This gift can of course only be given to those who are baptized, for it is a perfection of the first gift. It is receiving the gift of the Holy Spirit by the laying on of hands which, most probably, is referred to by Saint Peter in his assurance: "you shall receive the gift of the Holy Spirit."

Finally, with regard to Baptism, Saint Peter must have pointed out the following. Baptism is given "in the name of Jesus Christ," in the power of his Person. But the name of Jesus, as Saint Peter proclaimed, is "Lord"; that is, Jesus Christ *is* Lord. And so Baptism is given in the power of the Lord, and it is by this power that Baptism forgives sins and raises to the new life of sharing in the divine nature—and indeed, only the power of this name could do such things. To receive Baptism with faith in Jesus as Lord is then the fulfilment of the last part of what the prophet Joel prophesied about the last days: that there would be those in the last days who would call on the name of the Lord, and that all these would be saved. To receive Baptism, then, is to call on the name of the Lord. And on the Day of the Lord, then, those who have received Baptism with faith in Jesus Christ as Lord, and have not subsequently definitively rejected him, will be saved. This then, salvation, is "the promise to you and to your children and to all that are far off, every one whom the Lord our God calls to him."

We may suppose that already those of Saint Peter's hearers who were being saved, having heard all this, must have been very nearly ready to be baptized. And yet it must have been the case that Saint Peter would have explained something more to them before they could be baptized, namely, how they would be obliged to live if they received Baptism. And so his "many other words" must have also included something like the following.

There is one further effect of Baptism, because it is Baptism in the name of Jesus Christ. Now Jesus is the Christ, the Messiah, and by being baptized, and by that way calling on his name, we declare that we wish to be one of Jesus's Messianic kingdom. Part of the extraordinary revelation of these last days is that the Messianic kingdom begins not on the Day of the Lord, but already in these last days before the Day of the Lord. Yes, the Kingdom in the fullness of power and glory begins on the Day of the Lord. But it is already present now, and already began with the birth, in fact, with the conception of the Lord Jesus Christ, for his conception and birth were marked with wonders and signs, and from his very conception, as Isaiah prophesied.[43] He is God with us, and therefore his Kingdom is present with him, and all who believe and love him are already in his Kingdom. In his public ministry he made his Kingdom more explicitly present through his teaching, his institution of the sacraments, and in many other ways. After his Resurrection, while he was still with us, he made it still more present, and now, in these last days, the Kingdom is still more explicitly present, for now the Lord Jesus Christ is reigning from the right hand of his Father, the Holy Spirit has been poured out today to dwell within us, indeed the Lord and his Father also come to dwell in us spiritually.[44] Now the Father has begun to make the Lord's enemies a footstool for his feet, and this will be completed at his Second Coming. So it is that by being baptized, and by that way calling on the Lord's name, we declare that we wish to be one of the Lord Jesus's Messianic kingdom. Before we receive Baptism, then, we must know and accept how we are to live in Jesus's Kingdom.

And how are we to live in this Kingdom? Here Saint Peter must have given an initial explanation of the four elements which Saint Luke says characterized the first realization of the Kingdom after the Lord's pouring out the Holy Spirit. Referring to those who were baptized on that Pentecost Day, Saint Luke writes, "they persevered in the teaching of the Apostles, in the communion, in the breaking of the bread, and in the prayers."[45] For the purposes of this essay, we must consider very carefully how Saint Peter would have explained these four elements, for they are what the earliest monks understood to be the essential elements of the first Church of Jerusalem, and thus the essential elements of the monastic life.

First, we are to persevere in the teaching of the apostles. Saint Peter must have spoken along the following lines. To live in the Kingdom, we must first join the community of the Apostles,[46] sharing in particular their teaching and persevering in their teaching, because, to begin with, they are already in the Kingdom, having already been baptized, and now having received the Gift of the Holy Spirit, and then, because they were chosen by the Lord himself to preach and teach the whole of the Lord's revelation. At the same time, although this revelation cannot be added to after the death of the last Apostle, it can always be more and more fully and deeply understood, because it is a teaching about God, who is infinite. And since the reward of the righteous in the Kingdom of the Lord in power and glory will be union with God through knowledge and love, and since, as we shall see, the degree to which we shall be united to God in that Kingdom will depend on the degree to which we become united with God in this life by the love of God, and by such knowledge of God as accompanies and increases our love of God, then persevering in the teaching of the Apostles includes the obligation always to seek, guided by the love of God, to understand more and more deeply the teaching they give. Saint Peter must have expressed in his own words something of what Saint Paul says in numerous passages. For example:

> For this reason I bow my knees before the Father, from whom all fatherhood in heaven and on earth is named, that according to the riches of his glory he may grant you to be strengthened with might through his Spirit in the inner man, and that Christ may dwell in your hearts through faith; that you, being rooted and grounded in love, may have power to comprehend with all the saints what is the breadth and length and height and depth, and to know the love of Christ which surpasses knowledge, that you may be filled with all the fulness of God.[47]

The Apostles, in their "ministry of the word,"[48] both proclaim in the Spirit the fundamental truths of revelation, showing how these truths are fulfilments of the words spoken by the prophets, as in Saint Peter's first proclamation, and elaborate in the Spirit on these truths, as Saint Paul does in his letters. Saint Peter must have explained that this obligation always to seek, guided by the love of God, to understand more and more the teaching the Apostles have been given to pass on, will apply from the day of Baptism. And he probably will have explained that some of those persons who were with the apostles when the Holy Spirit descended—they together with the apostles numbered about one hundred and twenty persons—will begin to help the newly baptized to learn more and more.[49] (Very soon those who have the power to proclaim in the Spirit the fundamental truths of revelation as fulfilment of the prophecies will, it seems, be called prophets, and those who have the power in the Spirit to elaborate on those truths will, it seems, be called teachers.[50])

Saint Peter also must have explained that the newly baptized will need to perform three actions to grow in their knowledge of the teaching of the Apostles. They will need to listen to the apostles, and the prophets and teachers. They will need to read the Scriptures (and letters sent by the apostles or their authorized followers to the churches once the church begins to expand). And, for this hearing and reading to be effective, they will need to meditate on what they hear and read. Thus, the prophet David says that that one is blessed who meditates on the law of the Lord day and night, and so the baptized should meditate on the Scriptures and letters they read or hear read.[51] Saint Peter's hearers would know that this "meditation" consists first in constant repetition of what they hear or read in order to memorize it, then in constant repetition of it as they go about their other activities, and also in thinking about what they are repeating and so coming to understand it (with the help of apostles, prophets, teachers) more and more.

Second, we are to persevere in the communion. Saint Peter must have spoken along the following lines. There is this great truth: the Kingdom of the Lord Jesus Christ is not like earthly Kingdoms, with the members of the Kingdom being subjected by force to the King and living in fear of his power and of his punishments. No, his Kingdom is precisely what the prophets prophesied and what we have explained: it is a communion, a Kingdom of mutual knowing and mutual love between the King, his Father, and the Holy Spirit, and the members of his Kingdom, based on their sharing in the divine nature of the King, his Father, and the Holy Spirit, and their communion in all the gifts that divine nature brings. With whom, then, are we in communion? First, temporally speaking, with the Apostles, as we have just said. But then, absolutely speaking, and in the order by which we come to understand, with our Lord Jesus Christ the Son of God. And we have communion with his sufferings, becoming like him in his death, that we may attain communion with him in his resurrection from the dead.[52] We hardly dare speak of this and of what follows from it, so sublime are these truths. Our Lord Jesus Christ the Son of God is himself in communion, shares the divine nature, with his Father, who begets him from all eternity, and he and the Father are in communion with the Holy Spirit, who proceeds from both of them. Therefore, we are in communion with the Father, the Son, and the Holy Spirit. Their whole life is a communion in the divine nature, and now they share that communion with us.[53]

We are also in communion with one another. As we have just said, the Kingdom of the Lord Jesus Christ just is a communion of all of us with one another and with him and his Father and their Holy Spirit. We are in communion with one another also by being of one heart and soul,[54] of one heart and soul because we all share in the same love, the love of God and of neighbor on account of God, and in the same knowledge of the revelation the Apostles preach, to which all our other knowledge is referred. We also have communion with the Apostles in the Gospel,[55] and with one another in the mysteries of Baptism and of the Laying on of Hands for the Gift of the Holy Spirit, and in the other mysteries of salvation which the Apostles will reveal and through which we are given communion with the divine nature—and of the greatest of these we will speak shortly. And, we have communion with one another by having all material things in common, selling all our goods and possessions, all our lands and houses, bringing the proceeds of what we have sold and laying it at the feet of the Apostles, with distribution being made to each as any have need.[56]

Now, if we are baptized, then we are to live in this communion and to grow in this communion. In this communion we become aware of the knowledge and love of us of the Father, the Son, and the Holy Spirit, and we respond with knowledge and love of them, and of one another in them. You my hearers, men and women of Israel, already know that at Sinai the Lord entered into a communion with us, a communion confirmed by a covenant, and you know we were repeatedly unfaithful to that covenant, and that the prophets prophesied a new and eternal covenant.[57] And you know that the prophets prophesied that in the Kingdom of God in power and glory this communion will be immeasurably greater, because one of knowing God as he is and loving him as such, one to which Hosea prophesied that marriage would be an analogy. But it has been revealed to us that because we know who the Messiah is and see that he is already giving us his Spirit in these last days, a new communion, and a new covenant, already begun in these last days, truly the beginning of the communion of the Kingdom of God in power and glory. If we receive Baptism, we are given the power to live in this communion, and from then on we are obligated to live in this communion.

Third, we are to persevere in the breaking of bread. Saint Peter perhaps spoke along the following lines. There is another great mystery, besides Baptism and the Laying on of Hands, indeed there are five others. But greatest of them all, including Baptism, is the one to which we have just alluded, the Breaking of Bread. You must know that while we were at supper with the Lord Jesus on the night when he was betrayed he took bread, and, giving the Father thanks, he said the blessing, broke the bread and gave it to us, saying, "Take this, all of you, and eat of it, for this is my body, which will be given up for you." In a similar way, when supper was ended, he took the chalice, and giving the Father thanks, he said the blessing, and gave the chalice to us, saying, "Take this, all of you, and drink from it, for this is the chalice of my blood, the blood of the new and eternal covenant, which will be poured out for you and for many, for the forgiveness of sins. Do this in memory of me."[58] Because of what he said, we knew that by some incomprehensibly great miracle which he had worked the bread had been changed into his body, and that it was really present, but under the appearances of the bread, and that the wine had been changed into his blood, and that it was really present, but under the appearances of the wine. And we knew that since he was alive, his blood and his soul were present with his body under the appearances of the bread, and that since he is Lord, his divine nature was present as well.

Similarly we knew that his body and his soul were present with his blood under the appearances of the wine, and that his divine nature was present as well. And since he made present to us his body and blood as separated, and since he said, "This is my body, *which will be given up for you,*" and "This is the chalice of my blood...*which will be poured out for you and for many, for the forgiveness of sins,*" we knew he was making a reference to his being crucified, which we knew was going to happen soon, and we knew he was telling us that his death on the Cross, the separation of his body and his blood, would be a sacrifice for our sins and for the sins of a vast number of human beings, indeed, for the sins of all—we knew he was telling us this extraordinary, inconceivably gracious and merciful mystery he was going to do for the glory of his Father and for our salvation. And then he said, "Do this in memory of me." And we have done that. And now we realize that every time we do this, he not only makes really present his body and his blood, but, since he makes them present as separated, he is also making present his sacrifice on the Cross, and allowing us to add our own intentions—for praise, for thanksgiving, for forgiveness of sins, for every kind of petition—to accompany the sacrifice.

We now realize that the Breaking of the Bread is itself a sacrifice, his one sacrifice on the Cross, offered on the Cross in a bloody manner, offered in the Breaking of the Bread in an unbloody manner, but the same one sacrifice, with all its glorious blessings being renewed for us each time we offer it. And then, since he told us we were to eat his body and drink his blood, and since now his body and blood, and his soul, are glorified and will be for all eternity, we now realize that, when we eat his body and drink his blood, he is increasing our communion with him, bringing us into very union with him,[59] and therefore with the Father and the Holy Spirit, and therefore with one another in him, so as indeed to become one body with him, we the members, he the Head.[60] He is giving himself to us as nourishment for our souls, preserving and increasing our share in the divine nature;[61] he is giving us a pledge of heavenly bliss and of the future resurrection of our bodies.[62] In this life, we can in no way speak adequately of this great gift which the Lord Jesus has given us. But we know that it is the greatest source of our communion and the greatest realization of our communion.

Fourth, we are to persevere in the prayers. Perhaps Saint Peter spoke along the following lines: The Lord gave only one command as to when we should pray. His command was: "Pray without ceasing." He told a parable to the effect that we ought always to pray and not lose heart,[63] and when he spoke to us of these last days and of his coming on the clouds of heaven with power and great glory, he said that we must watch at all times, praying that we may have strength to escape all that will then take place, and to stand before him.[64] The Breaking of Bread is our greatest prayer. But we must also pray together at the three hours of daily prayer: morning, afternoon, and evening.[65] The Breaking of Bread and these daily prayers together are the strong moments of our prayer. But each of us must also try continually to pray throughout the day. How can we do this? I have already spoken to you of our effort to continue our meditation on the Word of God day and night, as the prophet put forward to us.[66] Now our prayer is a response to the Word of God. And so, as during our daily work and activities we try constantly to repeat to ourselves and think about some portion of the Word of God, we should as well allow prayer to spring up from us as our response to this Word. For example, we can constantly repeat the word he spoke to us, "they will see the Son of Man coming on the clouds of heaven with power and great glory," and after each repetition we can allow this prayer to spring up from our heart: "Come, Lord Jesus!" If our work is work of our hands, and of a sort such that, while our hands are working, we can be thinking of God and of the things of God, then we can be constantly meditating and praying as we work. If our work is of a sort that engages our attention in a way that makes it difficult to attend to other things, we can still pause frequently in this work for a few moments in order to meditate and pray. And it is also possible, if we advance, by grace, far in prayer, for us to combine meditation and prayer even with this latter kind of work, especially a very simple meditation together with the highest kind of prayer I am about to describe.

As for the kinds of prayer, there are supplications for forgiveness of our sins; there are promises we make to God; there are petitions for ourselves, but much more intercessions for others; there are thanksgivings, and these should always be mingled with supplications, promises, petitions, and intercessions.[67] Also there is praise, when with joy we simply proclaim the greatness and goodness and glory of God. Then there is the prayer the Lord himself taught us. This prayer of course, of all prayers in words, contains the plenitude of perfection. And yet the Lord, by the phrase of address, "Our Father," teaches us that we should aspire to one still higher state, consisting in a gazing on God alone—insofar as we are capable of such a gazing in this life—and in a great ardor of the love of God, of charity, in which state a disciple of the Lord communes with God most familiarly and lovingly as with one's own Father, and cries out, "*Abba*, Father,"[68] as we heard the Lord cry out.[69] And our Lord also showed us the form of this state when he retired alone to the mountain to pray, and all night continued in prayer to God.[70] Sometimes this is a prayer of darkness: we see in a mirror darkly.[71] Sometimes it is a prayer of light: God, the blessed and only Sovereign, the King of kings and Lord of lords, who alone has immortality and dwells in unapproachable light.[72] It is a prayer without words: the Spirit himself intercedes for us with sighs too deep for words.[73]

These, then, are the four essential elements of the Kingdom of the Lord Jesus Christ as it has begun on this Pentecost Day, or rather, the communion *is* the Kingdom of the Lord Jesus Christ, and perseverance in the teaching of the Apostles, in the Breaking of Bread, and in the prayers are the three essential elements of it. This is the Kingdom, the communion, into which the Lord Jesus Christ calls you, and in which, if you accept Baptism, you will be called to live, to persevere, and to grow. And we can express with one word how, so far as your part is concerned, you can live in, persevere in, and grow in, the communion. The word is "charity."[74] It is by exercising charity, the love of God and of neighbor on account of God, that, so far as your part is concerned, you live in the communion of the Kingdom, because love of God and neighbor effects the communion; that you persevere in it, because love of God and neighbor is not love unless it is unceasingly given; that you grow in it, because love of God and neighbor always wishes to grow greater and greater. We know that charity is in this way your whole obligation with regard to the communion of the Kingdom, because this is what the Lord himself taught us. When asked which is the great commandment in the law, he replied in this way: "You shall love the Lord your God with all your heart, and with all your soul, and with all your mind. This is the great and first commandment. And a second is like it: You shall love your neighbor as yourself. On these two commandments depend all the law and the prophets."[75] And the law, and the prophets who unceasingly exhort to the keeping of the law, depend on these two commandments, because the Lord said, "If you love me, you will keep my commandments,"[76] and his commandments are to keep all the laws of the Kingdom, all that are necessary to persevere in the communion, in the teaching of the Apostles, in the Breaking of the Bread, and the prayers.

The hearers may have felt a puzzle about the Double Commandment. For, if our great hope is to be united to God, and with and one another in God, by not only charity but also knowledge, why did not the Lord command us to know God, and our neighbor as the image of God, as well as command us to love God and our neighbor? Saint Peter must have added something along the lines of Saint Paul's celebrated formulation of the apostolic teaching in response to this question:

> If I speak in the tongues of men and of angels, but have not love, I am a noisy gong or a clanging cymbal. And if I have prophetic powers, and understand all mysteries and all knowledge, and if I have all faith, so as to remove mountains, but have not love, I am nothing. If I give away all I have, and if I deliver my body to be burned, but have not love, I gain nothing.
>
> Love never ends; as for prophecies, they will pass away; as for tongues, they will cease; as for knowledge, it will pass away. For our knowledge is imperfect and our prophecy is imperfect; but when the perfect comes, the imperfect will pass away. When I was a child, I spoke like a child, I thought like a child, I

> reasoned like a child; when I became a man, I gave up childish ways. For now we see in a mirror dimly, but then face to face. Now I know in part; then I shall understand fully, even as I have been fully understood. So faith, hope, love abide, these three; but the greatest of these is love.[77]

Of course it is true that love must always be accompanied by the sort of knowing of that toward which it is directed which is required by the sort of love it is; without this kind of knowing, love could not be elicited or exercised. The sort of love of God in the case of one who believes all that I am proclaiming to you is the love of God as Father—and so, as we have seen, our Lord teaches us to pray "Our Father..."—and it is also the love of God as Friend, for that is what our Lord told us at the Last Supper: "I no longer call you servants, but friends . . . ."[78] Therefore, it requires that one believe that God is one's Father and God is one's Friend. And this is to say that it requires faith. And so when our Lord gives us as the first and great commandment the love of God, he is implicitly commanding that we have faith. And similarly in his command to love one's neighbor as one's self, he is implicitly commanding that we have faith, the faith which believes that the neighbor is loved by God, is in the image of God, is capable of receiving God and must receive God if he is to come to beatitude. And indeed our Lord did explicitly command us to have faith. At the beginning of his earthly ministry he said, "Repent, and believe in the gospel."[79] At the end of his earthly ministry, at the Last Supper, he said, "Believe in God, believe also in me."[80] And we have also just taught that you must try always to grow more and more in the knowledge of God through hearing and reading and meditation of the Word of God. Why, then, did the Lord mention only love, and not faith, in his double commandment?

The reason is that any knowledge of God that we can have in this life, even that of the greatest gift of faith, is in itself imperfect, so imperfect that it does not grasp what God is, does not see God, but only sees in a mirror dimly, and so it cannot,[81] in and of itself, unite us to God. In and of itself, faith is dead.[82] Indeed, it can even be present in one who rejects God—for example, the mortal sinner who does not wish to be reconciled to God—and even in one who hates God—the demons believe, and shudder.[83] Whereas the love of charity, which always presupposes faith, transforms faith into living faith, and in this life can simultaneously reach beyond the limits of one's knowing by faith and unite one to God as to Father and Friend, but Father and Friend not yet seen, yet known as loving one and as he to whom one wishes to give oneself totally by love. Further, the love of charity is the best guide to ensuring that the greater knowledge of God by faith which we obtain by hearing, reading, and meditation is authentic, and is not mixed with error; and if we do fall into error in regard to this knowledge, then, if we are corrected, we will readily accept the correction because of our love of charity, with which humility is always joined. And further, from the love of charity, poured into our hearts by the Holy Spirit, there comes forth that wisdom which is the supreme gift of the Holy Spirit, still a knowledge of faith, but now very deep and quasi-experiential.[84]

Therefore, the only sure way in this age to draw closer to God and to begin to be in communion with him, in union with him, is by charity; thus, in this age, love of God takes precedence over knowledge of God. Whereas in the Kingdom in power and glory we will be united with God both by charity and, no longer by faith, but by knowledge, and in fact seeing God as he is and giving ourselves to him as so seen will be the substance of blessedness, while it will be the love of God which moves us to this seeing and giving and which rejoices in it when it is attained.[85] In this sense in the Kingdom knowledge of God will take precedence over love of God. Instructing us, then, for our life in this world, our Lord gives as his great commandment charity, which carries with it and enlivens faith, whereas faith is not necessarily accompanied by charity, and even when it is, does not of itself, unlike face-to-face vision of itself, unite us to God.

But now, given that by the Lord's own teaching the perfection of those who follow him is in the love of God and neighbor, Saint Peter must have next addressed this question: How then can we grow in the love of God and neighbor? To answer, he would first have described in some detail the spiritual struggle which each follower of Christ must undertake: we must by grace freely choose to use the virtues infused in us by Baptism, and in order to do that, we must by grace progressively uproot the old tendencies to sin which remain in us after Baptism, which the Lord chose to leave in us after Baptism in order that we may by grace fight against them and thus attain higher levels of virtue than we would have had these tendencies not remained. Here Saint Peter would again first have referred to the Lord's own teaching on this matter, which we now find throughout the Gospels, and in a certain way comprehensively summarized in the Sermon on the Mount of Matthew 5–7. He would also have given teaching such as we now find in numbers of passages of the letters of the Apostles, of Paul, and of apostolic men. A good example of such a passage is Col. 3:5–4:6. Again, Saint Paul in 1 Cor. 13:4–7 shows the kinds of evils the tendencies to which we must by grace get rid of if charity and the other virtues are to be fully released. The locus of evil tendencies, of vices, and also of good tendencies, of virtues, and of charity, is the heart, as the Lord shows in his teaching recorded in Mark 7:14–23. Therefore, the struggle after Baptism is the purifying of the heart, and purity of heart immediately gives rise to, or simply consists in, the fullness of charity, of love of God and neighbor, such as can be attained in this age. And since it is by the love of God and neighbor on account of God that we draw near to God, are united to God, the Lord proclaims in his Sixth Beatitude: "Blessed are the pure in heart, for they shall see God."[86] And here Saint Peter would have pointed out that this struggling, with the grace of the Lord, to come to purity of heart, to the fullness of charity will necessarily involve increasingly separating oneself from the world, in the sense of more and more separating oneself from the world's evil deeds and words and thoughts, from its evil example. He might have expressed this along these lines of Saint Paul:

> Do not be mismated with unbelievers. For what partnership have righteousness and iniquity? Or what fellowship has light with darkness? What accord has Christ with Belial? Or what

> has a believer in common with an unbeliever? What agreement has the temple of God with idols? For we are the temple of the living God; as God said,
>
> "I will live in them and move among them,
> and I will be their God,
> and they shall be my people.
> Therefore come out from them,
> and be separate from them, says the Lord,
> and touch nothing unclean;
> then I will welcome you,
> and I will be a father to you,
> and you shall be my sons and daughters,
> says the Lord Almighty."
>
> Since we have these promises, beloved, let us cleanse ourselves from every defilement of body and spirit, and make holiness perfect in the fear of God.[87]

This struggle towards purity of heart and charity, Saint Peter would in some way have said, is the first degree of "Therefore come out from them, and be separate from them, says the Lord."

Second, Saint Peter would have explained that the Lord taught that there were three practices which would make possible the most rapid and complete purification of the heart and attainment of unhindered charity, and that he counseled that we should undertake these practices if we were given the grace to do so. These practices consist in a further separation from the world, a separation this time not from evil practices of the world, but from practices in themselves good, but ones which, because of the weakness of our fallen nature as a result of original sin, can become the objects of inordinate desire and attachment on our part, and so hinder the love of God and of neighbor. These practices are the possession of material goods, marriage, and the free exercise of one's own will.

Thus, Saint Peter would have told his hearers, to the rich young man the Lord said, "If you would be perfect"—that is, perfect in charity—"go, sell what you possess and give to the poor, and you will have treasure in heaven; and come, follow me."[88] Here is the counsel to give up the possession of material goods. Saint Peter would have explained that the Apostles and those with them practiced this counsel by having a complete community of goods, and that any of his hearers who wished to receive Baptism would be asked to participate fully in this community of goods.

Also in the Lord's words to the rich young man is the counsel to give up the free exercise of one's will, and to be obedient to a superior whose directives are as from God. For by "follow me," the Lord meant that the young man should obey him and imitate him. Moreover, Saint Peter would have explained, the Lord said to the seventy whom he sent out to heal the sick and to proclaim the Kingdom of God, "He who hears you hears me,"[89] and this of course also applied to the Apostles, and to any on whom the Apostles and their successors laid their hands, or to whom they gave their blessing, to be superiors as representing the will of God to others. And so, Saint Peter would have explained, those who wished to be baptized would be asked to be obedient to Saint Peter and the Apostles, and to any superiors legitimately empowered for that service. And this would begin with their laying at the feet of the Apostles the proceeds of their sale of their goods.[90]

Then the Lord also said to his disciples, "Not all men can receive this word," that is, the word he is about to speak, "but only those to whom it is given. For there are eunuchs who have been so from birth, and there are eunuchs who have been made eunuchs by men, and there are eunuchs who have made themselves eunuchs for the sake of the kingdom of heaven. He who is able to receive this, let him receive it."[91] Here is the third counsel of the Lord, the counsel to celibacy for the sake of the Kingdom. Saint Peter, as we know from Saint Paul's First Letter to the Corinthians, would have counseled celibacy to those of his hearers who were unmarried and who wished to receive Baptism, and counseled those who were married and who wished to receive Baptism to make their marriage a school of charity and mutual obedience,[92] a school of chastity and of devotion to prayer,[93] a school for their children whom they are to bring up in the discipline and instruction of the Lord,[94] and to be in the world, but not of the world.[95] With the observance of these three counsels of giving up all material goods, of celibacy, and of obedience, we have the second degree of "Therefore come out from them, and be separate from them, says the Lord."

Finally, with regard to the implementation of the Double Commandment, Saint Peter would have taught his hearers with regard to the following matter: if our great hope is to be in communion with, united to, God, and with one another in God, and if what brings us into that union is charity, loving God and loving our neighbor, then does one of these loves bring us into greater union with God than the other? And if so, should we order our life toward it?

Saint Peter would have answered the first question along the following lines. Let us first ask what is the greatest act of charity. Our Lord taught us what it was, first, by giving us his example of it, the greatest of all the examples he gave us. What was this act of charity of which he gave us the example? It was the act of laying down his life out of love for his Father, that his Father's loving plan for the salvation of all of us might be fulfilled, and out of love for each one of us, too. This was the greatest act of charity ever performed. And also, at the last supper we had with him, he taught by his words what is the greatest act of charity. He said, "Greater love has no man, that a man lay down his life for his friends."[96] If he deigned at that supper to call us, marvelous to say, friends, then he, marvelous to say, is our friend, and so greater love no one has than this, to lay down one's life for him.

Brothers and sisters, the Lord suffered for you, leaving you an example that you should follow in his steps.[97] I understood this when he appeared to us on the shore of the Sea of Galilee. He turned to me and asked me three times, "Simon, do you love me?" Three times, by his love for me, by his grace, by his forgiveness, I said, "Yes, Lord, you know that

I love you." Then he said, "Follow me."[98] I knew then that I was to follow him all the way to the death he had died, that I was, that I am, to die for him. Brothers and sisters, let us all be prepared to die for him, out of love for him, out of love for his Father, out of love for their Holy Spirit, in witness to his truth, to his righteousness, for he is Truth, he is Righteousness. If persecution and tortures unto death should come our way, let us count it all joy,[99] let us rejoice that we are accounted worthy to suffer for his name.[100] If persecution unto death does not come our way, let us live as if tomorrow we are going to be put to death for him because we love him. Remember that in Baptism we die with him. Yes, I have been crucified with Christ; I live, and yet no longer I, but Christ lives in me, and that life which I now live in the flesh I live in faith, the faith which is in the Son of God, who loved me and gave himself up for me.[101] Since I am of Christ Jesus, I have crucified the flesh with all its passions and lusts.[102] Far be it from me to glory, save in the cross of our Lord Jesus Christ, through which the world has been crucified to me, and I to the world.[103] Let us, then, constantly keep our mind and heart on the Lord out of the love of charity for him, let us live as if all that is in this world is naught, all, that is, except our brothers and sisters, our neighbor, because for them, out of charity, we always have love also, love ready to help them in whatever way we can whenever the need for our love arises. Thus, the love of God is the greater love of charity, the love that brings us into greater union with God, but to be authentic that love of God must always have love of neighbor with it in readiness to serve. And thus, yes, we should order our life toward such love of God.

And without doubt the Lord himself taught that the love of God is the greater love, but that the love of neighbor must always been in readiness with it.[104] At the Last Supper he said, "He who loves me will be loved by my Father, and I will love him and manifest myself to him."[105] Now when he manifests himself to us, so that we see him as he is,[106] then we shall be in perfect union with him. Therefore, love of God in and of itself brings us into union with God, incomplete union in this life, and perfect union in the next. Whereas love of neighbor in and of itself does not bring us into union with God, but does so only if it is on account of God. And from this it follows that love of God in and of itself brings us into greater union with God than love of neighbor on account of God in and of itself does. For love of God in and of itself just is movement of oneself toward union with God by giving oneself utterly to God. Whereas love of neighbor in and of itself is not movement toward union with God, but is such only because the neighbor is loved on account of God, that is, because God loves the neighbor, because he has commanded us to love the neighbor. But our love of God is not the love of God of charity unless it includes the love of neighbor on account of God, and our love of neighbor is not the love of neighbor of charity unless it is motivated by the love of God.

Thus, given that love of God in and of itself brings us into greater union with God than love of neighbor on account of God in and of itself does, we should order our life toward love of God. In the Sermon on the Mount the Lord himself said, "But seek first [your heavenly Father's] kingdom and his righteousness, and all these things shall be yours as well"[107]; and again, after the feeding of the five thousand, he said to the people, "Do not labor for the food which perishes, but for the food which endures to eternal life, which the Son of man will give you; for on him has God the Father set his seal." Then they said to him, "What must we do, to be doing the works of God?" Jesus answered them, "This is the work of God, that you believe in him whom he has sent"[108]; Again, to Martha the sister of Mary he said, "Martha, Martha, you are anxious and troubled about many things; one thing is needful. Mary has chosen the good portion, which shall not be taken away from her."[109]

This answer of the Lord follows from his answer to the first question: given that love of God in and of itself brings us into greater union with God than love of neighbor on account of God in and of itself does, then we should order our life directly and immediately to the love of God, if we are given the calling and grace to do so, but that life must include love of neighbor as well. And that life includes the love of neighbor in this way: we principally intend and exercise the love of God, but whenever the needs of our neighbor require us to do so, we intend and exercise the love of neighbor.

And then Saint Peter would have pointed out the following: this life ordered directly and immediately to the love of God will require a still further separating of oneself from the world than is required by observing the counsels of giving up all possession of material goods, of celibacy and of obedience. For the love of God in and of itself can be hindered not only by the love of the good of external prosperity, by the love of the good of marriage and the family, and by the love of the good of the free use of one's will, but also by the love and even simply the distraction of anything in the world. And so for the fullest love of God in and of itself and the most rapid growth in it, and also the most rapid growth in the love of neighbor on account of God in and of itself, which flows from the love of God, the separating of oneself from the world itself, to the extent possible, is required. Thus, Saint Peter would have expressed in his own words the following: "From now on…let those who mourn live as though they were not mourning, and those who rejoice as though they were not rejoicing…and those who deal with the world as though they had no dealings with it."[110] And here is the third degree of "Therefore come out from them, and be separate from them, says the Lord."

And then Saint Peter must have added something along the following lines. My brothers, these are the last days. Just before our Lord ascended into heaven, we asked him, "Lord, will you at this time restore the kingdom to Israel?" He said to us, "It is not for you to know times and seasons which the Father has fixed by his own authority. But you shall receive power when the Holy Spirit has come upon you; and you shall be my witnesses in Judea and Samaria and to the end of the earth."[111] It is for us, then, to know that these are the last days, but not to know when the Lord will come again. Therefore, the only way in which we can live is to do our best, by grace, to be prepared for his Second Coming at every moment. And that is why he immediately directed our attention to the coming of the Holy Spirit, who will give us the power of grace to live as we must. Through the prophet Isaiah, the Lord said, "At the acceptable time I have listened to you, and helped you on the day of salvation."[112] Behold, now is the acceptable time; behold, now is the day of salvation.[113] When the Lord offers us his gifts, above all the Gift of the Holy Spirit, all the gifts of grace of the Spirit through our lives, the gift of salvation, we must always respond quickly; the Lord will not brook our delaying over accepting his infinite gifts of love.

And so, the acceptable time is always short, the day of salvation is always short. My brothers, after all I have said to you, do you not feel this love of God in and of itself rising up within you, as we feel it in ourselves? Do you not feel your mind and heart, as we feel our mind and heart, being drawn to gazing on the vision we have proclaimed to you: the Father, the Lord Jesus Christ at his right hand, the Holy Spirit being poured out upon us by him; he being both man and Lord; the communion with him now; his glorious coming in power and glory when he returns in his Second Coming? How can you not, as we cannot, keep mind and heart fixed on these wonders and glories? My brothers, the Holy Spirit, whom you will receive if you are baptized and we lay our hands on you, is himself the Love of God; the Holy Spirit, as we told you, will pour into your hearts the love of God; the Holy Spirit is the Spirit of Truth, and he will deepen more and more your vision of all these wonders and glories.[114] My brothers, this love of God, a flaming fire, will draw all other loves into itself, and so with the joy of this love you will gladly strive for purity of heart and charity, you will gladly follow the Lord's counsels, yes, you will gladly leave the world, and leaving behind all that belongs to this life, you will delight in giving yourself to the love of God.

And so my brothers, earnestly desire the higher gifts.[115] If you are baptized, you will die with Christ and be raised with Christ. And if you are raised with Christ, seek the things that are above, where Christ is, seated at the right hand of God. Set your minds on things that are above, not on things that are on the earth. For you will have died, and your life will be hid with Christ in God. When Christ who is our life appears, then you also will appear with him in glory.[116] My brothers, we look not to the things that are seen but to the things that are unseen; for the things that are seen are transient, but the things that are unseen are eternal.[117] My brothers—and here we may suppose he said as the Spirit gave him to say what Saint Paul said in this way:

> Whatever gain I had, I counted as loss for the sake of Christ. Indeed I count everything as loss because of the surpassing worth of knowing Christ Jesus my Lord. For his sake I have suffered the loss of all things, and count them as refuse, in order that I may gain Christ and be found in him, not having a righteousness of my own, based on law, but that which is through faith in Christ, the righteousness from God that depends on faith; that I may know him and the power of his resurrection, and may share his sufferings, becoming like him in his death, that if possible I may attain the resurrection from the dead. Not that I have already obtained this or am already perfect; but I press on that I may capture that for which I was captured by Christ Jesus. Brethren, I do not consider that I have yet captured it; but one thing I do, forgetting what lies behind and straining forward to what lies ahead, I press on toward the goal for the prize of the upward call of God in Christ Jesus.[118]
>
> My brothers, repent, and be baptized every one of you in the name of Jesus Christ for the forgiveness of your sins; and you shall receive the gift of the Holy Spirit. For the promise is to you and to your children and to all that are far off, every one whom the Lord our God calls to him. Save yourselves from this crooked generation.[119]
>
> So those who received his word were baptized, and there were added that day about three thousand souls.[120]

* * *

Taking the preceding as a summary of what the earliest monks understood the essential elements of the apostolic preaching to be and of what they understood the essential elements of the first Church of Jerusalem to be, which they saw as based on that preaching, we may note John Cassian's teaching as to the line of development which led from that Church to the first cenobitic communities of monks. In the passage from Cassian cited at the beginning of this essay, we see that the first Church of Jerusalem remained unchanged in its discipline up to the time of the death of the last Apostle around 100 A.D. But after the death of the Apostles, the faith of the multitude of believers began to grow cold. Cassian seems to include in this cooling the faith of the believers of the Church of Jerusalem, and seems to suggest that nevertheless initially the discipline of the Church remained unchanged. But he indicates that the cooling was much greater among the believers of Gentile origin, of whom by this time there were many Churches in the Roman world, and attributes this to the fact that all that the Apostles required of these believers were the abstinences noted in Acts 15:29. In his view, then, communion of material goods was not required of the members of these Churches even at the beginning of their Churches, but, he seems to suggest a few lines further on, was required of the leaders (*principes*) of these Churches. Then he notes that, apparently not much later, this liberty granted to the Gentiles began to mar the perfection of the Church of Jerusalem. He does not say how, but since the discipline he focuses attention on in this passage is that of the communion of material goods, one presumes it was especially, if not only, in this area.

A decisive point is reached when in this general cooling the leaders of the Churches began to relax for themselves the discipline of communion of material goods. At this point,

> those who still had the fervour of the apostles, mindful of that former perfection, left their cities and intercourse with those who thought that carelessness and a laxer life was permissible to themselves and the Church of God, and began to live in more remote places in the countryside around the towns, and there, in private and on their own account, to practise those things

> which they had learnt to have been ordered by the apostles throughout the whole body of the Church in general: and so that whole system of which we have spoken [viz., the system of cenobitic monks] grew up from those disciples who had separated themselves from the evil that was spreading.

Here for the first time a physical separation of some Christian disciples from their local congregations began. From the text it is difficult to determine whether Cassian thought these "disciples" were all celibates, or included some married disciples. What we now know about Church history suggests that they were all celibates. It is also clear that Cassian believes this separation from their local congregations of "those who still had the fervor of the apostles" was occurring in all the Churches of the Empire, not just in the Church of Jerusalem.

Then Cassian seems to suggest a further development which led to a still greater separation, in way of life and also physically: "And these, by degrees as time went on, were separated from the great mass of believers because they abstained from marriage and cut themselves off from intercourse with their kinsmen and the life of this world, and were termed monks or solitaries from the strictness of their single and solitary life." The development is gradual and over a significant period of time. Abstention from marriage, and perhaps also from intercourse with kinsmen, was already characteristic of "those who still had the fervor of the apostles." But cutting themselves off from the life of this world is something the members of the first Church of Jerusalem, because of their location, could do only by "dealing with the world as though they had no dealings with it,"[121] whereas Cassian's text seems to say that "those who still had the fervor of the apostles" were now practicing the same discipline physically rather than just spiritually. It is at the time when this further physical separation, not just into areas a little outside towns and cities, but into regions physically separated from the life of this world, occurred that "those who still had the fervor of the apostles" began to be called *monachi* in Latin, *monazontes* in Greek, a word which in Christian usage in the first part of the fourth century seems to have referred to someone who was celibate and who also lived in some form of separation from society.[122] Then, Cassian concludes,

> from the communion of their life together they were called cenobites and their abodes and dwelling places coenobia. That then alone was the earliest kind of monks, which is first not only in time but also in grace, and which continued inviolable for a very long period up to the time of Abbot Paul and Antony [up to the late third and into the early fourth centuries]; and even to this day [Cassian was writing this in the early fifth century] we see its traces remaining in strict coenobia.

Contemporary scholarship with regard to the origins of monasticism basically confirms the two developments of which Cassian speaks, the one separation from the local congregation and beginning to live as a distinct community, but close to the congregation and interacting with and serving it, and the second the further separation from society as a whole. The first separation seems to be beginning in the late second century, and the second, in the late third and early fourth centuries.[123]

One can clearly see how these early cenobites saw the form of their life to be the same as that of the first Church of Jerusalem.[124] As we said above, Saint Peter must have said that the first Church of Jerusalem was to be constituted by its members "persevering in the teaching of the Apostles and in the communion, in the breaking of the bread and in the prayers." The cenobites persevered in the teaching of the Apostles. And how? They could not hear the Apostles preach. But by their time the canon of the Old and New Testaments was largely in place, and so they could read what the Lord himself preached and taught, what the Apostles preached and taught, and what the Old Testament taught and how the Lord and his Apostles interpreted it. Thus, for these cenobites, and all subsequent monks, whether cenobitic or eremitical, the reading of Scripture, and reading it in a prayerful way, was of primary importance in their life. This kind of reading of Scripture was called in Latin *lectio divina*.

But further, by now many, and many great, writings of those whom we now call the Fathers of the Church had been written and were available. It can be said that all of them, without qualification, are based on Scripture, and very many of them are in the form of a commentary on this or that part of Scripture. Still further, the Magisterium of the Church was recognized, although not yet referred to by this term, and so the Scriptures and the Fathers were read in its light. Even if the term *lectio divina* was reserved to the reading of the Scriptures themselves, nevertheless the reading of the cenobites included the Fathers and magisterial sources as well. And this reading was a daily part of their life. But moreover, listening was still a daily, or almost daily, part of their life as well. For the Abbot—who, almost certainly, was a descendant of the "prophets" and "teachers" of the first Church of Jerusalem—gave instructions and exhortations freely, all based on the Scriptures, the Fathers, and the Magisterium.[125] And again, just as in the first Church of Jerusalem, all this reading and hearing was "ploughed" more deeply into the heart by the practice of meditation, the same practice of the Jerusalem Church. And as will be recalled, this meditation was practiced continually.

As for the perseverance of these cenobites in the communion: the notion of sharing in the life of the Most Holy Trinity, and of sharing in the life of one another through sharing in the life of the Most Holy Trinity, by way of mutual love and knowledge, is everywhere in monastic texts. In the passage from Cassian we have quoted, he says literally, "from the communion of their consortium they are called cenobites" (the latter from the Greek word *koinobion*, "common life"; hence, *koinobiotes* are "those who live in common, in communion"), implying that the concept of communion is the key concept of their spirituality.[126] Moreover, it should be noted that the hermits have their own kind of community, and of communion, too. And further, as part of their communion, the cenobites held all their material goods in common, just as did the members of the first Church of Jerusalem.

As for perseverance in the Breaking of the Bread and in the prayers: as for all Christians, the Eucharist was for the early monks the center of their life of prayer. In their writings they make little mention of it, because it was taken for granted, and because the legislation about its celebration was determined by the Church itself, and not by Abbots, or any other private group of persons. And as for the prayers: their whole day was punctuated by hours of common prayer, and they endeavored to continue in prayer privately during the times in between the common hours. For the purpose of private prayer they followed very precisely what was already going on in the first Church of Jerusalem. We spoke about how meditation could go on throughout the day, both in the case of manual work, and in the case of some sort of intellectual work. And we saw how frequent prayers were the responses to this continuous or frequent meditation. The kinds of prayer were those mentioned above for the Jerusalem Church. And as for that highest kind of prayer consisting in a gazing on God alone and in a great ardor of the love of God, in which state a disciple of the Lord communes with God most familiarly and lovingly as with one's own Father, the early monks called it "contemplation," *theoria* in Greek, *contemplatio* in Latin. The word in English, Greek and Latin signifies a simple gazing at or on, and in the case of this highest prayer, a simple, loving gazing on God.

Perseverance in these four elements was the essential structure of cenobitic (and indeed eremitical) monasticism, as it was of the first Church of Jerusalem. But further, the monks' way of life within that structure was the same way of life of the first Church of Jerusalem: the life of charity.[127] Further, the monks dedicated themselves to a life focused on the greatest and most rapid growth in charity, just as the first Church of Jerusalem had done. First, they dedicated themselves to the struggle to attain purity of heart.[128] Second, the monks practiced the three counsels the Lord gave for making growth in charity more rapid, counsels passed on by the Apostles: poverty, that is, community of temporal goods; celibacy; obedience.[129] Third, as between love of God and love of neighbor, although both are necessary, they dedicated themselves, as had the

Church of Jerusalem, to a life ordered directly and immediately to love of God, as the love which brings us in and of itself into greater union with God than the love of neighbor on account of God in and of itself, but a life in which they took up the works of love of neighbor whenever a neighbor needed them to do so.[130]

Moreover, the monks saw this way of life to which they dedicated themselves as their way of sharing in martyrdom, just as the first Church of Jerusalem had regarded it. Thus, to point out passages only from Cassian, and only two: the cenobites, he says—and he would certainly think the same of the anchorites—"are by patience and the strictness whereby they continue devoutly in the order which they have once embraced, so as never to fulfil their own will, crucified daily to this world and made living martyrs."[131] And in one of the passages in which he gives a summary statement of the nature of the whole of the monastic life, he recalls the Abba Pinufius giving this exhortation to a young monk whom he is receiving into the novitiate:

> Wherefore you ought in the first instance to learn the actual reason for the renunciation of the world, and when you have seen this, you can be taught more plainly what you ought to do, from the reason for it.
>
> Renunciation is nothing but the evidence of the cross and of mortification. And so you must know that today you are dead to this world and its deeds and desires, and that, as the Apostle says, you are crucified to this world and this world to you (Galatians 6:14). Consider therefore the demands of the cross under the sacrament of which you ought henceforward to live in this life; because *you* no longer live but *He* lives in you who was crucified for you (Galatians 2:20). We must therefore pass our time in this life in that fashion and form in which He was crucified for us on the cross so that (as David says) piercing our flesh with the fear of the Lord, we may have all our wishes and desires not subservient to our own lusts but fastened to His

> mortification. For so shall we fulfil the command of the Lord which says: He that takes not up his cross and follows me is not worthy of me (Matthew 10:38). But perhaps you will say: How can a man carry his cross continually? Or how can any one who is alive be crucified? Hear briefly how this is.
>
> The fear of the Lord is our cross. As then one who is crucified no longer has the power of moving or turning his limbs in any direction as he pleases, so we also ought to affix our wishes and desires—not in accordance with what is pleasant and delightful to us now, but in accordance with the law of the Lord, where it constrains us. And as he who is fastened to the wood of the cross no longer considers things present, nor thinks about his likings, nor is perplexed by anxiety and care for the morrow, nor disturbed by any desire of possession, nor inflamed by any pride or strife or rivalry, grieves not at present injuries, remembers not past ones, and while he is still breathing in the body considers that he is dead to all earthly things, sending the thoughts of his heart on before to that place whither he doubts not that he is shortly to come: so we also, when crucified by the fear of the Lord ought to be dead indeed to all these things, i.e., not only to carnal vices but also to all earthly things, having the eye of our minds fixed there whither we hope at each moment that we are soon to pass. For in this way we can have all our desires and carnal affections mortified.[132]

"You are henceforward to live in this life under the *sacrament* (*sacramentum*) of the Cross"—there could not be a clearer statement of the monks' seeing their life as a "white martyrdom," as it was to be called in the subsequent tradition.

In the monastic tradition already by the fourth century the part of the monastic life dedicated to attaining purity of heart was called the "active life" and the part dedicated to rapid growth in love of God, accompanied by love of neighbor by *praeparatio mentis*, was called the "contemplative life"; both parts together could also be called the contemplative life, since that was the ultimate end of the entire monastic life. The first part of the life was called the "active life" because it consisted in acts directed toward the uprooting of the vices and in acts directed toward exercising the virtues implanted by charity and being released and developed by the uprooting of the vices and the practicing of those virtues.

As for the "contemplative life": Contemplation is the simple intellectual gazing on a truth, or a thing which is and which is made manifest by a truth.[133] We saw above that the love of God presupposes a knowledge of God by faith—and we now add, by faith in this life, by vision in the life to come. Therefore, an act of love of God must be accompanied by an act of contemplating God as known by faith or by vision. And so we could say that a life ordered directly and immediately to love of God is also a life ordered directly and immediately to the loving contemplation of God as known by faith or by vision. But we can also say simply that it is the life of contemplation, or the contemplative life. For the faith in question is living faith, and so it is informed by charity, and the vision of God makes the love of charity indefectible. And what principally belongs to the life of contemplation can only be the contemplation of God, for this contemplation is the purpose and perfection of human life. But there can belong to it also, secondarily and as disposing to the principal contemplation, the contemplation of the effects of God, as leading us to the knowledge of God. The effects of God are good in themselves, and the contemplation of the effects of God is, in itself, good. But, if it is not also used as leading to further knowledge of God, then it is simply the exercise of the vice called in the ancient and medieval eras "curiosity."[134] And so it is excluded from the contemplative life.

Finally, as the inevitable effect of ordering their life in this way, the monks practiced the separating of themselves from the world, what began to be called the flight from the world, involved in pursuing the active life, the further flight from the world involved in observing the counsels, and the further flight from the world, one of physical separation, involved in pursuing the contemplative life; the first two flights were exercised by the first Church of Jerusalem (with celibacy being practiced actually by some, spiritually by others), the third only spiritually.

I present the preceding as an account of the nature of the Christian monastic life and of its goals and ultimate goal, in all ages, including our own. For it is this nature and goal of the monastic life which Saint Basil proposes in the *Asketikon,* which became the foundational document for all of Eastern monasticism to the present, and which Saint Benedict proposes in his *Rule,* which became the foundational document for all of Western monasticism to the present. Moreover, the very recent magisterium of the Church has, for both East and West, reconfirmed this as the nature and goal of monasticism.[135]

In the light this account of the monastic life, let us now examine the two essays by Saint John Henry Newman.

II. Saint John Henry's "The Mission of Saint Benedict"

WE NEED as a preliminary to note first who are the readership of the two essays by Saint John Henry. Both appeared in the *Atlantis,* the first in January 1858, the second in January 1859. The *Atlantis* was the scholarly journal of the Catholic University of Ireland, of which Saint John Henry was one of the founding group, and of which he was Rector from 1854 to 1857. Its founders intended that readership would be the entire scholarly community and the articles would demonstrate that Catholic scholars produced work equal in quality to that of any other body of scholars. Thus, contributors would tend to deal with subjects of interest to any scholarly community, and to avoid topics of interest only to Catholic scholars.

From this point, a second preliminary follows. This statement in the first essay needs to be given special attention: "I trust the reader will be so good as to keep in mind that I am all along speaking of the Benedictine life *historically,* and as I might speak of any other historical *fact;* not venturing at all on what would be the extreme presumption of any quasi-doctrinal or magisterial exposition of it, which belongs to those only who have actually imbibed its tradition."[136]

I am giving an exposition of the Benedictine life as one who by grace has made an effort over a long period of his life to imbibe its tradition as best he can, and my exposition is certainly not magisterial, although it is perhaps quasi-doctrinal. But because of the difference between the exposition which Saint John Henry is giving in a truly magisterial way and the exposition I am giving as best I can, it should not be surprising that the two expositions have little in common so far as their content is concerned. I am describing the life from the point of view of someone trying by grace to live it; the saint is describing the life from the point of view of someone who is outside the life, and who is considering it only with respect to one specific matter, viz., what teaching or education it gave "in the time of [its] ascendancy,"[137] which might be said to be from about the middle of the sixth century to the middle of the twelfth century.[138]

As a final preliminary with regard to this first essay, we need to bear in mind the following statement of Saint John Henry: "[Saint Benedict] found the world, physical and social, in ruins, and his mission was to restore it in the way, not of science, but of nature, not as if setting about to do it, not professing to do it by any set time or by any rare specific or by any series of strokes, but so quietly, patiently, gradually, that often, till the work was done, it was not known to be doing."[139] Saint John Henry would agree with all interpreters of Saint Benedict that it had never entered Saint Benedict's mind that his mission was "to restore…the world, physical and social, in ruins…." What he understood his mission to be was to establish a school in which the students could learn to grow in charity so as to attain eternal life.[140] Of course, it may be correctly said that the Lord knew and intended, according to his providence, that Saint Benedict's work would begin the restoration of a world in ruins. But it is this sense of "mission," not the former sense, which Saint John Henry has in mind in his first essay.

Proceeding now to the first essay, we find that Saint John Henry on the very first page states his fundamental thesis, that what the Benedictines in the time of their ascendancy primarily taught was Poetry, what the Dominicans in the time of their ascendancy primarily taught was Science, and what the Jesuits in the time of their ascendancy primarily taught was Prudence.[141] It will be our purpose in the following to comment on this thesis.

Saint John Henry proceeds to describe the "unity of idea," in effect, the common essence, "which...is to be found in all monks in every part of Christendom" as consisting in "a unity," in effect, a commonness, "of object [that is, of purpose], of state, and of occupation." He begins with observations which could be misunderstood: "Monachism...was a reaction from...secular life"[142]; "[the monks'] one idea...their one purpose, was to be quit of [the secular world, especially as it existed at the end of antiquity, in great corruption]"[143]; "early monachism was flight from the world, and nothing else." I have proposed that the monks' "one purpose" was not flight from the world, but communion with God and with one another in God, the contemplative love of God and the love of neighbor flowing from it, and thereby salvation, eternal life, and that flight from the world was for them not an end in itself, but a means to attain these sublime goals. Further on, Saint John Henry speaks in more complete terms, and this passage can indeed be taken as a summary of his understanding of the essence of monasticism:

> Monachism was, as regards the secular life and all that it implies, emphatically a negation, or, to use another word, a *mortification*; a mortification of sense, and a mortification of reason. Here a word of explanation is necessary. The monks were too good Catholics to deny that reason was a divine gift, and had too much common sense to think to do without it. What they denied themselves was the various and manifold exercises of the reason; and on this account, because such exercises were excitements. When the reason is cultivated, it at once begins to combine, to centralize, to look forward, to look back, to view things as a whole, whether for speculation or for action; it practises synthesis and analysis, it discovers, it invents. To these exercises

> of the intellect is opposed simplicity, which is the state of mind which does not combine, does not deal with premisses and conclusions, does not recognize means and their end, but lets each work, each place, each occurrence stand by itself—which acts towards each as it comes before it, without a thought of anything else. This simplicity is the temper of children, and it is the temper of monks. This was their mortification of the intellect; every man who lives, must live by reason, as every one must live by sense; but, as it is possible to be content with the bare necessities of animal life, so is it possible to confine ourselves to the bare ordinary use of reason, without caring to improve it or make the most of it. These monks held both sense and reason to be the gifts of heaven, but they used each of them as little as they could help, reserving their full time and their whole selves for devotion—for, if reason is better than sense, so devotion they thought to be better than either; and, as even a heathen might deny himself the innocent indulgences of sense in order to give his time to the cultivation of the reason, so did the monks give up reason, as well as sense, that they might consecrate themselves to divine meditation.[144]

This passage distinguishes two operations of the reason; I prefer the term "intellect." The first operation consists in "the various and manifold exercises of the reason," in the exercises of reason "when the reason is cultivated." In my interpretation, Saint John Henry calls this operation of reason "Science," naming it from its product, which is science; I prefer to name it "the scientific operation of the intellect." Since Saint John Henry holds that "Science" is what the Dominicans taught, I propose to make use here of the Dominican account of this scientific operation of reason; that account consists, of course, in Aristotelian logic, as perfected by Saint Thomas and others.[145]

The scientific operation of the intellect consists in the operations of that liberal art of the trivium called logic, and in particular of that branch of it called demonstrative logic. Thus, "combine" seems to refer to the second act of the mind, judgment; "premisses" and "conclusions" are technical terms used in explicating the third act of the mind, reasoning, the act of mind which "discovers" new truths from presently known ones. In the later passage on this topic, Saint John Henry says of this set of operations that "its mission is to destroy ignorance, doubt, surmise," and so the type of reasoning he has in mind here is apparently demonstration, the type of reasoning through premises and conclusions in which the conclusion reached is certain, not just probable. Moreover, he seems to have in mind demonstration in the strict sense, demonstration which assigns the actual cause of an attribute's inherence in a subject; thus, in the later passage, he says that the characteristic of this operation of the intellect is that it knows the causes of things. In this Aristotelian-Thomistic logic, the result of demonstration is called "science," in the sense of certain knowledge.

Many acts of demonstration with reference to the material that is being considered result in a habit of mind which is also called "science," and further, the body of truths attained by the one with the habit is also called a "science." Thus, in the saint's expression "to view things as a whole, whether for speculation or for action," it would seem that "to view things as a whole" refers to science, and that "whether for speculation or for action" refers to the distinction in this logic between speculative science and practical science. The expression "to centralize" may refer again to science, in that all of the truths of a science are derived by demonstration from a few, or one, supreme principle. And, when he writes, "Science results in system, which is complex unity," he seems again to have in mind by "system" that which is derived by demonstration from few, or one, supreme principle. His expressions "to look forward" and "to look back" may be taken to signify respectively the consideration by practical science, e.g., ethics, of "means and their ends" and the consideration by speculative science of causes. And by "invent" the saint may have in mind the making of some useful product by a technological art, which must make use of a speculative science.

In the later passage, Saint John Henry says that "reason," i.e., the intellect when operating in this discursive way, "investigates, analyses (in the sense I believe of dividing a perceived whole into its parts), numbers, weighs, measures, ascertains, locates, the objects of its contemplation." He may be referring to operations not of demonstrative logic, but of dialectical logic, the other part of logic, which attains only probable truth. Its function in developing a science is to put forward an "hypothesis," a probable truth from which many consequences can be deduced, and then to test the hypothesis by examining whether the consequences are confirmed in actual reality. In this procedure the goal is to transform the hypothesis into a principle: a proposition immediately evident from the facts, and therefore certain, which principle can then be used as a premise for a demonstration. If this interpretation is correct, then we have in this first set of operations of the intellect, except for "invent," dialectical logic being used to obtain principles for demonstrative logic, whose result is science.

The second operation of the intellect recognized in this passage is the "simple" operation of the intellect. The only positive description of this operation the saint gives at this point is this: "[it] lets each work, each place, each occurrence stand by itself—[it] acts towards each as it comes before it, without a thought of anything else." This "simple" operation of the intellect seems to be one species of the operation or act of contemplation, characterized as consisting in the simple, that is, nondiscursive, consideration of a truth. According to my interpretation, this operation of the intellect the saint calls "Poetry," again taking the result of an operation of the intellect as the name of the operation. I prefer to call this operation the poetic operation of the intellect.

We next note that the passage says that these two operations of the intellect are "opposed." Certainly the two operations are different, but they not are opposed except in the sense that they cannot be in act simultaneously. But surely the same human being can exercise both these operations, one now at this time, the other at another time. Then the saint seems to be saying that the monks denied themselves the scientific operation of the intellect, and did so because it was an "excitement," and an excitement would be a hindrance to their ultimate purpose, which is first described as "devotion," and then as "divine meditation." It is clear here that the saint does not intend that flight from the world, or mortification of sense and reason, is the ultimate purpose of the monks, but rather the means, indeed the proximate means, to the ultimate purpose ("devotion" or "divine meditation").

In accordance with this, when Saint John Henry says "they [the monks] used each of them [sense and reason] as little as they could help," he must be interpreted to mean that the monks used sense only to the extent necessary to secure "the bare necessities of animal life," and that they used reason only to the extent that "every man who lives, must live by reason," and this degree of reasoning need involve no more than "the bare ordinary use of reason." The structure of the passage seems to require holding that "the bare ordinary use of reason" is synonymous with "the poetic operation of the intellect," i.e., the "simple" operation of the intellect. But we cannot make this equivalence. Surely living by reason necessarily involves not just the simple operation of the intellect but also at least some use of the scientific operation of the intellect: some reasoning as to the causes of things, about means to an end, and so on, just to secure, along with sense, the bare necessities of animal life. In addition, since the life in question is the life of a man, there will be other needs for the scientific operation of the intellect, e.g., the demands of love for neighbor, such as caring for the sick or teaching the newcomer about monastic life, which will require more than the simple operation of the intellect. In fact, all of us surely exercise the scientific operation of the intellect every day of our lives. Of course, we are not required to have any understanding of the operations of logic which constitute the scientific operation of the intellect, but use them we do and we must. Moreover, these uses just for living, and for living as a human being, do not seem to be "excitements." Perhaps trying to understand logic is an excitement, but surely using it is often not. By "the bare ordinary use of reason," then, the saint must understand some use both of the scientific operation of the mind, and of the "simple," or poetic, operation of the mind.

But we can certainly agree with Saint John Henry that in the monastic life the scientific operation of the intellect is not to be elaborated to the point of its becoming an "excitement," and so a distraction, from the ultimate purpose of "devotion" or "divine meditation." And we can also certainly agree that from this primacy in the monastic life of "divine meditation" so much of the nature of monastic life necessarily flows.

In the next sentence after the preceding passage the saint expresses the "unity of idea," that is, the common essence, of monasticism:

> Now, then, we are able to understand how it was that the monks had a unity, and in what it consisted. It was a unity, I have said, of object, of state, and of occupation. Their object was rest and peace; their state was retirement; their occupation was some work that was simple, as opposed to intellectual, viz., prayer, fasting, meditation, study, transcription, manual labour, and other unexciting, soothing employments.[146]

It is surprising, in view of the passage immediately preceding this sentence, that the saint says that "their object was rest and peace." Surely he had just established that their purpose was what he calls "devotion" and "divine meditation," and that "rest and peace" attained by the "mortification" of sense and reason was not the monks' ultimate purpose, but the means to the end. Perhaps Saint John Henry later stops with *summa quies*, "perfect quietness," as he calls "rest and peace," because his chief interest is not in the ultimate purpose of monasticism, since that would carry him into a "quasi-doctrinal" exposition of monasticism. Rather, it is in that characteristic of it, viz., the mortification of sense and reason in order to achieve perfect quietness so as to make possible the "simple" or poetic operation of the intellect: the poetic life, which is in his view that which the monks taught during the period of Benedictine ascendancy.

It is also surprising that in this passage Saint John Henry, in giving examples of the occupations of monks, does not consider prayer, meditation, and study to be intellectual occupations; I believe this is because in this sentence he uses the term "intellectual" to signify, not the scientific operation of the intellect *simpliciter*, but that operation exercised in such a way that it is an "excitement." In any case, happily, when at the beginning of §6, after the long digression of §§4 and 5, he restates his view of the "object" of ancient monachism, he expresses himself as follows: "I have now said enough both to explain and to vindicate the biographer of St. Maurus, when he says that the object, and life, and reward of the ancient monachism was *summa quies*—the absence of all excitement, sensible and intellectual, and the vision of Eternity." Here he seems to use the expression *summa quies* to signify both the mortification of sense and reason and the vision of Eternity, that is, what he earlier called "devotion" or "divine meditation," whereas I believe it would be clearer if he spoke of the vision of Eternity as that for the sake of which the monks practiced the twofold mortification. However this may be, one can certainly accept the characterization of the ultimate purpose of monasticism as "the vision of Eternity," that is, the contemplative love of God, which is eternal life: "And this is eternal life, that they know thee, the only true God, and Jesus Christ whom thou has sent."[147]

In the passage of which this sentence is the beginning, the remainder of §6, the saint now turns his attention to explaining what he means by "poetry," that is, the "simple" or poetic operation of the intellect; he had only given the very briefest explanation of this in the passage from §3 on which we commented at length above. "Poetry," he writes, "...is always the antagonist to *science*. As science makes progress in any subject-matter, poetry recedes from it. The two cannot stand together; they belong respectively to two modes of viewing things"—that is, two modes of intellection of things, "which are contradictory of each other." As noted above, "two modes of viewing things" cannot be contradictory of each other in any way other than that they cannot be exercised simultaneously; otherwise, surely, they are complementary.

The passage goes on to list various operations constituting the scientific operation of the intellect—commented on above in treating the passage from §3, with the exception of the following: "The aim of science is to get a hold of things, to grasp them, to handle them, to comprehend them; that is (to use the familiar term), to *master* them, or to be superior to them. Its success lies in being able to draw a line round them, and to tell where each of them is to be found within that circumference, and how each lies relatively to all the rest." Here, the second sentence only speaks metaphorically of the nature of the unity of a science, a matter addressed above. (I shall return later to the first sentence.) Turning to the poetic operation of the intellect, Saint John Henry begins in this way: "But as to the poetical, very different is the frame of mind which is necessary for its perception." Here he calls the poetic operation of the intellect a perception." We would then expect that he would elucidate what kind of "perceiving" it is and what operations make it up. But this he does not do; in fact, he had said above, "I have no intention of committing myself here to a definition of poetry."

For the rest, he seeks to manifest what this perception is not by describing its constituent operations, but by describing its formal object, that is, by describing what it is a perception of, and this he calls "the poetical." (The following passage in which he does this is of great interest, and I shall return to it.) First, I propose that a definition, as best I can manage, is needed in order to understand the poetic operation of the intellect, and again, since Saint John Henry holds that the Dominicans taught us Science, I propose to call on their help to produce a definition—and defining is a scientific act of the intellect—of the poetic operation of the intellect. The Dominicans would refer me to Aristotle's *Poetics*.

And so I say that the poetic operation of the intellect is the operation of the first liberal art of the trivium, the art we call grammar or poetics, that is, the representation through words, orally, or in a written work, what we call a "work of literature," of a beautiful human action, with thought and character, and perhaps consisting only in a process of the poet's thought, the consideration of which action quiets the restless emotions of the hearer or reader by conforming these emotions to reason and bringing them to rest in the beauty of the action, and thus enables the hearer or reader to recognize that the beautiful action is an example which can be generalized into a universal and great truth about life which the hearer or reader then considers.[148] However, for the saint's purposes, it is important to note that the beginning of the poetic operation of the intellect consists in the poet's own consideration of a beautiful human action, the consideration of which quiets the restless emotions of the poet by conforming these emotions to reason and bringing them to rest in the beauty of the action, and thus enables the poet to recognize that the beautiful action is an example which can be generalized into a universal and great truth about life which the poet then considers. From this, when the full liberal art is exercised, follows the representation of the action through words, orally, or in a written work, what we call a "work of literature."

With this definition in mind of the poetical operation of the intellect, let us now consider what Saint John Henry has to say about its formal object, the "poetical." He continues thus:

> It [the poetical] demands, as its primary condition [for its perception], that we should not put ourselves above the objects in which it resides, but at their feet; that we should feel them to be above and beyond us, that we should look up to them, and that, instead of fancying that we can comprehend them, we should take for granted that we are surrounded and comprehended by them ourselves. It implies that we understand them to be vast, immeasurable, impenetrable, inscrutable, mysterious; so that at best we are only forming conjectures about them, not conclusions, for the phenomena which they present admit of many explanations, and we cannot know the true one.

The formal object, the poetical, of the poetic operation of the intellect is not a quality residing in material objects but rather a beautiful human action, with thought and character, and perhaps consisting only in a process of the observer's thought, the consideration of which action quiets the restless emotions of the observer by conforming these emotions to reason and bringing them to rest in the beauty of the action, and thus enables the observer to recognize that the beautiful action is an example which can be generalized into a universal and great truth about life which the observer then considers. By "the poetical," the saint is referring to the beautiful action, and to the truth of life which the beautiful action exemplifies, and, as part of that truth, to the "objects," that is, the realities, of which that truth speaks or which it implies. It is these realities that we should not put ourselves above, but at their feet; that we should understand to be above and beyond us, to be vast, immeasurable, impenetrable, inscrutable, mysterious, and so on. The saint is saying that in the authentic poetic operation of the intellect, the beautiful action, and the truth of life which the intellect considers, always point in some way to divinity, to divine mystery, and that therefore an authentic poetic work in words must do the same.

It was Augustine's view that *in creaturarum consideratione non vana et peritura curiositas est exercenda, sed gradus ad immortalia et semper manentia faciendus*; that is, "in the study of creatures we must not exercise an empty and futile curiosity, but should make them the stepping-stone to things unperishable and everlasting."[149] I submit that he would hold that the same is true in the particular *consideratio creaturarum* which belongs to the poetic operation of the intellect and that therefore an authentic poetic work must always open the way to and invite this *gradus*. Further, I submit that the monks whom Saint John Henry is considering would have thought the same. The saint completes his treatment of the poetic operation of the mind by this sentence: "Poetry does not address the reason, but the imagination and affections; it leads to admiration, enthusiasm, devotion, love." That is, the poetic operation of the intellect, the consideration of the beautiful action, does not engage the scientific operation of the intellect, but activates the imagination and affections, and leads to admiration, enthusiasm, devotion, love. To iterate the point above, the beautiful action quiets restless emotions by conforming them to reason and resting them in its beauty.

Let us return now to the ultimate purpose of the monastic life. This purpose Saint John Henry has so far characterized as "devotion," or "divine meditation," or "the vision of Eternity." That operation of the intellect which is the ultimate purpose of the monastic life, and is the operation, together with all that flows from it, which the monks taught during the period of Benedictine ascendancy, is best characterized not as devotion, or divine meditation, or the vision of Eternity, but as *contemplation*. Contemplation is the operation of the intellect consisting solely in the simple consideration of a truth, or a thing which is and which is made manifest by a truth. Moreover, the primary object of contemplation is God, as known in himself, to the extent possible, and the secondary objects are the effects of God, which are contemplated in themselves, but also as leading to fuller knowledge of God. Further, the contemplation of God presupposes, in this life, faith, and in the life to come, vision, and therefore is always accompanied by the love of charity. If contemplation is understood in this sense, then the poetic operation of the intellect is a species of it, one of the species which considers an effect of God and God through that effect. In a word, it is the species which considers God's effect of the beautiful action which quiets one's restless emotions by resting them in its beauty and which exemplifies a truth about life which itself ultimately points to God, which truth, and then God, one considers.

Another species of contemplation is the contemplation of a conclusion arrived at through the scientific operation of the intellect. For example, the consideration of the effect of God consisting in the material universe, of its enormous size, and at the same time of the fact that its behaviors can be modeled by most precise and elegant mathematical formulations—this consideration is also a species of contemplation, for from it we see and consider the infinite power and wisdom of God. We noted earlier the saint's statements that, on the one hand, "[t]he aim of science is to get a hold of things, to grasp them, to handle them, to comprehend them; that is (to use the familiar term), to *master* them, or to be superior to them"; whereas, on the other hand, "[the poetical] demands, as its primary condition [for its perception], that we should not put ourselves above the objects in which it resides, but at their feet; that we should feel them to be above and beyond us, that we should look up to them, and that, instead of fancying that we can comprehend them, we should take for granted that we are surrounded and comprehended by them ourselves. It implies that we understand them to be vast, immeasurable, impenetrable, inscrutable, mysterious."

I consider that what the saint proposes to be the qualities of the poetic contemplation of reality are also the qualities of the scientific contemplation of reality. Perhaps what the saint says of science is true of science when it is pursued for the sake of technology. But it is not true of speculative science, science for the sake of knowing God's beautiful universe; here, the conditions required for the scientific operation of the intellect are the same as those required for its poetical operation. In this way the scientific operation of the intellect can lead to contemplation just as the exercise of the liberal art of poetics can. And if the scientific operation of the intellect which enables the understanding of the conclusion that God is infinitely powerful and infinitely wise, and even the scientific operation of the intellect which arrives at this conclusion, can be exercised by a monk without "excitement," in Saint John Henry's sense, then the door is fully open to the possibility that the scientific operation of the intellect and its conclusions can be fully part of the monastic life just as the poetic operation of the intellect and the conclusion of its argument are. The monks, then, ultimately sought and taught contemplation in its fullness, together with all that leads to it and flows from it, that is, the contemplative life, including certainly the species of contemplation which is a poetic operation of the mind. In fact the saint has already authorized the identification of contemplation as the ultimate purpose of monastic life by quoting with approval at the end of §5 the two magnificent passages, one from Saint Basil the Great, the Father of Eastern monasticism, and one from Pope Saint Gregory the Great, one of the great Fathers of Western monasticism, which put forward that contemplation of God is the ultimate purpose of the monastic life.

Returning to §6, we find that, after Saint John Henry has completed his account of the formal object of the poetic operation of the intellect, he writes: "I have now said far more than enough to make it clear what I mean by that element in the old monastic life, to which I have given the name of the Poetical. Now, in many ways the family of St. Benedict answers to this description, as we shall see if we look into its history." From this point on, most of the essay is devoted to a sketch of monastic history in the West in gross, and then with respect to some of its most important elements, so as to demonstrate the existence in it of "the Poetical," that is, to demonstrate that the history as a whole, and each of these elements of it, is a beautiful action, perhaps only a process of one's thought, which quiets one's restless emotions by resting them in its beauty and which exemplifies a truth about life which one then considers.

To begin, in the remainder of §6, he sketches the development through history of the Order as a whole, and shows that the development, as it were, the life of the Order, is a beautiful action of the kind of which I speak; in §7, he selects a particular great abbey, the Abbey of Saint Hubert in the Ardennes, for more detailed consideration, and shows that its life through history is such a beautiful action, and comments at the end of his treatment: "Can we imagine a more graceful union of human with divine, of the sweet with the austere, of business and of calm, of splendour and of simplicity, than is displayed in a great religious house after this pattern, when unrelaxed in its observance, and pursuing the ends for which it was endowed?"

Then, in §8, he considers the element of monastic history consisting in the monks' manual labor to transform the vast wildernesses of Europe which existed at the beginning of the time of their ascendancy into gardens and great stretches of fruitful agricultural lands: another beautiful action. Further on, he chooses certain individual monks engaged in this manual labor of transforming the land for closer consideration, and begins: "How romantic then, as well as useful, how lively as well as serious, is their history, with its episodes of personal adventure and prowess, its pictures of squatter, hunter, farmer, civil engineer, and evangelist united in the same individual, with its supernatural colouring of heroic virtue and miracle!" So we hear of the lives of Saint Columban, of Saint Gall, of Saint Ronan, of the monks of Saint Dubritius, of Saint Sequanus, of Sturm, and of others—all beautiful lives, beautiful actions; then, especially, the beauty of the lives of Herluin, of Saint Bernard, of Easterwine.

Then, in §9, Saint John Henry tells of the works of mercy of the monks, to their neighbors and to those who came to their guest house—beautiful actions, all—and concludes with his marvelous passage on the beautiful poetry Virgil would have written on all this, had he seen and known it. Saint John Henry does all this in his own magnificent, and poetic, prose. The beauty of all these actions, these lives, these histories, depends on this, that the actions performed, the lives and histories lived all so humanly and richly, were performed and lived by men who, all the while they were engaged in earthly actions, were at the same time seeking to keep their minds and hearts fixed on God and the things of God through contemplative love. So much of the beauties which Saint John Henry describes was dependent on the inward and secret contemplative love of God, yet the presence of that contemplative love of God would have been manifested to the outside observer in the one great work of poetics and fine art which the monks brought forth and gave to the whole Church, the sacred liturgy. Saint John Henry does not deal with this (although note the allusion to "the poetry of ceremonies—of the cowl, the cloister, and the choir"[150]), but this would certainly be the supreme poetic beauty with which the monastic life is luminous. All that the saint describes, together with this great addition, contribute to the understanding of what I have been told, that in Croatian, the word for "monks" is a word which means "the beautiful ones."

Finally, in §§10 and 11, and as a transition to the second essay, Saint John Henry speaks of the literary labors of the Benedictines; in §12, the last section, he summarizes his views on the nature of Benedictine life. §10 speaks of the work of the monks of transcribing manuscripts, illuminating them, wrapping them or binding them in covers, in short, of making books, already a major work of ancient monks, and this gives him occasion to note some of the many contributions of the monks to the development of the fine arts. Then, at the beginning of §11, the saint writes as follows:

> While manual labour, applied to these artistic purposes, ministered to devotion, on the other hand, when applied to the transcription and multiplication of books, it was a method of instruction, and that peculiarly Benedictine, as being of a literary, not a scientific nature. Systematic theology had but a limited place in ecclesiastical study prior to the eleventh and twelfth centuries; Scripture and the Fathers were the received means of education, and these constituted the very text on which the pens of the monks were employed. And thus they would be becoming familiar with that kind of knowledge which was proper to their vocation, at the same time that they were engaged in what was unequivocally a manual labour; and, in providing for the religious necessities of posterity, they were directly serving their own edification. And this again had been the practice of the monks from the first, and is included in the *unity* of their profession. St. Chrysostom tells us that their ordinary occupation in his time was "to sing and pray, to read Scripture, and to transcribe the sacred text." As the works of the early Fathers gradually became the literary property of the Church, these, too, became the subject-matter of the reading and the writing of the monks. "For him who is going on to perfection," says St. Benedict in his *Rule*, "there are the lessons of the Holy Fathers, which lead to its very summit. For what page, what passage of the Old or New Testament, coming as it does with divine authority, is not the very exactest rule of life? What book of the Holy Catholic Fathers does not resound with this one theme, how we may take the shortest course to our Creator?"

In this passage we note that according to Saint John Henry the reading of the Scripture and the Fathers was "a method of instruction...of a literary, not a scientific nature." Then we are told that the result of this reading was that the monks became "familiar with that kind of knowledge which was proper to their vocation," that is, a literary knowledge. Further along we are told that "the works of the early Fathers [that is, all the Fathers, all of whom were early relative to the period of history here being considered] gradually became the literary property of the Church."

Note here a use of the expression "of...a scientific nature" that was not evident in the treatments by Saint John Henry in §§3 and 6 of the scientific operation of the intellect. Surely in the sense of "scientific" of those sections, a great number of passages of all the Fathers reflect the use of the scientific operation of the intellect, and in numbers of cases a use of it of a profundity not surpassed even at the present day. For example, the *De principiis* of Origen, and so many of his works; quite generally the works of Saint Augustine; the commentaries on Scripture of the Fathers; their works of controversy with heretics; and on and on. The forms of reasoning of demonstrative logic are used frequently, as are the forms of dialectical logic, e.g., in the controversies with heretics. If one wishes to say that the works of the Fathers are of a "literary" kind, because they almost always involve appeal to the emotions, either in the way of poetics or in the way of rhetoric, then that is one's choice. But not to note the scientific operation of the intellect evident everywhere in the Fathers is to miss an essential element of their thought and is to miss the scientific character of so much of the study and the teaching of the Benedictines in the time of their ascendancy.

Furthermore, the Scriptures themselves have numerous passages which have a dialectical or even demonstrative form: for dialectics, the debates of Saint Paul with Jews and with pagans; for demonstration, a great number of teachings which are derived from the certain premises consisting in the articles of faith. Also, reference is made by Saint Paul, the Book of Wisdom, and elsewhere to the fact that the existence of God can be known with certainty through the things he has made.[151] One of the things Saint John Henry has in mind when he uses the word "scientific" in this passage is systematic exposition of thought. Thus, "systematic theology had but a limited place in ecclesiastical study prior to the eleventh and twelfth centuries"; and again, later in §11: "The *Summae*

Sententiarum...were lessons or instructions arranged according to a scheme or system of doctrine." Certainly the works of the Fathers are rarely systematically written, although the thought of the Fathers is often highly systematic.

In any case, reading systematically expressed theology, or teaching it, does not seem necessarily to be an "excitement." But there is a further notion in the saint's mind, when he uses the expression "scientific" in this passage. In speaking of the labors of the monks which resulted in the catenae and in the *Summae Sententiarum*, he writes: "where there was nothing of original research, nothing of brilliant or imposing result, there would be nothing to dissipate, elate, or absorb the mind, or to violate the simplicity and tranquility proper to the monastic state." This recalls his use of the word "excitement" in the passage from §3. My commentary on that passage proposed that the use of the scientific operation of the intellect in living as a human being in the way the monks did is necessary, and appears not to be "exciting." And I agreed that in the monastic life the scientific operation of the intellect is not to be elaborated to the point of its becoming an "excitement," and so a distraction, from the ultimate purpose of "devotion" or "divine meditation," not to the point that it is no longer still compatible with, or rather, still promoting, the primary goal, that is, contemplation, and contemplation of God.

But now Saint John Henry seems to be saying that original research, or arriving at a brilliant and imposing result, certainly can, and often does, "dissipate, elate, or absorb the mind," and "violate the simplicity and tranquility proper to the monastic state." With respect to the saint, it is worth considering whether, on the part of a monk, original research, or arriving at a brilliant and imposing result, like reading systematic theology and expounding it, have the effects mentioned depends on the monk in question, on the degree of his intellectual ability and of his monastic virtue. For why should original research or arriving at such a result in and of themselves be excluded from the monastic life? Similarly with regard to monks writing history[152]: Saint John Henry writes of, in his opinion, "that laborious research and excitement of mind which is demanded of the writer who has to record a complex course of history, extending over may centuries and countries, and who aims at the discovery of truth, in the midst of deficient, redundant, or conflicting testimony." Must such excitement of mind be present in a monk writing this sort of history who has the requisite level of intellect and virtue? And as to why the monks at the time of the Benedictine ascendancy wrote such simple histories, as opposed to the kind of history the saint describes, it bears asking whether this is due more to the paucity of materials available to them than to any necessary incompatibility with their vocation.

Reading and teaching theology and philosophy, systematically expounded, and original research, or arriving at a brilliant and imposing result, and the laborious research of the historian, and the use of the scholastic method to learn, and even do research in, and teach theology and philosophy, are not necessarily "exciting" for the teacher or the learner. What is decisive for showing that these exercises are not necessarily "exciting," and can therefore be appropriate to the monastic state, is demonstrating that, in the case of those monks with the necessary intellectual abilities and monastic virtue, during these exercises the actions of meditation, prayer, and contemplation can be maintained, either by pausing during the exercises in order to elicit these actions, or, for the advanced, by in some way carrying on the actions in the course of the exercises. These actions can be maintained during these exercises by those monks.

Again, on this question of what sort of use of the intellect is appropriate for monastic life, the views, with the exception of one, which Saint John Henry reports as those of Mabillon are helpful. Saint John Henry writes:

> For instance, he [Mabillon] frankly concedes, or rather maintains, that the scholastic method of teaching theology and philosophy is foreign to the profession of a Benedictine, as such. "Why," he asks, "need we cultivate these sciences in the way of disputation? Why not as positive sciences, explaining questions and resolving doubts as they occur? Why is it not more than

enough for religious pupils to be instructed in the more necessary principles of the science, and thereby to make progress in the study of the Scriptures and the Fathers? What need of this perpetual syllogizing in form, and sharp answers to innumerable objections, as is the custom in the schools?" Elsewhere he contrasts the mode of teaching a subject, as adopted by the early Fathers, with that which the Schoolmen introduced. "The reasonings of the Fathers," he says, "are so full, so elegantly set forth, as to be everywhere redolent of the sweetness and vigour of Christian eloquence, whereas scholastic theology is absolutely dry and sterile." Elsewhere he says that "in the study of Holy Scripture consists the entire science of monks." Again, he says of Moral Theology, "As monks are rarely destined to the cure of souls, it does not seem necessary that they should give much time to the science of Morals." And though of course he does not forbid them the study of history, which we have seen to be so congenial to their calling, yet he observes of this study, when pursued to its full extent, "It seems to cause much dissipation of mind, which is prejudicial to that inward compunction of heart, which is so especially fitting to the holy life of a monk." Again, observing that the examination of ancient MSS. was the special occupation of the Maurists in his time, he says, "They who give themselves to this study have the more merit with God, in that they have so little praise with men. Moreover, it obliges them to devote the more time to solitude, which ought to be their chief delight. I confess it is a most irksome and unpleasant labour; however, it gives much less trouble than transcription, which was the most useful work of our early monks." Elsewhere, speaking of the celebrated Maurist editions of the Fathers, he observes, "Labour, such as this, which is undergone in silence and in quietness, is especially compatible with true tranquillity of mind and the mastery of the passions, provided we labour as a duty, and not for glory."

We note that according to the views of Mabillon, as represented here, theology and philosophy are *sciences*; that is, he would have meant, given the time in which he lived, bodies of knowledge which result from demonstration, the first principles of the demonstrations of theology being the articles of faith, and the first principles of the demonstrations of philosophy being self-evident to the human intellect, or evident from facts as the result of the operations of dialectical logic. And so the scientific operation of the intellect is indispensable for both sciences, although the expositions of theology of the Fathers also contain much of eloquence, that is, of results of the operations of the liberal arts of poetics and of rhetoric.

Thus, what "is foreign to the profession of a Benedictine, as such" is *the scholastic method of teaching* theology and philosophy, that is, by way of *disputation*. What, rather, is appropriate to the Benedictine vocation is the teaching of these sciences as "positive" sciences. The adjective "positive" as applied to these sciences can have various meanings, but I think the meaning Mabillon intends is clear: they are taught positively when they are taught without disputation, that is, "perpetual syllogizing in form, and sharp answers to innumerable objections," and are taught by "instruction in the more necessary principles of the science," "explaining questions and resolving doubts as they occur," as a result of which the students are enabled "to make progress"—on their own—"in the study of the Scriptures and the Fathers." This teaching, and the progress in understanding Scriptures and the Fathers, that is, in theology, and also the progress in understanding of philosophy, are, Mabillon holds, appropriate for the Benedictine life. Further, with regard to his statement that "in the study of Holy Scripture consists the entire science of monks," he likely intends that in the study, under the guidance of the Magisterium, of Scripture and Tradition consists the entire science of monks in the sense that Scripture and Tradition, when interpreted in the light of the Magisterium, are the two sources of theology.

As to his statement that "as monks are rarely destined to the cure of souls, it does not seem necessary that they should give much time to the science of Morals," he is likely thinking of the casuistic form of moral theology. Moral theology as found in, say, the works of Augustine, or in the Second Part of Saint Thomas's *Summa theologiae*, certainly needs to be given a good deal of time by monks.

The opinions of Mabillon which Saint John Henry presents actually support the view that Benedictine monks, in the learning and teaching of the Fathers, and of the Scriptures, and now, Mabillon adds, of philosophy, some of which was available to the medieval monks, most certainly use the scientific operation of the intellect, and do so frequently, and do so appropriately to their vocation, provided that they study and teach the Scriptures and theology and philosophy as positive sciences. Therefore, *pace* the saint, the method of instruction and of learning of the monks is incorrectly described as "being of a literary, not a scientific nature," the knowledge proper to their vocation is not only literary but also scientific, and the works of the Fathers are not best described as "literary." With regard to Mabillon's view, according to the saint, that the scholastic method of teaching theology and philosophy is foreign to the profession of a Benedictine, as such, I propose, again, that if a monk's intellectual attainments and level of virtue permit him to teach, to learn and even do research in, theology and philosophy by using the scholastic method, without "excitement" for himself or for his students, then surely there is no ground for saying that they are incompatible with the monastic vocation.

Saint John Henry concludes §11 thus:

> I think I may interpret Mabillon to mean that (be the range of studies lawful to a monk what it may) still, whatever literary work requires such continuous portions of time as not to admit of being suspended at a moment's notice, whatever is so interesting that other duties seem dull and heavy after it, whatever so exhausts the power of attention as to incapacitate for attention to other subjects, whatever makes the mind gravitate towards the creature, is inconsistent with monastic simplicity.

With this, all would of course agree. But he then proceeds to illustrate this principle as follows:

> Accordingly, I should expect to find that controversy was uncongenial to the Benedictine, because it excited the mind, and metaphysical investigations, because they fatigued it; and, when I met such instances as St. Paschasius or St. Anselm, I should deal with them as they came and as I could. Moreover, I should not look to a Benedictine for any elaborate and systematic work on the history of doctrine, or of heresy, or for any course of patristical theology, or any extended ecclesiastical history, or any philosophical disquisitions upon history, as implying a grasp of innumerable details, and the labour of using a mass of phenomena to the elucidation of a theory, or of bringing a range of multifarious reading to bear upon one point; and that, because such efforts of mind require either an energetic memory devoted to matters of time and place, or, instead of the tranquil and plodding study of one book after another, the presence of a large library, and the distraction of a vast number of books handled all at once, not for perusal, but for reference.

With this, I will only say that, with all respect to the saint, he goes too far, for the reasons I have presented above.

In §12, Saint John Henry provides a resume of the essay, in his poetic, beautiful, inimitable prose. Commending this section, then, to the reader's rereading of it, I proceed to the consideration of the second essay.

III. Saint John Henry's "The Benedictine Schools"

THE ESSAY begins with a reminder to the reader that—what is certainly true—an essential element of the monastic life is flight from the world. In reviewing the first essay, I proposed that the reader should take care not to suppose that Saint John Henry thought that "rest and peace" in and of itself was the final purpose of the monk, although a number of his statements could indeed seem to suggest that. Rather, the saint actually held that the purpose of "rest and peace" is not just escaping from all that was bad in the society of the time, but rather "devotion," or "divine meditation," or, "the vision of Eternity"—these are so many expressions of the monks' ultimate purpose.

Here at the beginning of the second essay Saint John Henry seems to suggest that another reason some or many of the monks had for their flight from the world was the belief that the end of the world was imminent. He notes a number of Church Fathers who in their writings seem to be expressing such a belief on their part. To my knowledge, this motive for flight from the world does not appear in the *Life of Saint Antony* by Saint Athanasius, the *Asketikon* of Saint Basil, the works of Evagrius of Pontus, the *Institutes* and *Conferences* of John Cassian, the works of Saint Augustine, the *Rule* of Saint Benedict and Saint Gregory's *Life* of him—that is, in the works mentioned of Saint Athanasius and of the principal monastic Fathers both of the Greek and the Latin Church. The teaching, then, that a reason for flight from the world is the imminent end of the world is not part of the foundations of monasticism, or of its essence, or, in Saint John Henry's expression, its "idea."

Saint John Henry next draws our attention to the fact that, already starting with Saint Gregory, monks are no longer entirely confined to their cloisters, but indeed are found to be missioners, to be teachers, even to hold political positions, etc., and holds that at least some of these positions, notably being a teacher and being an "apostle," that is, a missioner, not to mention holding political office, seem quite opposed to the monastic vocation. The problem with holding political office is clear. He ultimately suggests a way in which such works can be compatible with the vocation. But I would suggest that if we attend to the fact that the monks saw their origins in the first Church of Jerusalem, then there is surely no problem with monks being teachers, because "teachers," as we saw, were figures of the first Church which the New Testament mentions. New members of the Church would need much teaching, and also children of Christian parents would need to be taught—and in this case, probably by the mother. In Desert monasticism, new entrants to that way of life would have to be taught, and so we see that, for example, Cassian's *Conferences* are "memoirs" of long teachings of abbots which the young Cassian had heard. There is also the fact that Saint Benedict calls his entire institute a school—a "school of the Lord's service," in which the Abbot was teaching all the time; studies of newly received monks are also mentioned in the Rule.[153] And as to missioners—the Apostles themselves were such.

Continuing to our main concern: in §§3 and 4 Saint John Henry presents his learned and helpful exposition of the nature of the monastic schools, including the curriculum they taught. The Benedictines, through their teaching of the contemplative life, not only bequeathed to subsequent generations, as the saint demonstrates, "classical studies and tastes,"[154] and a theology which was "a loving study and exposition of Holy Scripture, according to the teaching of the Fathers,"[155] but also the understanding of the nature and order—both the order of learning and the order with respect to the hierarchy of being—of the arts and sciences, and also the understanding of that order as the schema of the ascent of the mind and heart to God.

In the monastery itself, Saint John Henry tells us,[156] was an infant school, a grammar school, and a seminary. In the infant school, no doubt, the little ones were taught their letters and the beginnings of reading and writing—here was the beginning of the liberal art of poetics. Then, as required by the Mass and the Divine Office, they had to be taught to sing—the beginning of the liberal art of music. And further, they surely were given the first instructions in numbers and in calculating—the beginning of the liberal art of arithmetic.

Then, as Saint John Henry tells us, at the age of seven, they come to the grammar school of the monastery (what corresponds more or less to our grammar school and the first year or two of high school), where, after learning the Psalter by heart, they undertake a full study of the first liberal art, grammar, that is, in my terminology, poetics, consisting in grammar in the strict sense and poetics in the strict sense of knowing how to understand and to produce works of imaginative literature. But also, although the saint does not mention this, in the monastery's grammar school they must have begun to learn, from the Latin authors they read, the second liberal art, rhetoric, which will be so important for them as both the homily and the sermon are forms of rhetoric. In all this the admirable goal is to learn to speak and to write Latin well, and to exercise in that language the liberal arts of poetics and rhetoric. In the learning of poetics, the beauties and the glories of Virgil, to which the saint has movingly referred, are seen, culminating, insofar as the ascent of the mind to God is concerned, in the visions in the Eclogues of the Boy who is about to be born, of the Woman, of the New Age. Then, in the study of Cicero, the study of rhetoric will already have begun. Moreover, the *pueri* will read some of the Latin historians, and this will further their knowledge of the liberal arts of both rhetoric and poetics, for history is both a narration, and hence an exercise of poetics, and a mode of narrating intended to persuade the reader to choose virtue in the personal, familial, economic, and political spheres, and hence an exercise of rhetoric. And, as the Saint says,[157] in the grammar school there would also have been religious instruction.

At the end of the monastery's grammar school, they will have gained in the Latin language what Saint John Henry calls "scholarship, that is, such an acquaintance with the literature of a language as is implied in the power of original composition and the *vivâ voce* use of it. Thus Cassiodorus defines it to be 'skill in speaking elegantly, gained from the best poets and orators'; St. Isidore, 'the science of speaking well'; and Raban, 'the science of interpreting poets and historians, and the rule of speaking and writing well.'"[158] The list which the saint provides of the Latin authors the monk scholars will have read is impressive, and he says that it all led "to possessing a thorough knowledge of the Latin tongue." Further on, it is true, he describes the classical attainment of the Benedictine classical scholar as "a fair or a sufficient acquaintance with Latin literature,"[159] but here he is comparing it to the standards of a classical don of mid-nineteenth-century Oxford. His conclusion may be taken as this: "whatever the monks had not, a familiar knowledge and a real love they had of the great Latin writers,"[160] and this and its not inconsiderable standards they passed on to the generations after the time of their ascendancy.

Then, as the saint explains, for the more gifted of those who are monks, there begins at the age of fourteen the study of at least some of the seven liberal arts, a deeper study of those already begun, and/or a study of equal depth of those not yet begun, perhaps also the study of some other subjects, in a period corresponding to the last two or three years of our high school and indeed in certain subjects to at least a portion of our undergraduate education. These studies require going to other monasteries where specialists in one or another of these liberal arts are to be found.

It is important to note carefully the saint's paragraphs on this higher education.[161] In the paragraph beginning, "This curriculum, derived from the earlier ages of heathen philosophy," he tells us that the study of the seven liberal arts of grammar, rhetoric, and logic, and of arithmetic, music, geometry and astronomy, became standard for those preparing to study theology, on the authority of Saint Augustine, in his *de Ordine*. This is certainly true, and because of the greatness of that authority of Saint Augustine during all the centuries of Benedictine ascendancy, and after that up to our own time, it will be helpful to examine in some detail what he says in *de Ordine* about the matters with which we are concerned.[162]

In this dialogue, Saint Augustine lays down as one fundamental principle this: "Reason desires to transport itself to that most blessed contemplation of divine things."[163] This is the principle of the natural desire for God in every human being. In the very first lines of the dialogue,[164] he lays down a second fundamental principle: "In order to see [that is, not only to believe, but to understand, insofar as this is possible] divine things one must have both merit of life and erudition [that is, both the moral virtues and learning]." In these two principles we already find the two fundamental principles of all Catholic education. In this dialogue, his concern is with what learning or erudition is needed; of course, there are great treatments throughout many of his works of what constitutes merit of life.

In what, then, does this erudition consist? First, he states why this erudition is necessary: "But lest reason fall off those heights [viz., of "that most blessed contemplation of divine things"], it sought to go upwards by steps, and contrived for itself out of its own possessions an orderly way for ascending by steps."[165] Erudition, then, consists in the possession of this orderly way upwards.

What is this way? His method for dealing with this question is "to talk about an *Order of Study*, by which one can advance from corporeal things to the incorporeal,"[166] and thus he addresses the question both of the order of study or learning of the disciplines which constitute the way and also their order with respect to the hierarchy of being. As to the order of study, he in fact speaks of the order in which the human reason developed these disciplines, but that sequence is also the best order for their study.

First, then, he holds,[167] comes *grammatica*, the art of speaking and writing well, because all human life requires society, and the existence of society requires communication of thoughts, and the means for doing that is language, both oral and written. He notes that grammar's first stage is simple literacy, after which grammar in the strict sense began to be developed. Then he points out that, as its name suggests, grammar is especially concerned with writing, and so "whatever is worth committing to memory in writing is also part and parcel of grammar." He only mentions history as an example of what became a part of grammar, but of course all of what we would call imaginative literature became part of it too.

He puts forward that also at this first stage of the development of the liberal arts not only is grammar being developed, but also what he calls *numeri*. I believe that in Saint Augustine's time the word *numeri* could mean what we call mathematics, but as used by the saint it clearly signifies what at some point in the Latin tradition of the liberal arts will always be signified by *arithmetica*, simply a borrowing of course of the Greek word. He gives a profound reason as to why this first of the mathematical arts was developed: reason could not begin to understand anything "if things, as limitless as they appear, had not been given some kind of fixed limit, and so the need for numbering was seen as paramount."[168] And so he holds that at least the beginning of the art of arithmetic was at this stage.

Then, after this first stage in the development of the arts, reason "sought to take care of itself" and so "to distinguish, bring out and order the tools of its own trade," and so it brought forth "the discipline of disciplines," *dialectica*. But because only few have the capacity to attain "what is right, useful, and good" in human affairs by being presented with purely intellectual arguments, reason then developed the art of *rhetorica*, by which it presents intellectual arguments as to what should be done, but also draws its hearers to assent to what should be done by arousing their emotions. He calls rhetoric a "part" of reason, and says that in this part of itself reason is raised to its highest level. Obviously, then, he holds that rhetoric follows dialectic.[169]

Then, according to Saint Augustine,[170] reason wanted to take off immediately from this point to "the most blessed contemplation of divine things. It desired to see that beauty, which it alone and in a state of utmost simplicity, would be able to see, and see without bodily eyes; but the senses stood in the way." Reason determined that hearing and seeing were the senses which most distracted it and most forcibly blocked, by the sensory images they produced, its vision of that divine beauty. Therefore it began to study these two senses especially, and sought to determine how, instead of being seen as producing images which blocked the higher vision, they could be seen as producing images from which the reason could ascend to higher vision. Reason first turned its attention to hearing, and to its object, sound. It distinguished sound into three kinds: that of the human voice singing, as in the case of "tragedians, comedians, choirs, and all those who in one way or another sing"; that of wind instruments, and that of percussion instruments. It saw that "all of this was worth very little without regular timing and a variety of high and low pitch sounds." Here again number was appearing. From reason's tracking down all the numerical relations present in singing, "reason gave birth to poets." Then reason began to realize that "number was supreme and all-encompassing" and was indeed "divine and eternal". And so reason "grievously tolerated that the splendor and purity of number should be somewhat clouded by the material sound of voices."

At which point, he seems to say, reason turned its attention to the sounds from instruments, sounds free of the human voice. Without going into detail as to how reason found number in instrumental sounds, he simply says, concluding, that the discipline found by considering singing and instrumental sounds, "which participates in both sense and intellect," was called *musica*. It should be noted that thus poetry is considered by Saint Augustine to be a part of music, not a separate art. He does not use the word *poetica*, which would be the name of an art, but simply speaks of "poets."

Then, after considering hearing, the reason turned to vision.[171] "[I]t found that nothing but beauty pleased it, and in beauty it found figures, in figures dimensions, in dimensions, numbers. It asked itself whether there could be in this world such a line, or rotundity, or other form or figure as that which the intellect could comprehend. It found all that the eyes could see far inferior to what the mind could see. It distinguished the various forms and figures the mind could see and arranged them all in a discipline, and called that discipline *geometria*." Similarly, reason was drawn to the motion of the heavens, "and there too it understood that nothing other than dimensions and numbers dominated. And so by defining and sorting out all these reason gave birth to *astrologia*, a great argument for those who are religious but a torment for those who are merely curious."[172]

Saint Augustine recognized that these last four arts all dealt with what he called "number," as the first three all dealt with language. And in his seeing their chief function as helping us to raise our intellect to the consideration of incorporeal forms, the Platonic influence on his thought is clear. At this point, however, he warns us of a deadly pitfall which some thinkers did not avoid. He says that seeing the power of number, the reason of these thinkers became proud and presumptuous; their reason came to believe that it itself was the numerical principle by which all reality was ordered, or at least to believe that knowing this numerical principle was the ultimate aim of the intellectual journey. But, he says, false images of the things which we number, which things flow from "that most hidden *principle by which we number*," drew the minds of these thinkers to themselves [that is, to the false images] and often these thinkers lost the knowledge they had.[173] He may be speaking here of thinkers who embraced that form of Pythagoreanism or Neo-Pythagoreanism which did indeed teach that number was "the principle binding the world together, both cosmologically and ethically."[174] In teaching this, Saint Augustine is saying, they failed to consider the principle *by which we number*, that is, the Truth by which we know any truth at all, the Truth which is God.

After warning against this error, Saint Augustine is ready to tell us that with these seven arts in hand, reason is now ready to seek "the divine things." He writes, "If someone brings together all those things that are taught by these [seven] disciplines into one, simple, true, and certain whole," that is, into the whole which consists in the orderly way for ascending by steps toward the divine things which is provided by these disciplines in their proper order, the whole which he calls "erudition," then "that person can without rashness seek divine things." And here, following the paragraph of Saint John Henry we are considering, we would think Saint Augustine means "that person can without rashness undertake the study of theology." But that is not what he means. What he actually says is, "that person can without rashness seek divine things, *now not only as to be believed, but also as to be contemplated, understood, and retained*."[175]

Here the distinction between divine things as to be believed and divine things as to be contemplated, understood, and retained is the distinction between divine things as presented by theology and divine things as presented by philosophy; or, the distinction between divine things as presented by a kind of positive theology simply as articles of faith and divine things as presented by theology making use of philosophy in order to make these divine things, insofar as it is possible for us in this life, understandable, and therefore more retainable, and more luminous objects of contemplation. Thus, a discipline now appears on the scene after the liberal arts and just before theology: philosophy. Saint John Henry, in the paragraph we are considering, mentions "philosophy," and says that in the Alexandrian tradition "philosophy" was considered to consist in logic plus the four mathematical arts. That is certainly not what Saint Augustine understands "philosophy" to be. In the section from which we have just quoted (II.44), he clearly says that philosophy, and also theology, come *after* one has learned the liberal arts. What, then, is the discipline which Saint Augustine calls philosophy?

In II.16, he writes:

> Twofold is the way we follow when the obscurity [of divine things] holds us back, the way of reason and the way of certain authority. Philosophy puts forward reason, but liberates very few, causing them not only not to contemn divine mysteries, but to understand them insofar as they can be understood. True and genuine philosophy has no other business than to teach that there is a principle without a principle of all things, that there is great intellect in it, and to teach what emanates from it for our great benefit without any decrease in it. Which principle the venerable mysteries teach to be the one God omnipotent and tripotent, Father and Son and Holy Spirit, and these mysteries, by a sincere and unshaken faith [on the part of the ones who believe these mysteries], liberate whole peoples, neither by confusing them, as some say, nor by doing violence to them, as some others maintain. And how great also is this, that God for our sake deigned to assume this human body of ours, and the more demeaning it seems, the more merciful it is, and the more remote from the pride of those with clever minds.

In this passage, Saint Augustine first distinguishes philosophy and theology by distinguishing the two lights by which they proceed. Philosophy proceeds by the light of reason alone. Theology proceeds by the light of faith. Philosophy knows its first principles by the light of natural reason alone, and proceeds to know other matters by reasoning from those principles by that same light. Theology knows its first principles, that is, the articles of faith, by the light of faith, by which it grasps the revelation of God, and it proceeds to know other matters following from those articles by the same light of faith. Theology, then, is superior to philosophy, which is itself superior to all other sciences known by the natural reason, and so theology is the queen of the sciences. Theology can, however, make use of philosophy, not because it is dependent on philosophy, but in order to make more manifest to our intellects what is contained in theology; our intellects, by what they know through philosophy, are led by the hand to know more manifestly what is contained in theology.[176]

Second, Saint Augustine distinguishes philosophy and theology by this, that although philosophy knows some divine things by the light of natural reason, there are many divine things theology knows by the light of faith which philosophy does not know and cannot know by the light of natural reason alone. Philosophy can know that there is a first principle of all things, itself without any principle, that in it is great intellect, that from it comes many benefits for the human race. Theology knows all this, but knows as well the mystery that the inner life of God is triune—that there is one God, the Father, the Son, and the Holy Spirit. Again, theology knows the mystery of the Incarnation. Connected with the mystery of the Trinity and the mystery of the Incarnation there are a great many other mysteries which theology knows and philosophy cannot know.

What, then, is the subject matter of philosophy? At several points in *de Ordine* Saint Augustine says it is God and the human soul.[177] One's first reaction to this might be to ask how it is that the other topics philosophy considers are all related to these two topics, although it is granted that the first is beyond any measure pre-eminent and the second is at least quite important. Passages in *The City of God* help one to understand Saint Augustine's thought.[178] Speaking of "the city which is above," the city of God, he says, "It is; it sees; it loves."[179] Although he does not do so explicitly, one sees that this last statement can be applied to the human soul. He then suggests that three questions arise from these three operations—existing, knowing, loving—of the soul: What is the cause of existence? What is it by which the intellect understands truth? What is the end to which all love tends? Then he says that Plato, whom he considers to be the greatest of the philosophers, is said to have been the first to discover and promulgate a threefold division of philosophy corresponding to these three questions: the first part, seeking the cause of the existence of all things, is the physical; the second part, seeking that by which the intellect understands truth, is the logical; the third part, seeking the end to which all love tends, is the ethical. He says that the three Latin equivalents of these denominations—natural, rational, and moral—have by his time been naturalized into Latin, and so in Latin one can say that philosophy is divided into natural philosophy, rational philosophy, and moral philosophy. And he says that Plato, and those who most closely followed him, "do perhaps entertain such an idea of God as to admit that in Him are to be found the cause of existence, the One in whom all truth becomes certain to us, and the end in reference to which the whole life is to be regulated."[180]

One is hesitant to make any comment on such profound thought. But perhaps it would be helpful at least to point out that what Saint Augustine calls logical or rational philosophy is, or at least has as its central and largest component, the liberal art of logic. And again, that what he calls natural philosophy has as its highest part metaphysics or divine science, the science which seeks to understand God, insofar as that is possible by the light of natural reason. And finally, that therefore another threefold division of philosophy that one finds in the tradition is that of natural philosophy, moral philosophy, and metaphysics, with what Saint Augustine calls rational philosophy being considered as not part of philosophy but its immediate propaedeutic.

Saint John Henry tells us that Saint Augustine's teaching in *de Ordine* with respect to the liberal arts, and with respect to their being "the fitting and sufficient preparation for theological learning" "was transferred to the use of the Church on the authority of St. Augustine."[181] I think we should be happy, with one proviso, to accept this on the authority of Saint John Henry, whose many natural attainments certainly included scholarship as to Church history. The proviso is this. I think it is clear that the theological learning Saint Augustine has in mind is what is expressed in the passage from *de Ordine* I quoted above: knowledge of "divine things, *now not only as to be believed, but also as to be contemplated, understood, and retained.*" And it is clear that in his view this theological learning consists in possessing a theology which makes use of philosophy to make more manifest the teachings of the faith it presents. Therefore, the attaining of the capacity to understand and indeed to produce philosophical reasonings which are part of a theological work and are used to make more manifest its teachings must also be part of the preparation for acquiring theological learning as Saint Augustine conceives it. And it also true that he holds that the liberal arts are a fitting and sufficient way of attaining this capacity, as well as the capacity to understand and to produce the other parts of theology.

I think in what follows I can add a few additional points, a number of which also come from Saint John Henry, about how, actually, the curriculum of the liberal arts was transferred to the use of the Church on the authority of Saint Augustine.

The next figure of importance for this is Boethius (480–524), one of Theodoric's ministers, who strongly confirms Saint Augustine's teaching about the mathematical arts. True, Martianus Capella, a pagan writer, produced in the early fifth century an allegorical work putting forward as the liberal arts the same ones which Saint Augustine puts forward, and true, his work was widely read in the Middle Ages. However, one often sees the claim that Martianus's work is the first to put forward this view. This cannot be true, because Saint Augustine was writing *de Ordine* in 386. Furthermore, the quality of Martianus's treatment cannot even be compared with that of Saint Augustine. Boethius, however, makes the great contribution of pointing out that all four mathematical arts are about *abstract quantity*. He also confirms Saint Augustine's ordering of the four arts as arithmetic, music, geometry, and astronomy. Of course, as we saw, in Saint Augustine's treatment of these arts, logic and rhetoric come between arithmetic and music.

In speaking, however, of the first stage of the development of the arts, when grammar and arithmetic begin to be developed, Saint Augustine says that at first only the "infancy of grammar" was attained, and I think it very probable he thought the same about arithmetic. Further, he speaks explicitly of reason developing music, geometry, and astronomy, and doing so after it had developed logic. Therefore, I think Saint Augustine would have agreed that in their mature forms, the mathematical arts should be ordered as arithmetic, music, geometry, and astronomy, and placed after the language arts. This ordering was to hold for the Middle Ages and indeed up to the Renaissance. Then, returning to Boethius, his *de Arithmetica* was a remarkable work for its time, and very influential in the Middle Ages. And it was he who coined the term "quadrivium" for these four arts.

As for the language arts, for the Middle Ages "the text that defined the relationship between the two sciences of constructing arguments"—that is, rhetoric and dialectic—"was Boethius's *De topicis differenciis*. In this very influential work…the matter of rhetoric is the hypothesis [or specific question], which is tied to circumstances [concrete circumstances of place, time, etc.,], while that of dialectic is the thesis or general question, which is not…." "[Moreover,] the rhetorician uses incomplete syllogisms (enthymemes), while the dialectician uses complete syllogisms."[182] Therefore, dialectic is more certain, more general, more abstract, and less tied to matter than rhetoric, and so in Boethius's view—which is the view of a philosopher—dialectic is the higher art. Therefore, the order of the three language arts in Boethius's view is grammar, rhetoric, and dialectic—their order according to the philosophical tradition of antiquity. Whereas Saint Augustine's order of these arts is according to the rhetorical tradition of antiquity. It was in fact Boethius's understanding of the order of the language arts which was to prevail in the Middle Ages. As for the term "trivium" for these arts, this term was not to come into use until several centuries later. It began to be used by Alcuin and his circle of scholars in the palace school of Charlemagne.[183]

The next figure of importance with respect to how the curriculum of the liberal arts was actually transferred to the use of the Church on the authority of Saint Augustine is Cassiodorus (c. 484–c. 584). He, like Boethius, was aware that the West was heading to a complete loss of the Greek language and with that a great loss of the treasures of Greek intellectual culture. Boethius had indeed set himself the enormous task of translating into Latin all of the works of Plato and Aristotle, but his falling out of the favor of Theodoric put an end to his efforts almost before he had started. Nevertheless, we have just seen how important the work was which he did accomplish. Cassiodorus, who was also a minister under Theodoric, after a secular career set up a monastery called Vivarium intended to be a center of Christian scholarship and of which he was the superior. There he wrote his *Institutiones* for the instruction of his monks; it was to become a major instruction of Latin monks through the period of Benedictine ascendancy. The *Institutiones* consisted in two books, the first concerned with the *litterae divinae,* and dealing with ways of studying and understanding the Scriptures. The second book was concerned with the *litterae humanae,* and dealt with the seven liberal arts, ordered in the same way as Boethius had done.[184]

Then there was Saint Isidore, Bishop of Seville (570–636), "who was the author most read in the early Middle Ages."[185] The first three books of his *Etymologiae* treat of the seven liberal arts, ordered again as grammar, rhetoric, dialectics or logic (Isidore makes this equivalence), arithmetic, music, geometry, astronomy.

Every monastery in the Latin West would have had in its library the works of Saint Augustine, the *Institutiones* of Cassiodorus,[186] and the works of Saint Isidore, and many would have had the works of Boethius. This throws great light on how the teaching of *de Ordine,* with Saint Augustine's authority accompanying it, was in fact "transferred to the use of the Church," as Saint John Henry says. But now we return to Saint John Henry himself for guidance, and note the first two paragraphs of §3. Here is a very illuminating and fascinating account of the next stages of the transference, from the appointment of Theodore as Archbishop of Canterbury to Alcuin and the schools of Charlemagne and then on through Cluny and her dependencies up to Abbo of Fleury

(c. 945–1004). And not long after him are to come Lanfranc and Saint Anselm.

Then, returning to §4, let us observe what Saint John Henry tells us as to the subjects, other than the liberal arts, which monks could study at this or that school intended for those who had completed their own monastery's grammar school. The subjects the saint mentions are the following: Greek, Hebrew, and Arabic; physics; philosophy; *leges et canones*; medicine; painting, engraving, carpentry, stone work. Were these subjects related to the liberal arts, and if so, how? Of course, Greek, Hebrew and Arabic—and any language—could be the matter of the three language arts. As for Gerbert's physics, it appears to me that his studies were in astronomy rather than in natural philosophy or natural science. *Leges et canones* were taught in connection with rhetoric, under its division of "judicial."[187] Medicine during the period in question primarily followed the theory of the balancing of the four humors, which is an application of an arithmetical concept, and in addition celestial bodies were thought to have effects on health, and music was thought to have beneficial effects on health, and so astronomy and music were related to medicine as well. Painting, engraving, carpentry, and stone work are fine arts, and the ones mentioned are not directly connected with the liberal arts.

As to philosophy, Saint John Henry points out that "St. Abbo of Fleury (A.D. 990), after mastering, in the monastery of that place, grammar, arithmetic, logic, and music, went to Paris and Rheims for philosophy and astronomy." Now "philosophy" appears as a higher subject. And the term "philosophy" here evidently is not synonymous with the quadrivium, as, according to Saint John Henry, it sometimes was, because in the case of St. Abbo, before coming to Paris and Reims he had already studied arithmetic and music, at Paris and Rheims he studied "philosophy" and astronomy, so "philosophy" cannot include arithmetic, music, and astronomy, and after his time at Paris and Reims he "taught himself rhetoric and geometry," and so "philosophy" does not include geometry, either. What was this "philosophy"? By the time of Saint Abbo, Boethius's *The Consolation of Philosophy*, which had been little read up to the time of

Charlemagne,[188] began to be widely read, and as a result the notion that philosophy is an independent discipline which can be studied in and of itself must have been spreading. And so the philosophy in question could have been a subject studied in this way. Of course, it is clear that what Saint Augustine calls philosophy is a subject of this kind. But, with regard to the period prior to Charlemagne, it appears unlikely that philosophy was known or studied in any way other than by reading and studying philosophical passages in the Fathers.

What we find here is that the curriculum of the medieval universities was already beginning to take shape through all these monastic studies and the order which was understood to exist among them. First came the liberal arts, as the way to higher knowledge. Then, from one of the language arts, comes law, and from several mathematical arts comes medicine. Then, from the liberal arts comes philosophy, first as known by way of studying the Fathers, but then beginning to be developed in and of itself, with that eventually leading to Saint Anselm. And as a discipline in and of itself, the division of Saint Augustine was known, of natural philosophy, rational philosophy, and moral philosophy. And then theology, the queen of the sciences. Here we have the curriculum of the medieval university. Cassiodorus, as we have seen, in his *Institutiones* divides his work into two books, the first concerned with the *litterae divinae*, the second book with the *litterae humanae*. In the University of Oxford throughout the twentieth century almost to the end of that century there were four faculties: the faculty of Literae Humaniores, comprising the liberal arts and philosophy, the latter having generated a great number of disciplines which today we would see under the headings of natural science and moral science; the faculty of law; the faculty of medicine; and the faculty of theology. Thus indeed, as Saint John Henry says, the schools of Charlemagne "may be considered the shadow, and even the nucleus of the Universities which arose in a subsequent age."[189] Again, "Nor is it too much to say that the Colleges in the English Universities may be considered in matter of fact to be the lineal descendants or heirs of the Benedictine schools of Charlemagne,"[190] although in this second quotation, but not in the first, the saint is referring in particular to these colleges' teaching of the Latin classics.

Saint John Henry continues: "These manual arts [certain *fine* arts], far more than the severer sciences [that is, everything beyond poetics], were the true complement of the Benedictine ideal of education, which, intellectually considered, was, after all, little more than a fair or a sufficient acquaintance with Latin literature." As the reader now knows well, my opinion differs from that of the saint on this matter which is so important both for the nature of the Benedictine life and for what Benedictines taught. In fact, the saint refutes himself. He goes on to say, "the school-task of the boy [monk]"—that is, poetics, i.e., Latin literature—"became the life-long *recreation* [emphasis added] of the man."[191] Again: "As far as they allowed themselves in any recreation, which was not of a sacred nature, they found it in these beautiful authors, who might be considered as the prophets of the human race in its natural condition."[192] Again: "I have distinctly said that, after their school years, the monks were as little taken up with the classics, *exceptis excipiendis,* as member of parliament or country gentlemen at the present day. They had their serious engagements, as statesmen have now, though of a different kind, and to these they gave themselves. Theology was their one study; to theology secular literature ministered, first as an aid and an ornament, then as a relaxation, amid the mental exertion which it involved."[193]

Saint John Henry has said all this far better than I can. And I must add at this point that, precisely because of what the saint says in the last sentence of his just quoted, it is very odd that he should have said earlier on that if one were asked whom the Benedictine would teach, one's answer would be: children. Children, adolescents, yes, in that that is when the teaching of languages and their literatures rightly begins. But surely, if theology was the one study of Benedictine men, to which secular literature ministered, then must it not have been the case that in every monastery the Benedictine men more advanced in theological study would be teaching other Benedictine men this discipline? And indeed, as we saw, the saint says that each monastery had not only an infant school and a grammar school, but also, as he calls it, a seminary. For the reasons I have already put forward in this essay, I see no restriction as to the ages of the students for whom Benedictines would be excellent teachers.

In §5 of the essay, Saint John Henry proposes that, although theology was indeed the monks' great study, their study of it, and their writings of it, involved no "creative action of the intellect." I would dispute this claim with regard to the catenae and glosses produced by the monks, and especially with regard to the *Summae Sententiarum*—see the accounts of these by the saint in §11 of the first essay. As Saint John Henry himself says, "The *Summae Sententiarum*...opened the way to the intellectual exercises of the scholastic period."[194] And indeed, the Sentences of Peter Lombard (he was not a monk, but he was a canon, and his work was of the kind being considered) was the great theological textbook for several centuries, and every university theologian had to comment on them. But, whether or not there was a "creative action of the intellect" involved in writing these works, what I have urged before is that if there was no such action, this was not because such an action is contrary to the Benedictine vocation.

In §6, the essay illustrates the way in which, from the latter part of the eighth century onwards, in order to meet attacks against the faith, a method of theology began to be needed which could defend the faith in the midst of fierce controversy, and a true and complete philosophy as a discipline in and of itself began to be needed which could serve as a correct and powerful instrument for manifesting the truths of theology. Saint John Henry will say that both the method and the philosophy needed will be those of scholasticism, but that the Benedictines initiated both developments. Thus his conclusion (§7), ends with these words:

> And thus the period, properly Benedictine, ended; this honour being shown by Providence to the great Order from which it is named, in reward for its long and patient services to religion, that, though its monks were not to be immediately employed by the Church in the special sense in which they had been her

> ministers for some hundreds of years, still they should be the first to point out, and that they should hansel, those new weapons, which Orders of a different genius were destined to wield against a new description of opponents.[195]

The "Orders of a different genius" are of course the Dominicans and other others like them, the Dominicans being the "emblem" of all of them.

With this view of the saint, I think we can most certainly agree. But what I want to note for our purposes is that, as he says, the Benedictines first saw the need for the method and the philosophy, and developed the first beginnings of each. Of course, I differ from the saint in this; in my view the Benedictines did not fully develop this method and this philosophy because for its development the gathering of a large number of researchers, teachers and students—that is, the university—was necessary, which gathering could occur only in towns and cities. These towns and cities were beginning to arise in the eleventh and twelfth centuries, and so the great new movement began. There is a reason, then, arising from the nature of the monastic life, that the Benedictines did not *develop* the method and the philosophy: namely, that an essential element of the monastic life is some degree of physical separation from the world, either by the monastery being located outside a city or town, or if in one, observing a set of strict rules about a monk's leaving the monastery's enclosure. But the reason is not that the development of the method and the philosophy, or their use, are necessarily "excitements" of the intellect, in Saint John Henry's sense.

It bears emphasizing that, as Saint John Henry's own treatment shows, the Benedictines in the time of their ascendancy not only saw the necessity of and developed the beginnings of the method and philosophy in question, but also made the following contributions to the education of future generations: the confirmation of the liberal arts as the way to higher knowledge, and a competence in them good for its time; quite a thorough knowledge of Latin and of its literature; a wide-ranging and thorough knowledge of the Scriptures and of the Latin Fathers; and finally, the basic understanding of the nature and the order of the arts and sciences, and so of the whole structure of the curriculum of the universities which were to arise, and the understanding that the arts and sciences, in their proper order, are the path for the ascent of the mind and heart to God.

IV. Conclusion

IN VIEW of the preceding, I now consider Saint John Henry's fundamental thesis, that what the Benedictines in the time of their ascendancy taught was Poetry, what the Dominicans in the time of their ascendancy taught was Science, and what the Jesuits in the time of their ascendancy taught was Prudence.

My contention is that Saint John Henry's thesis requires adjustment.

By way of summary: As Saint John Henry says, the monks exercised the poetic operation of the intellect in their reading and their teaching, and also in their work, so that their work and indeed their life had the "poetical" character. I have proposed that it is most accurate to say that the monastic life was ultimately ordered toward, not "devotion," or "divine meditation," or "the vision of Eternity," but the loving contemplation of God, first through his effects, but then in himself, insofar as this is possible in this life.

I have also held that the monks clearly exercised the scientific operation of the intellect, not only in their ordinary life, but especially in their reading and teaching of the Scriptures, of the Fathers, and of philosophy. Moreover, I have held that "the bare ordinary use of reason," which involves to some extent the scientific operation of the intellect, is certainly not usually "exciting," in the saint's use of that term, and that reading and teaching theology, and philosophy, systematically expounded, and original research, or arriving at a brilliant and imposing result, and the laborious research of the historian, and the use of the scholastic method to learn, and even do research in, and teach theology and philosophy, are not necessarily "exciting" for the teacher or the learner, either.

I have also said that what is decisive for showing that these exercises are not necessarily "exciting," and can therefore be appropriate to the monastic state, is that, in the case of those monks with the necessary intellectual abilities and monastic virtue, during these exercises the actions of meditation, prayer, and contemplation can be maintained, either by pausing during the exercises in order to elicit these actions, or, for the advanced, by in some way carrying on the actions in the course of the exercises. I have held that these actions can be maintained during these exercises by those monks and that the truth reached as the conclusion of a demonstration, which was itself perhaps preceded by dialectics, may indeed itself be an object of contemplation, and of divine contemplation, for every truth ultimately comes from God, who is himself Truth, and who created all finite beings according to the Truth which he is.

I have also maintained that the Benedictines bequeathed to those beyond the time of the Benedictine ascendancy an excellent knowledge of the Latin classics, an excellent knowledge of Holy Scriptures and the teaching of the Fathers, and the understanding of the nature and the order of all the arts and sciences, and therefore the entire schema of the education the universities were to offer, and also the vision of the pursuing of these arts and sciences as the ascent of the mind and heart to God.

I have also submitted that the Dominicans, although building on the method of the *Summae Sententiarum* which the Benedictines initiated, developed and taught the highly effective method of learning, "researching in," and teaching philosophy and theology which is called the scholastic method, involving disputation, demonstration, and systematic exposition. (And here I am speaking of the Dominicans, as well as of the Benedictines, as Saint John Henry suggests, as the "emblems" of the many others as well who were involved in what each of these orders taught.)

As to the Jesuits, Saint John Henry does not develop his thoughts at any length, and therefore it is difficult to know precisely what he has in mind. But I suspect his thought is along the following lines.

Saint Ignatius established that it was the purpose of the Society of Jesus to serve only God and the Roman pontiff in whatever the present or other Roman pontiffs order that concerns the saving of souls and the spread of the faith. In view of this one purpose, the members of the Society needed to be as free as possible of any other purposes or obligations, so that they would always be ready, at a moment's notice, to undertake what the Roman pontiff asked of them. This meant, as Saint John Henry notes, that they must be free of the obligations "of the cowl, the cloister, and the choir," that is, of any elaborated ceremony in the celebration of the liturgy of the church, of any kind of stability in community (except, as it is today, stability in their province), and of celebration in choir of the Liturgy of the Hours and of the Mass. It also meant that, in effect, they must be free of any sort of rule, other than the most general. Therefore, a very high degree of the virtue of prudence is needed on the part of each member of the Society so that, in the absence of the assistance of all these sorts of structure, he may still conduct himself in perfect and total obedience to his superiors, to the Roman Pontiff, and to God. And it can be said that the Spiritual Exercises of Saint Ignatius are precisely a method of coming to a prudent decision under God as to an action to be taken or course of action to be taken. Certainly the Spiritual Exercises, if not the first of their genus of spiritual teaching, are one of the most celebrated. Further, in such a very active life as all of this will result in for a member of the Society, and since some degree of contemplation is needed in every Christian life, he will need to have the prudence to see how to be, as one of Saint Ignatius's first companions, Jerónimo Nadal, put it, *simul in actione contemplativus*—"a contemplative in the midst of action".

I suggest that it is this line of thought that leads Saint John Henry to say that what the Society of Jesus has taught in the time of its ascendancy is Prudence. And here again, as in the case of the development of the scholastic method, there was a need for a further development in the teaching of the Church, and a need which, because of their vocations, the Benedictines and Dominicans were not most suited to fulfill. This time the need was for teaching as to how to make a prudent decision under God in the midst of the intensely active life which was developing in the Church and in European society—and the direction of intellect involved in such a life is what Saint John Henry means by "that peculiar movement of mind [which] commenced [at] the Reformation, [and] the issue of which is still to come." The Benedictines and Dominicans were less free to bring about the needed development of teaching because of the obligations to the choir, to their rule, and so forth, which were essential to their vocation. But at the same time, their vocations did not prevent them from adopting the development and teaching it as well.

As Saint John Henry points out, the Church maintains alive every development of teaching she has received over the centuries, and therefore so do her religious institutes. Today, then, Benedictines, Dominicans, and Jesuits teach the same curriculum, the structure of which, as I have put forward, was developed by the Benedictines. It may be the case that to some extent each of these institutes gives a certain emphasis to that part of Catholic teaching which it especially developed: the Benedictines to the ascent of the mind and heart to God; the Dominicans to a scientific precision, certitude, and clarity in philosophy and theology, which results in an unsurpassed excellence in those disciplines; and the Jesuits, to prudence in an active life.

Yet it is not the case that each form of education is suited only to those whose disposition corresponds to the emphasis in that form of education. It can be that the student of an intensely active disposition is best educated precisely by a contemplative education before he enters the life he is disposed to, that the one of contemplative disposition is best educated by an education for action before turning to contemplative education and life, and that scientific philosophy and theology are best as the first education for either one. All this is a matter for discernment with respect to the unique human being in question.

Therefore, I suggest the following amended form of Saint John Henry's thesis:

The Benedictines, in the time of their ascendancy, taught the consecrated contemplative life, and as to teaching in the strict sense, the understanding of the nature and order of the arts and sciences, the development of some of them quite fully, of the rest at least with regard to their fundamental principles, and the vision of the order of them as the ascent of the mind and heart to God.

The Dominicans, in the time of their ascendancy, taught the consecrated active life of preaching, teaching, and study as flowing from contemplation, and as to teaching in the strict sense, the method for the sciences, including the natural sciences that were to develop, and a highly developed and excellent theology and philosophy.

The Jesuits, in the time of their ascendancy, taught the consecrated active life of whatever actions for the saving of souls and the spread of the faith the Roman pontiff ordered, while being in those actions a contemplative in the midst of action, and as to teaching in the strict sense, moral theology and moral philosophy, and a method for the practical intellect, starting from these sciences, to arrive at a prudent choice of action.

In short:

The Benedictines taught:	*contemplari*
The Dominicans taught:	*contemplata aliis tradere*
The Jesuits taught:	*simul in actione contemplativus esse*

That is:

The Benedictines taught:	the contemplative life
The Dominicans taught:	the active life of handing on to others the things contemplated
The Jesuits taught:	the active life of, in the midst of action, being contemplative

In conclusion, I offer this brief presentation of that vision of the ascent of the mind and heart to God which is to guide the Benedictine teacher. I begin, then, with the thesis of the first section of this essay, that the vocation of the monk is to live, together with his brothers, the life of the first Church of Jerusalem. I recall that in that first Church there were "prophets" and "teachers." It seems that those who had the power to proclaim in the Spirit the fundamental truths of revelation as fulfilment of the prophesies were called "prophets," and those who had the power in the Spirit to elaborate on those truths were called "teachers." What, then, in the light of this, is that vision of the ascent of the mind and heart to God which is to guide the Benedictine teacher?

As frequently noted in this essay, for the Christian, any knowledge, and any increase in knowledge, must always be such as to be accompanied by charity and to promote growth in charity. But, we also pointed out that there are frequent exhortations in the apostolic preaching always to seek, guided by the love of God, to understand more and more deeply the teaching the Apostles give, and we gave references to such exhortations. Of course, charity is the reason for such exhortations. For love always seeks an ever deeper and clearer knowing of the one whom it loves, of the one to whom it wishes utterly to give itself. Therefore, the love of charity is the motive force of this ascent of the mind and heart to God, and we should allow this love of charity to become an ardent, vehement, yes, impetuous love in us. Moreover, the Lord will always show us, perhaps through others, when our journeying toward union with God by knowledge and love begins to stray from the path marked out by love, begins to become an increasing of knowledge not accompanied by and promoting love, that is, begins to become "curiosity," in the sense of a vice. Therefore, in this glorious journey, love must always lead the way.

To these exhortations of the Apostles to this journey we could add numerous exhortations of the Fathers as well. Let us only recall what Saint Augustine taught us in his *de Ordine*. First, "Reason desires to transport itself to that most blessed contemplation of divine things." Thus the Lord has already instilled in us this desire to ascend by mind and heart to God. Second, "In order to see divine things one must have both merit of life and erudition." These two teachings correspond to the exhortation of the Apostles to make the ascent by way of love and knowledge. As we also saw, Saint Augustine held that once we had erudition, we could proceed to philosophy, that is, the love of wisdom, and having reached its goal, we will have wisdom. And then in theology we attain the supreme wisdom, sacred wisdom. So we could say: "In order to see divine things, we must have both merit of life and erudition followed by wisdom."

Guided, then, by charity, the vision of the beautiful ascent, according to my inadequate description, opens up before us. In describing this vision, I will follow the way marked out by Saint Augustine, but according to the teaching of Saint Thomas Aquinas, by which he adds scientific precision and rigor, and systematic exposition, to the description of the way.[196] I believe that, for the reasons given earlier in this essay, in calling on Saint Thomas I will still very much remain a Benedictine teacher, and I believe that Saint John Henry will grant me this, and still allow me to consider myself his faithful son.

First, then, we notice the distinction between the moral virtues and the intellectual virtues: the moral virtues are habits of the will, or of the sensory appetite governed by the will, by which the will makes a good choice, while the intellectual virtues are habits of the intellect by which it generates true knowledge. We have spoken earlier as to how the moral virtues (indeed, we call them "supernatural" moral virtues, because they flow from grace), and the virtues of faith, hope and charity, and the gifts of the Holy Spirit, are all given to us at Baptism, and we have spoken about the "active" life, in which we struggle to cooperate with grace to uproot the vices and release the virtues and gifts. I will not repeat all of this here, but attend now to the intellectual virtues, the ascent via erudition and wisdom.

The first great division of the intellectual virtues is between the theoretical and the practical virtues, the first concerned with knowing the truth of things, the second concerned with knowing in order to do or make something. The very first intellectual virtue is the virtue of understanding, by which we understand first principles of thought, e.g., "A thing is not both *x* and *not x* simultaneously." Understanding is considered a theoretical virtue, but these first principles are presupposed by all subsequent thought, theoretical or practical. Then there is the practical virtue of prudence, concerned with doing things, and which, with the moral virtues and the other virtues and the gifts aiding the will in place, chooses a good action. Then come the arts and sciences. The sciences are all theoretical virtues, concerned with knowing the truth of things for its own sake; the arts are all concerned with making things, and from that point of view are all practical. However, there is one set of arts which, as we shall see, because they are all closely connected with the sciences, are considered theoretical.

The first of the arts are those which make something useful for maintaining our life, such as medicine (here what is "made" is the state of health), agriculture, tailoring, building, etc. Saint John Henry has brought out the great contribution of the monks to agriculture, and to some of the others of these arts. When these arts are secured, human beings naturally turn to the arts concerned with making things which give us pleasure, relaxation, recreation, and these arts are called the "fine" arts. The very great contribution of the monks toward all these arts, which Saint John Henry does not speak of, but which I have referred to, was brought about by what is needed for the celebration of the sacred liturgy.

Consider which fine arts are required for the celebration of the supreme liturgical act, the Holy Mass. First, there is poetics (which is also, as we know, a liberal art), since the most essential constituent of the Mass is words. These words are almost all provided by the Scriptures themselves: the prose narratives which constitute the readings of the Mass, and poetry of the psalms and canticles of Scripture, used at various places during the Mass. The church itself has provided by the art of poetics other elements: the prayers, the antiphons, the texts of hymns and sequences, and so forth. But there are also the words of the homilist, and for this the homilist must have the art of rhetoric, and ideally poetics as well. (We will speak of the category of rhetoric further on.) Then, there is also music, another fine art which is also a liberal art. This art provides sound which represents emotion, and is very important for the Mass. There are also fine arts pertaining to what is seen during the celebration of the Mass. First what is seen is the motion of the human bodies of those who are celebrating the Mass, ministering in it, or participating in it; this motion in fact is a very slow, and grave, dance, and so we have the fine art of dance. But then what is seen during the Mass is the setting of the action of the Mass, and here the fine arts come in of architecture, of all the visual arts, e.g., mosaic, painting, sculpture, of the arts we call crafts—for example, the furniture used during the Mass, the vestments, and so on. To all these arts, in their sacred use, the monks made very great contributions.

After attaining the arts of maintaining life—and these, when they make use of natural science, we now call "technologies," from the Greek word for art—and the fine arts, human beings ascend to the level of seeking knowledge not for doing something, as in the case of prudence, or for making something, as in the technologies and fine arts, but for the sake of knowing the truth of things, that is, they begin to seek the sciences. And for this are required the liberal arts. First the arts of the trivium are needed. Logic is the art of reasoning, or arguing, correctly, and of course this is required for gaining any kind of knowledge. Rhetoric includes argument, but also tries to draw its hearers to assent to a truth by appealing to their emotions. In the case of rhetoric, the truth argued for is practical rather than theoretical, and a little further on we must explain why rhetoric is needed for science. And poetics, as we have seen, involves generalizing an example, viz., the beautiful action, so as to obtain a universal truth about human life, which is strictly speaking theoretical, and this generalizing is also an argument, albeit very simple. The order of these arts in the ascent to God, both in learning and with reference to the hierarchy of being, is poetics, rhetoric, and logic. In the order of the hierarchy, poetics is the most material, logic the most abstract, and rhetoric holds the middle position. In the order of study poetics obviously comes first, but then it is easier to study and begin to produce persuasive speech that to learn logical theory.

Then there are required the mathematical arts, which, as we have seen, in ancient and medieval times were considered to consist in four arts, the arts of the quadrivium. The necessity of these arts is due to the fact that the most fundamental property of material beings is quantity. Everything in the material universe has quantity, and quantity can be divided into two kinds, discrete quantity and continuous quantity. Therefore, if we are to come to a knowledge of the truth of material things, we will need to understand quantity. Now the subject matter of the mathematical arts is simply, as Boethius pointed out, abstract quantity; mathematical objects are simply abstractions derived from quantity. Most fundamentally, numbers are abstractions derived from discrete quantity, and geometrical objects are abstractions derived from continuous quantity.

Mathematics, then, will help us to understand the truth of material things. The most fundamental forms of mathematics, corresponding to numbers and to geometrical objects, are arithmetic and geometry. Because of the great simplicity of these mathematical objects, the principles of mathematics can be quite certain, and from them many conclusions, theorems, as they are called, can be derived with certainty. The knowledge of these theorems, and of how they are demonstrated, can be considered in and of themselves, and so mathematics can be considered as a science. Today we call this pure mathematics. But mathematics can also be used to construct models of material entities; we call this applied mathematics. For the ancients and medievals, there were two arts of applied mathematics, music, applying numbers to model the sounds which, together with silence, constitute music; and astronomy, applying numbers and geometrical objects to model the motions of the heavenly bodies. And the order of these arts, the order of study and the order with reference to the hierarchy, is this: arithmetic first, for numbers are needed in the three subsequent arts; then music, which applies arithmetic; then geometry, since it and arithmetic will both have to be applied in astronomy. Today, of course, there are many more arts of both pure and applied mathematics.

As to the order of the mathematical arts: mathematical objects are incorporeal, but they are only abstractions in the intellect, abstracted from corporeal, or material, beings, and in this sense are less real than corporeal beings, and so mathematics in the hierarchy of being precedes the sciences of material being, that is, the natural sciences. And in the order of study, although mathematics is highly abstract, its arguments, precisely for this reason, are very clear and very certain, and require no experience of the natural world either by observation or by experiment, and so mathematics can be learned even by boys, boys who are not yet ready to think about our experience of the material world. Hence, in both the order of the hierarchy and the order of study mathematics precedes the natural sciences. But it also must follow the trivium, because for both its articulation and its learning it requires logic.

These verbal and mathematical arts are called "arts" because they do indeed make something, but no longer in matter, but in the intellect, although what is made in the intellect is communicated by material words. Thus, taking the verbal liberal arts, grammar-poetics makes a story or narrative (this is true of poetry as well as of prose literature), rhetoric makes a "speech," as we call it, designed to persuade, and logic makes an order in the reasoning of our intellect, with dialectical logic, as we have seen, making a discussion or debate or an argument with a probable conclusion, and demonstrative logic making a proof, or demonstration, or argument with a conclusion which is certain. Whereas of the mathematical liberal arts, arithmetic makes a count by way of numbers of discrete quantity, geometry makes a measurement by way of geometrical objects of continuous quantity, music makes a model by way of numbers of sound and silence, and astronomy makes a model by way of numbers and geometrical objects of the motions of the heavenly bodies.

On the other hand, these arts, although they make something, are called "theoretical," because they are ordered to the sciences. As we noted, rhetoric appears to be an exception, because it is immediately ordered to persuading others to some action, especially some action for the good of political society. However, political society itself is ordered to a just society, at the center of which would be freedom for the worship of God and for advancing in the knowledge of God and of his creation, and these knowledges would fall under the category of the theoretical. Rhetoric is needed, then, to persuade political society to order itself in this way, and in this sense rhetoric can be said to be ordered to the sciences and so called a theoretical art. Recall also that poetics does make an argument, and the truth about human life which the argument puts forward is contemplated for its own sake (and also is to be seen as pointing to divine things), and therefore poetics is also a contemplative, that is, theoretical, art. Last, these arts are called "liberal," that is, free, because they are directed to knowledge for its own sake, and not for the sake of *serving* the doing or making of something, and also because their developers and practitioners must have at least some degree of leisure, that is, of freedom from doing things all for the purpose of *serving* the doing of something else or making something else, and so can devote themselves to seeking to know truth for its own sake.

Now, with the liberal arts in place, humankind is ready to proceed to the full range of the sciences, that is, to the knowledges of the truth of things. In ancient times, as we saw from Saint Augustine, and for a time in the Middle Ages, all these sciences were understood to be parts of philosophy. Saint Augustine recognized natural philosophy and moral philosophy, but also rational philosophy, identified with the liberal art of logic. But, in the course of the Middle Ages it became more common to see logic as propaedeutic to philosophy, and to distinguish metaphysics or divine science from the rest of natural philosophy, and so the division of philosophy became natural philosophy, moral philosophy, and, using the Latin term, divine science. Today we tend to reserve the term "philosophy" to the highest of the sciences attainable by the natural reason, viz., divine science, which considers the principles of all the other sciences, the nature of being itself, both material and immaterial, and some of the attributes of God, as God can be known by the natural reason. For us, then, the great division of the sciences is natural science, moral science, and divine science. The natural sciences are knowledges about the natural world. In fact, these sciences ultimately demonstrate, by way of causal arguments, the existence of God, and the existence in human beings of an immaterial soul. Then, the moral sciences, concerned with personal, family, and economic and political morals, are the theoretical sciences which determine what are good and bad acts, whereas prudence, as we have seen, is the practical intellectual virtue which, presupposing the possession of the moral virtues, chooses a good way to act. Last, as we have said, comes divine science.

By the time we have arrived at this point, we have already obtained a sublime and beautiful vision of God and of the world God has created. All created beings are finite manifestations of the sublimity and beauty of God. The only ultimate purpose of a human being, so far as natural reason can know it, is the natural love of God and the natural contemplation of God, and the natural love and contemplation of all these finite manifestations of his sublimity and beauty—above all, other human beings—and the ordering of his personal life, his family life, and the economic and political life, to some kind of remote, but true, manifestation of the sublimity and beauty of God.

Then comes sacred theology, that is, the theology which takes the revealed articles of faith as its principles. And then the whole world of supernatural marvels, the world we have tried to suggest in the first section of this essay, opens up before us. Aristotle said that God was too distant to be our friend. Now God calls us to be God's friends. There is this extraordinary mystery: the Persons of God wish to share their life with persons who are not God. A great and beautiful light is shed over all the arts and sciences. Benedictine teachers teach whichever of them we are called to make a specialty. We teach the liberal arts, both verbal and mathematical, which are fundamental today as they were in the past. We teach the verbal arts in the language of the place where we live, but also there is taught in our schools the verbal arts of the classical languages. For, as our civilization has been formed by the joining of Christianity, the Greco-Roman heritage, and the Germanic heritage, so the Greek and Roman classics always remain of fundamental significance. We teach history, but now knowing that the history of the Church will prove, on that "Day," to be the key to the meaning of all history. The teaching of the natural sciences occurs in our schools with excellence and enthusiasm. And we see that the supposed unbridgeable separation between mathematics and the natural sciences on the one hand, and history, philosophy, literature, and the fine arts on the other hand, has no basis whatsoever in the wisdom of the ancients and medievals, and in the truth of natural and of revealed theology. Moral science and its divisions are taught in our school, for precisely because our Benedictine school has a contemplative orientation, the questions of personal morality, and morality of the family, of the economic and political community, are of vital importance for giving us the possibility of attaining, by the Lord's grace, the contemplative end to which he has called us. Therefore we teach all these moral sciences, and from the view of the moral teaching of the Church, including all its social teaching. Nor do we hesitate to engage with the moral issues that most concern our fellow human beings and us today, issues in personal morality, in family morality, moral issues in the political and economic realms, and we engage in them in a very detailed and practical way. Last, of course, and during the whole course of studies, we teach sacred theology, in the way appropriate to the ages and circumstances of those whom we are teaching.

In earlier times metaphysics or divine science was called not just a science, but "wisdom," because it was knowledge which unified all the other sciences, and considered God himself. All the more was and is sacred theology called "wisdom," because it considers all that metaphysics or divine science considers, and vastly more, the whole revelation of God, and because it considers all of this by the light of revelation, and not just by the light of natural reason.

Now we come to the final degree, in this life, of the ascent of our mind and heart to God. All the preceding stages of our ascent to God have consisted in the stages of the ascent of the intellect through the arts and sciences, then through the wisdom by the light of natural reason, and then through the wisdom by the light of faith, with the whole ascent guided by charity. But, as we saw in the first section of this essay, and have had occasion to recall more than once, it was the teaching of the apostles that, as formulated by Saint Paul, "our knowledge is imperfect and our prophecy is imperfect; but when the perfect comes, the imperfect will pass away."[197] It is still the case, then, that we see only as in a mirror, darkly. But there is one further step that we can take in this life: it is by way of the wisdom which is one of the gifts, the supreme gift, of the Holy Spirit, and the gift which especially accompanies charity, which, we recall, is poured into our hearts by the Holy Spirit. By this gift of wisdom we are taught, as the great Eastern monk known as Dionysius the Areopagite says, "not only by learning, but also by experiencing divine things"[198]—and the word here translated "experiencing" could also be translated "suffering"—suffering divine things. At this last stage of the ascent of the mind and heart to God, the heart, which has accompanied the mind all along, now takes over. It is through love-knowledge, the divine kind of knowing, the kind of knowing we participate in by the gift of wisdom, that we make the final ascent possible in this life.

Note this sublime truth of Christianity, this sublime truth the Lord taught us: even a brother or sister in Christ who has been deprived of education, who, let us say, is illiterate, even this brother or sister, without ever having ascended any of the previous steps, can now soar beyond us, for the gift of wisdom is given in proportion to the degree of our charity. The ancient philosophers could see no way to avoid the conclusion that wisdom, and therefore what happiness can be had in this life, could be had only by those with intellectual power and education. But the merciful Lord grants a wisdom the philosophers do not know to all who come to him. It is this sublime truth of Christianity which leads the great Saint Augustine, in *de Ordine*, to say to his beloved mother, who has been present during the dialogue, but who has made the ascent to God by a way other than that of the philosophers: "Mother, 'philosophy' means the 'love of wisdom.' You have a wisdom, I know, which is not that of the philosophers. You love this wisdom. As a matter of fact you love it far more than you love me, and do I know how much you love me! You love it so much, indeed, that neither setbacks of any kind nor death itself holds any terror for you. The learned are of the opinion that to achieve this most difficult state is the inner core of philosophy itself. Should I not therefore be your willing disciple?"[199] And shortly we shall see how he and his mother together are lifted up for the briefest moment toward a glimpse of that Divine Beauty which the wisdom of charity knows. At the same time, those of us whom the Lord has blessed with the gift of teaching, must know that the Lord asks us to make this ascent of mind and heart by the way of the arts and sciences, and to teach it to others, for that is the vocation he has given us in his Church, but also to make it by the gift of love-wisdom, the gift he gives to all. And we are all joined together in him, and one in him.

What is this wisdom that suffers the things of God? It cannot be put into words. It can be, to a small degree, pointed to in words. Great saints, and working in and through them the Lord, have pointed to it in words. Let us close, then, with a few words from the monastic Fathers, from the Apostles, and from the Lord himself.

The Monastic Fathers

Saint Basil

> What is more marvelous than the divine beauty? What thought has more charm than the magnificence of God? What loving desire of the soul is so keen and intolerable as that which comes from God upon the soul which is cleansed from all evil and cries with true affection, "I am wounded by love"?[200] Wholly indescribable and inexplicable are the flashes of the divine beauty; speech cannot express them, hearing cannot receive them. Though you speak of the rays of the morning star, of the brightness of the moon or the light of the sun, all are worthless in comparison with its glory and fall short as far, compared with the true Light, as the deep shades of a moonless night compared with the glow of the noonday sun. This beauty is unseen by fleshly eyes, and comprehended only by the soul and mind when, if at all, it has illumined one of the saints, and left in them the sting of intolerable loving desire. Saints like these, weary of the present life, cried, "Woe is me, that my dwelling is prolonged,"[201] "When shall I come and appear before the face of God?"[202], and, "To depart and be with Christ, for that is far better,"[203] and "My soul thirsts for God, the strong, the living

> One,"[204] and, "Lord, now let your servant depart."[205] Oppressed by this life as if it was a prison, those whose souls were touched by the divine loving desire could hardly restrain their impulses. Yes, they had an insatiable desire to behold the divine beauty and prayed that their contemplation of the sweetness of the Lord might last on into life eternal.[206]

Evagrius of Pontus

> That prayer of our Lord must be fulfilled in which he prays, "Father, grant them that they also in us should be one, as you and I are one." Since God is one, when he comes into each one, he makes all one,[207] and number falls away through the coming of the Onlyness.[208]

(Evagrius says that in heaven each of us, although retaining our personal identity unimpaired, will be so united to God that it will be as if only God is; this state he calls the "Onlyness.")

John Cassian

> For then will be perfectly fulfilled in our case that prayer of our Saviour in which He prayed for His disciples to the Father saying "that the love wherewith Thou lovedst Me may be in them and they in us"; and again: "that they all may be one as Thou, Father, in Me and I in Thee, that they also may be one in us," when that perfect love of God, wherewith "He first loved us" has passed into the feelings of our heart as well, by the fulfilment of this prayer of the Lord which we believe cannot possibly be ineffectual. And this will come to pass when God shall be all our love, and every desire and wish and effort, every thought of ours, and all our life and words and breath, and that unity which already exists between the Father and the Son, and the Son and

the Father, has been shed abroad in our hearts and minds, so that as He loves us with a pure and unfeigned and indissoluble love, so we also may be joined to Him by a lasting and inseparable affection, since we are so united to Him that whatever we breathe or think, or speak is God, since, as I say, we attain to that end of which we spoke before, which the same Lord in His prayer hopes may be fulfilled in us: "that they all may be one as we are one, I in them and Thou in Me, that they also may be made perfect in one"; and again: "Father, those whom Thou hast given Me, I will that where I am, they may also be with Me." This then ought to be the destination of the solitary, this should be all his aim that it may be vouchsafed to him to possess even in the body an image of future bliss, and that he may begin in this world to have a foretaste of a sort of earnest of that celestial life and glory. This, I say, is the end of all perfection, that the mind purged from all carnal desires may daily be lifted towards spiritual things, until the whole life and all the thoughts of the heart become one continuous prayer.[209]

Saint Augustine

And being thence warned to return to myself, I entered into my inward self, Thou leading me on; and I was able to do it, for You had become my helper. And I entered, and with the eye of my soul (such as it was) saw above the same eye of my soul, above my mind, the Unchangeable Light. Not this common light, which all flesh may look upon, nor, as it were, a greater one of the same kind, as though the brightness of this should be much more resplendent, and with its greatness fill up all things. Not like this was that light, but different, yea, very different from all these. Nor was it above my mind as oil is above water, nor as heaven above earth; but above it was, because it made me, and I below it, because I was made by it. He who knows the Truth knows that Light; and he that knows it knows eternity. Love knows it. O Eternal Truth, and true Love, and loved Eternity! You are my God; to You do I sigh both night and day. When I first knew You, You lifted me up, that I might see there was that which I might see, and that yet it was not I that did see. And Thou beat back the infirmity of my sight, pouring forth upon me most strongly Your beams of light, and I trembled with love and fear; and I found myself to be far off from You, in the region of dissimilarity, as if I heard this voice of Yours from on high: I am the food of strong men; grow, and you shall feed upon me; nor shall you convert me, like the food of your flesh, into you, but you shall be converted into me. And I learned that You correct man for iniquity, and You make my soul consume away like a spider. And I said, Is Truth, therefore, nothing because it is neither diffused through space, finite, nor infinite? And You cried to me from afar, Yea, verily, "I Am that I Am." And I heard this, as things are heard in the heart, nor was there room for doubt; and I should more readily doubt that I live than that Truth is not, which is clearly seen, being understood by the things that are made.[210]

And I viewed the other things below You, and perceived that they neither altogether are, nor altogether are not. They are, indeed, because they are from You; but are not, because they are not what You are. For that truly is which remains immutably. It is good, then, for me to cleave unto God, for if I remain not in Him, neither shall I in myself; but He, remaining in Himself, renews all things.[211] And You are the Lord my God, since You stand not in need of my goodness.[212]

Again:

She [his mother Monica] and I stood alone, leaning in a certain window, from which the garden of the house we occupied at

Ostia could be seen; at which place, removed from the crowd, we were resting ourselves for the voyage, after the fatigues of a long journey. We then were conversing alone very pleasantly; and, forgetting those things which are behind, and reaching forth unto those things which are before,[213] we were seeking between ourselves in the presence of the Truth, which You are, of what nature the eternal life of the saints would be, which eye has not seen, nor ear heard, neither has entered into the heart of man. But yet we opened wide the mouth of our heart, after those supernal streams of Your fountain, the fountain of life, which is with You; that being sprinkled with it according to our capacity, we might in some measure weigh so high a mystery.

And when our conversation had arrived at that point, that the very highest pleasure of the carnal senses, and that in the very brightest material light, seemed by reason of the sweetness of that life not only not worthy of comparison, but not even of mention, we, lifting ourselves with a more ardent affection towards the Selfsame, did gradually pass through all corporeal things, and even the heaven itself, whence sun, and moon, and stars shine upon the earth; yea, we soared higher yet by inward musing, and discoursing, and admiring Your works; and we came to our own minds, and went beyond them, that we might advance as high as that region of unfailing plenty, where You feed Israel for ever with the food of truth, and where life is that Wisdom by whom all these things are made, both which have been, and which are to come; and she is not made, but is as she has been, and so shall ever be; yea, rather, to have been, and to be hereafter, are not in her, but only to be, seeing she is eternal, for to have been and to be hereafter are not eternal. And while we were thus speaking, and straining after her, we slightly touched her with the whole effort of our heart; and we sighed, and there left bound the first-fruits of the Spirit[214]; and returned to the noise of our own mouth, where the word uttered has both

> beginning and end. And what is like Your Word, our Lord, who remains in Himself without becoming old, and makes all things new?[215]
>
> We were saying, then, If to any man the tumult of the flesh were silenced—silenced the phantasies of earth, waters, and air—silenced, too, the poles; yea, the very soul be silenced to herself, and go beyond herself by not thinking of herself—silenced fancies and imaginary revelations, every tongue, and every sign, and whatsoever exists by passing away, since, if any could hearken, all these say, We created not ourselves, but were created by Him who abides for ever: If, having uttered this, they now should be silenced, having only quickened our ears to Him who created them, and He alone speak not by them, but by Himself, that we may hear His word, not by fleshly tongue, nor angelic voice, nor sound of thunder, nor the obscurity of a similitude, but might hear Him—Him whom in these we love—without these, like as we two now strained ourselves, and with rapid thought touched on that Eternal Wisdom which remains over all. If this could be sustained, and other visions of a far different kind be withdrawn, and this one ravish, and absorb, and envelope its beholder amid these inward joys, so that his life might be eternally like that one moment of knowledge which we now sighed after, were not this Enter into the joy of Your Lord?[216]

Again:

> Too late did I love You, O Beauty, so ancient, and yet so new! Too late did I love You! For behold, You were within, and I without, and there did I seek You; I, unlovely, rushed heedlessly among the things of beauty You made. You were with me, but I was not with You. Those things kept me far from You, which, unless they were in You, were not. You called, and cried aloud, and forced open my deafness. You gleamed and shine, and

chase away my blindness. You exhaled odours, and I drew in my breath and do pant after You. I tasted, and do hunger and thirst. You touched me, and I burned for Your peace."[217]

Saint Benedict

Does he truly seek God?[218]

The Apostles

Saint Paul

Now the Lord is the Spirit, and where the Spirit of the Lord is, there is freedom. And we all, with unveiled face, beholding the glory of the Lord, are being changed into his likeness from one degree of glory to another; for this comes from the Lord who is the Spirit.[219]

For what we preach is not ourselves, but Jesus Christ as Lord, with ourselves as your servants for Jesus' sake. For it is the God who said, "Let light shine out of darkness," who has shone in our hearts to give the light of the knowledge of the glory of God in the face of Christ.[220]

When all things are subjected to him, then the Son himself will also be subjected to him who put all things under him, that God may be all in all.[221]

Saint John

See what love the Father has given us, that we should be called children of God; and so we are. The reason why the world does not know us is that it did not know him. Beloved, we are God's children now; it does not yet appear what we shall be, but we know that when he appears we shall be like him, for we shall see him as he is.[222]

They shall see his face, and his name shall be on their foreheads. And night shall be no more; they need no light of lamp or sun, for the Lord God will be their light, and they shall reign for ever and ever.[223]

The Lord

He who eats my flesh and drinks my blood abides in me, and I in him.[224]

This is eternal life, that they know thee the only true God, and Jesus Christ whom thou hast sent.[225]

I have manifested thy name to the men whom thou hast given me out of the world.... And not for them only do I pray, but for them also who through their word shall believe in me, that they all may be one, as thou, Father, in me, and I in thee; that they also may be one in us....[226]

Father, I desire that they also, whom thou hast given me, may be with me where I am, to behold my glory which thou hast given me in thy love for me before the foundation of the world.[227]

All authority in heaven and on earth has been given to me. Go therefore and make disciples of all nations, baptizing them in the name of the Father and of the Son and of the Holy Spirit, teaching them to observe all that I have commanded you; and lo, I am with you always, to the close of the age.[228]

Notes for the Interpretive Essay

1. Acts 4:32; 2:45; 4:34, 35. In my text, all quotations from and references to the Bible will be taken from and made to the Revised Standard Version unless otherwise noted, and the numbering of the Psalms will be as in the RSV.
2. Acts 15:29.
3. John Cassian, *Conferences*, XVIII.v. In. Philip Schaff and Henry Wace, eds., *Nicene and Post-Nicene Fathers—Second Series*, Vol. 11 (Grand Rapids, MI: Eerdmans, 1991). Translation slightly altered by myself.
4. Acts 2:14–36.
5. Amos 5:18, and, e.g., Malachi 3:19–23; Isaiah 26:20–27:1; 33:10–16. In this first section of the essay, I am much indebted to the footnotes and cross-references of *The New Jerusalem Bible*, Standard Edition (London, 1985), and to the "Alphabetical Table of the Major Footnotes" of that Bible, pp. 2079ff; also to L. Ott, *Fundamentals of Catholic Dogma* (Rockford, IL: TAN Books, 1974).
6. Daniel 12:1–3.
7. Daniel 7:1–28.
8. Isaiah 65:17; 66:22.
9. Psalm 27:4.
10. Ibid., 42:1–2.
11. Deuteronomy 6:4–5.
12. Hosea 6:6.
13. Jeremiah 9:23–24.
14. Isaiah 11:9.
15. Habakkuk 2:14.
16. Jeremiah 31:34.
17. Wisdom 3:9.
18. Isaiah 40:5; cf. Psalm 97:6: "all the peoples behold his glory."
19. Isaiah 52:8
20. Ibid., 66:18.
21. Daniel 7:1–28
22. Genesis 1:31.
23. Ibid., 12:1–5; 15:1–6.
24. Exodus 3:1–4:20.
25. Genesis 1:26.
26. Hosea 2:19,20,23.
27. Daniel 7:22; 7:14.
28. 2 Samuel 7:4–17; Isaiah 9:1–7; 11:1–9.
29. Daniel 7:13.
30. Isaiah 7:14.
31. Ibid., 9:6.
32. Acts 2:41.

33. Acts 2:37.
34. Ibid., 2:38–40.
35. 1 Peter 3:18.
36. 1 Corinthians 15:3–4.
37. Romans 3:23–25.
38. Isaiah 52:13–53:12; See also Acts 8:32–35.
39. Romans 6:3–11.
40. 2 Peter 1:4.
41. Isaiah 11:1–3.
42. Romans 5:5.
43. Isaiah 7:14.
44. John 14:23.
45. Acts 2:42, my translation.
46. 1 John 1:3.
47. Ephesians 3:14–19. See also, for more examples: Hebrews 5:11–6:1a, Colossians 1:9–10; 1 Corinthians 2:6–13; Romans 11:33–36.
48. Acts 6:4.
49. Ibid., 1:15.
50. Ibid., 13:1.
51. Psalm 1:2; 1 Timothy 4:15.
52. Philippians 3:10–11.
53. For our communion with our Lord Jesus Christ, see 1 Corinthians 1:9; with the Father, 1 John 1:3; with the Holy Spirit, 2 Corinthians 13:14
54. Acts 4:32.
55. Philippians 1:5.
56. Acts 2:44–46; 4:32, 34–36.
57. Jeremiah 31:31–40.
58. See Matthew 26:26–28; Mark 14:22–34; Luke 22:15–20; 1 Corinthians 11:23–26; and *The Roman Missal*, E.T. according to the 3rd Typical Edition (Washington, DC, 2011), "Words of Consecration," p. 639.
59. John 6:57.
60. 1 Corinthians 10:17.
61. John 6:51.
62. Ibid., 6:54.
63. Luke 18:1.
64. Luke 21:36.
65. See C. W. Dugmore, *The Influence of the Synagogue upon the Divine Office* (London: Faith Press, 1964), pp. 11–25, 59–64.
66. Psalm 1:2.
67. 1 Timothy 2:1–8; 1 Thessalonians 5:16–18.
68. Romans 8:15.
69. Mark 14:36.

70. Luke 6:12.
71. 1 Corinthians 13:12.
72. 1 Timothy 6:14–16.
73. Romans 8:26–27.
74. Cf. Saint Thomas Aquinas, *Summa Theologiae* [hereafter *ST*] II-II, q. 184, a. 1.
75. Matthew 22:37–40.
76. John 14:15.
77. 1 Corinthians 13:1–3, 8–13.
78. John 15:15.
79. Mark 1:15.
80. John 14:1.
81. 1 Corinthians 13:12.
82. James 2:17.
83. Ibid., 2:19.
84. 1 Corinthians 2:6–13.
85. *ST* I-II, qq. 1–5.
86. Matthew 5:8.
87. 2 Corinthians 6:14–7:1.
88. Matthew 19:21.
89. Luke 10:16.
90. Acts 4:35.
91. Matthew 19:11–12.
92. Ephesians 5:21–33.
93. 1 Corinthians 7:9, 5.
94. Ephesians 6:4.
95. John 14:15–16.
96. John 15:13.
97. 1 Peter 2:21.
98. John 21:15–19.
99. James 1:2.
100. Acts 5:41.
101. Galatians 2:20.
102. Ibid., 5:24.
103. Ibid., 6:14.
104. With the rest of this paragraph, cf. *ST* II-II, q. 182, a. 2, and cross-references.
105. John 14:21.
106. 1 John 3:1–2.
107. Matthew 6:33.
108. John 6:27–29.
109. Luke 10:41–42.
110. 1 Corinthians 7:29–31.
111. Acts 1:6–8.

112. Isaiah 49:8.
113. 2 Corinthians 6:2.
114. John 16:13.
115. 1 Corinthians 12:31, 14:1.
116. Colossians 3:1–4.
117. 2 Corinthians 4:18.
118. Philippians 3:7–14)
119. Acts 2:38–40.
120. Ibid., 2:41.
121. 1 Corinthians 7:31.
122. Timothy Fry, O.S.B., et al., *RB 1980: The Rule of St. Benedict in Latin and English with Notes* [hereafter *RB*] (Collegeville, MN: Liturgical Press, 1981), p. 310.
123. See Owen Chadwick, *Western Asceticism*, General Introduction, in *The Library of Christian Classics*, Vol. 12 (Westminster: John Knox Press, 1958).
124. For the remainder of this first section of my essay, I have been helped by Adalbert de Vogue, *The Rule of Saint Benedict: A Doctrinal and Spiritual Commentary*, trans. John Baptist Hasbrouck (Kalamazoo, MI: Cistercian Publications, 1983), relevant chapters.
125. *RB 1980*, pp. 330–32.
126. See also Cassian's *Conference* I, on the end and goal of monastic life, and *Conferences* XVI and XVII, on monastic friendship. For the Pachomian tradition it was certainly the key term and the key concept. For Saint Basil, see the famous Longer Rule VII of the *Asketikon*, and note the references to Acts 2 and 4. And for Saint Benedict, see, for example, Chapter 1 of the *Rule*, where he calls the cenobites "the strong kind of monks"; Chapters 33 and 34 of the Rule, and note the references to Acts 4; Chapter 2:20 ("we are all one in Christ"); and the whole of Chapter 72, the grand summary of the Rule, which, although it does not use the word "communion," is a most beautiful presentation of the whole concept.
127. Charity is the goal for Saint Basil: *Asketikon*, Longer Rules 1, 2, and 3. Charity is the goal for Cassian: *Conferences* I, XVI, XVII. Charity is the goal for Saint Benedict: Prologue 47, 49, Chapter 4:1–2, Chapter 7:67–70, Chapter 72.
128. *RB* 7:70.
129. Ibid., 33:2–4.
130. Saint Basil, Longer Rules 1, 2, 3; Cassian, *Conferences*, I.viii.1, x.5; Saint Benedict, *RB* 4:21, 35:6.
131. *Conferences*, XVIII.vii.7.
132. *Institutes*, IV, 33–35.
133. cf. *ST* I, q. 16, a. 1, c., quoting Saint Augustine.
134. For the preceding, see *ST* II-II, q. 180, a. 4, c.
135. see Pope Saint John Paul II, *Orientale lumen*, sections 9–16, and Pope Benedict XVI, *Address to the Congregation for Institutes of Consecrated Life and Societies of Apostolic Life*, November 20, 2008.

136. John Henry Newman, "The Mission of Saint Benedict," in *A Benedictine Education: The Mission of Saint Benedict & The Benedictine Schools*, ed. Christopher Fisher (Providence, RI: Cluny Media, 2020), p. 47.
137. Ibid., p. 3.
138. D. Knowles, *Christian Monasticism* (New York, 1977), p. 37, 83.
139. Newman, "The Mission of Saint Benedict," p. 37.
140. *RB*, Prologue; 4:1; 72.
141. Newman, "The Mission of Saint Benedict," pp. 3–6.
142. Ibid., p. 9.
143. Ibid., p. 10.
144. Ibid., p. 11–12.
145. For the rest of this paragraph, cf. William Wallace, *The Elements of Philosophy* (New York: Alba House, 1977), ch. 2; Benedict Ashley, *The Arts of Learning and Communication* (Dubuque, IA: Priory Press, 1961), Part One, chs. 2 and 3.
146. Newman, "The Mission of Saint Benedict," p. 12.
147. John 17:3.
148. Cf. Ashley, *Arts of Learning and Communication*, pp. 264, 280–1.
149. As quoted in *ST* II-II, q. 180, a. 4, c. (English translation is from the translation of Fathers of the English Dominican Province, published by Benziger Brothers.)
150. Newman, "The Mission of Saint Benedict," p. 7.
151. Romans 1:20; Wisdom 13:1–9.
152. Newman, "The Mission of Saint Benedict," pp. 43–44.
153. *RB* 58:5.
154. Newman, "The Benedictine Schools," in *A Benedictine Education*, p. 87.
155. Ibid., p. 90.
156. Ibid., p. 76.
157. Ibid., p. 79.
158. Ibid.
159. Ibid., p. 81.
160. Ibid., p. 83.
161. Ibid., pp. 79–82.
162. In the following I will make use of the edition of *de Ordine* by Silvano Borruso, with his English translation (South Bend, IN: St. Augustine's Press, 2007). In some quotations I will adjust his translation in order that it conform more closely to the literal text.
163. *De Ordine*, II.39.
164. Ibid., I.1.
165. Ibid., II.39.
166. Saint Augustine, *Retractationes*, as quoted in Borruso, p. xiii.
167. *De Ordine*, II.35–37.
168. Ibid., II.35.
169. Ibid., II.38.
170. Ibid., II.39–41.

171. Ibid., II.42.
172. Ibid., II.42.
173. Ibid., II.43.
174. Bruce Kimball, *Orators and Philosophers* (New York: Teachers College Press, 1986), p. 23.
175. *De Ordine*, II.44.
176. cf. *ST* I, q. 1, a. 5 ad 2.
177. *De Ordine*, II.16–17, 24, 47.
178. *The City of God*, trans. Marcus Dods (New York: The Modern Library, 1950), xi.24–25; viii.4.
179. Ibid., xi.24.
180. Ibid., viii.4.
181. Newman, "The Benedictine Schools," p. 80.
182. *The Seven Liberal Arts in the Middle Ages*, ed. David Wagner (Bloomington, IN: Indiana University Press, 1986), pp. 101–102.
183. Kimball, *Orators and Philosophers*, p. 51. For this paragraph, and the preceding two, see ibid., pp. 46–48, and Wagner, *Seven Liberal Arts in the Middle Ages*, pp. 150–55.
184. Kimball, *Orators and Philosophers*, pp. 44–46.
185. Ibid., p. 46.
186. Cf. Lucy Beckett, *In the Light of Christ* (San Francisco, CA: Ignatius Press, 2006), p. 141.
187. Pierre Conway and Benedict Ashley, "The Liberal Arts in Saint Thomas Aquinas," *The Thomist*, Vol. 22, No. 4 (October 1959), p. 53,and fn. 122.
188. Kimball, *Orators and Philosophers*, p. 48; pp. 55–6; p. 55, fn. 34.
189. Newman, "The Benedictine Schools," p. 80.
190. Ibid., p. 83.
191. Ibid., p. 82.
192. Ibid., p. 84.
193. Ibid., p. 89.
194. Newman, "The Mission of Saint Benedict," p. 43.
195. Newman, "The Benedictine Schools," pp. 98–99.
196. In the following, I am indebted to Conway and Ashley, "The Liberal Arts in Saint Thomas Aquinas."
197. 1 Corinthians 13:9–10.
198. *ST* II-II, q. 45, a. 2.
199. *De Ordine*, I.32.
200. Song of Songs 2:5.
201. Psalms 120:5.
202. Psalms 42:2.
203. Philippians 1:23.
204. Psalms 42:2.
205. Luke 2:29.
206. *Asketikon*, Longer Rule 2.

207. Cf. Saint Paul, "And God will be all in all" (1 Corinthians 15:28).
208. *Letter on Faith*, n. 25.
209. *Conferences*, X.vii.
210. Romans 1:20.
211. Wisdom 7:27.
212. *Confessions*, VII.10.16–17.
213. Philippians 3:13.
214. Romans 8:23.
215. Wisdom 7:27.
216. Matthew 25:21; *Confessions*, IX.10.23–25.
217. *Confessions*, X.27.37.
218. *RB* 58:7.
219. 2 Corinthians 3:17–18
220. Ibid., 4:5–6.
221. 1 Corinthians 15:28.
222. 1 John 3:1–2.
223. Revelation 22:4–5.
224. John 6:56.
225. Ibid., 17:3.
226. John 17:6, 20–21, Douai-Rheims 1899 American Edition.
227. John 17:24.
228. Matthew 28:18–20.

CLUNY MEDIA

Designed by Fiona Cecile Clarke, the CLUNY MEDIA *logo depicts a monk at work in the scriptorium, with a cat sitting at his feet.*

The monk represents our mission to emulate the invaluable contributions of the monks of Cluny in preserving the libraries of the West, our strivings to know and love the truth.

The cat at the monk's feet is Pangur Bán, from the eponymous Irish poem of the 9th century. The anonymous poet compares his scholarly pursuit of truth with the cat's happy hunting of mice. The depiction of Pangur Bán is an homage to the work of the monks of Irish monasteries and a sign of the joy we at Cluny take in our trade.

"Messe ocus Pangur Bán,
cechtar nathar fria saindan:
bíth a menmasam fri seilgg,
mu memna céin im saincheirdd."

Made in the USA
Middletown, DE
10 June 2021